THE CRYSTAL CABINET

Mary Butts

THE CRYSTAL CABINET

my childhood at Salterns

Foreword by Camilla Bagg
Afterword by Barbara Wagstaff

Beacon Press · Boston

Beacon Press
25 Beacon Street
Boston, Massachusetts 02108

Beacon Press books
are published under the auspices of
the Unitarian Universalist Association of Congregations.

95 94 93 92 91 90 89 88   8 7 6 5 4 3 2 1

Library of Congress Catalog Card Number 87-47974
ISBN 0-8070-7038-6

Contents

List of Illustrations

The publishers are grateful to Camilla Bagg for making these
photographs available.

Foreword

WHEN *The Crystal Cabinet* first came out, in 1937, a note informed its readers that, earlier in the year, Mary Butts had died suddenly, at the age of forty-four. It is now known that she was forty-six.

Many years later it was said to me, her daughter and only child, that such a sad event would hardly be likely to happen these days. It was the combination of an undiagnosed condition, a sudden haemorrhage, life in a remote village, the passing of several hours before being found, no telephone at hand, no easy transport, the nearest hospital ten miles away and the day of the routine blood transfusion not yet arrived – all these together spelt disaster. Today, Mary Butts might well have been put back on her feet in no time, to go on writing, developing her undoubted gifts and living to achieve and enjoy the recognition she deserves.

Readers of *The Crystal Cabinet* were not aware that the book was a much edited version of the manuscript which was finished in 1936. It is dedicated to Angus Davidson, a writer who, in his youth, had been one of the minders of the Hogarth Press for Leonard and Virginia Woolf. He was a translator from the Italian and the author of a biography of Edward Lear. After coming to live in the same Cornish village as Mary Butts had settled in – Sennen Cove, by Land's End – he became a good friend to my mother and she leant on him for company and advice.

Would a woman today automatically turn to a man for comment on her work? As I understand it, she turned to two. Men, in those days, were still considered to be the ones who *knew*; knew about the world and what you could or could not do, once you ventured out into it to sell your wares. Women, however talented and clever but still unsure of themselves, listened humbly.

Her other adviser was, I believe, Father Bernard Walke, the vicar of St Hilary, Marazion. Mary attended his church, having found its particular style of extreme Anglo-Catholic worship (some said Popery) suited her, and she valued her friendship with 'Ber' Walke. It can be seen in the manuscript that she herself closed off, by brackets in red ink, passages which a man of God could not possibly have advised her to publish without giving serious thought to what she was doing. They were passages about people, particularly about her mother, which Christian charity, not to mention good taste – once so important – must surely have precluded.

Angus Davidson, kind and conventional, would have agreed. But, when he so unexpectedly became Mary's literary executor, he found himself faced with the problems of editorship. Though there were clear directions about the painful and embarrassing parts to be excluded, many minor points still had to be considered. What was to be done with the signs of hasty writing, debatable punctuation, careless quotations, irrelevancies, repetitions? Considering the difficulties he made a good job of it, but about a quarter of the book was not used with the result that some of its powerful impact was weakened.

It is not possible to say if Mary herself would have done much revision; in her last months she cannot have been feeling well. The editors of this edition have tried to interfere as little as possible but a certain amount of tidying up was felt to be desirable, with the more obscure allusions clarified and collected into an appendix. At the same time, to give a little of the flavour of the period, a few older spellings have been kept because they would have been familiar to her. And 'gay', in this book, means only what it used to mean – light-hearted or merry.

To have done more, in the cause of absolute correctness of grammar, syntax and punctuation, might have altered her style which reflects something of her personality – a breathless eagerness to go into raptures over the wonders of life and living. Not unlike the way in which she sometimes spoke.

The reception of *The Crystal Cabinet* appears to have been tepid – mainly of interest to people who lived in Dorset, particularly by Poole Harbour. An anonymous review in *The Times Literary Supplement* reveals a hint of bafflement, taking refuge in telling the readers much of the story of the book, calling attention to its shortcomings and, at the same time, casting round to do justice to the author. Eighteen months later, the Second World War put Mary Butts and her book into total eclipse. By the time it was over no one was bothering about such a little-known writer. Her novels and short stories, with their setting of taken-for-granted money, no necessity to find a job, cultivation of the mind, frequent assumptions that the reader was well up in French and the

iv

classics, and no interest whatever in ordinary people – after so much turmoil and suffering they were no longer of interest. The world had moved on.

At sixteen, I was too young to understand any wider view but, at the domestic level, I observed that the book brought little pleasure to my mother's family. My great-aunts, Ada and Irlam, discussed it, not *sotto voce* 'lest the child should hear' but, because Irlam was very deaf, at the top of their voices. Thus I discovered that, though they agreed that the book was not without merit, they were shocked. It pained them that the death of their younger sister, Monica, had been brought up; they were outraged that their beloved mother, for so long a widow and now, mercifully, deceased, had been criticized for her rumoured treatment of her daughter. As for Mary's hinting that some of the blame for the tragedy lay with the old lady – the aunts were distraught with grief.

They could not approve of the references to friends and neighbours, even if complimentary – 'such poor taste'; still less of what was said about their connections by marriage, the Hydes. They found their niece inaccurate about dates, names, places. For instance, surely she knew that Aubrey had died at twenty-four, not twenty-two, and that Irlam's famous picture, *The Young Violinist*, had been shown 'on the line' at the Royal Academy in the nineties, not the eighties. Gratifying though it might be for people to think that Ada had published several novels it was not true – there was only one. Salterns was not anywhere near one hundred acres – more like fifty. And there were indignant expostulations that it had *never* been a boarding-house though it might at times have taken a paying-guest – a difference which was felt to be important.

The conversations usually ended something like this: 'Poor Mary! How could she have departed so from all she was brought up to?' Or, to me: 'Your poor mother! Such sad disregard for the truth.' Today we maintain that, to some people, it is not facts which are so significant as what is perceived and utterly believed to be the truth. That was not the thinking fifty years ago, at least not in my great-aunts' world, the foundations of which lay in the teachings of the Church. No amount of fine writing about the beauties of nature and the deeply felt sufferings of growing up could outweigh the duties of charity and fortitude. Just as well they did not know about the full manuscript.

By 1937 I had spent nearly ten years in the same place, with some of the same people, following in my mother's steps. I even went to the same school, Sandecotes, and did not move on to St Andrews but stayed till I was seventeen. After leaving me in Parkstone my mother never came there again; she had been heard to say it made her feel ill – the long creeping process of the suburbanization of a landscape which had been sacred to her. She found some sort of substitute when she settled at the far end of Cornwall, consoled by the magnificence of the cliff scenery and, inland, the remains of Celtic 'magic'.

At the time I did not know how my mother felt about the places of her childhood but, thirty years later and independently, I developed my own attitude towards them, not so much of passionate despair as of resigned depression. I could see for myself how beautiful the district must once have been, and that already it was too late. Everything natural was disappearing because so many people wanted to live there in that mild, sunny climate, with two kinds of sea conveniently near each other: Poole Bay, off the English Channel, on one side of the Sandbanks, and on the other the quieter waters of the Harbour. I was told it was the largest in the world; from its narrow entrance with all its inlets and promontories, a hundred miles round. On the Parkstone side there was just enough left of the past to make the scene all the more sad.

There were still some unmade roads where as you walked you could scuff the sandy soil. There were still bits of heath and woodland remaining between the building plots. The pine-trees shed their slippery bright brown needles or lay fallen in the sun, intoxicatingly resinous. There was a long country lane going past a disused sandpit which I was warned was dangerous. There were patches of derelict land covered with bramble which masked the pools of milky water where once there had been thriving clay workings and pottery kilns. The last vestiges of what Parkstone must have been like came through to me without influence from Mary Butts. She was not there to exert any.

Across the waters of the Harbour could be seen the extraordinary Isle of Purbeck, not a real island but a large part of Dorset isolated by the indentations of the Harbour. It lay long, low, and not in the least like 'a naked god laid down asleep', as she was to write in this book. More like a pair of sofa-backs. At such a distance, against the westering sun (for I was never free to see it early in the day), it was difficult to pick out detail but the sofa-backs ran for miles along the dim horizon, curving down towards each other. Where they would have met on the plain there rose up a mound. And on it there was something sticking up. Faint image of a castle! Astonishing – how it was wedged there between the soaring downs.

On the rare occasions when I could go to Corfe the outing went to my head but later, at the prospect of having to leave, brought on a fit of the sulks. To be there was so glorious – so free. Around the enormous walls of the ruined castle rose the grassy slopes of the downland; they were steep, and slippery because the grass was short and dry. Auntie said I was to be careful not to fall and squash the bee-orchids. At the top of the long climbs, sitting in the brilliant light, cooled by breezes off the sea and surrounded by small bright blue butterflies, I wished I did not have to return through the boring streets to the shut-in house on the fringe of Upper Parkstone.

Discontented schoolgirl that I was, I despised my great-aunt's modest home, a long way from the sea and the handsome houses set in large wooded gardens. Salterns was rarely mentioned. I was never taken to see it or encouraged to find it. My grandfather, 'the Captain', had died in 1905; Granny's second husband was dead, and about him I was told nothing; she and Uncle Tony moved to London after the First World War. I was born in 1920 and arrived in Parkstone in 1928. The great days were over and my great-aunt Ada was determined that I should grow up without illusions of grandeur.

There was a variation on the theme: 'Poor, dear Mary', and this referred to my great-aunts' only married sister, the mother of Mary Butts. It is sad to count the number of people who, so she declares in *The Crystal Cabinet*, did not like her mother. It is impossible to believe.

My grandmother was the victim of her daughter's obsession against her and was subjected for years to much unkind criticism, reproaches and downright hurtfulness. From reading family letters there is no evidence that Granny was anything but kind and forgiving to her diffficult child; she loved her Lord and tried to follow His precepts, turning the other cheek, pouring oil, and sacrificing her comfort in order to help financially as much as she could. Foolish she had undoubtedly been in letting the family possessions slip away from her but she remained loving and generous, patient and resigned to hard times. All the same she was not without a hold on reality. In her letters to her daughter the most severe censure I can find is:

> *I have always loved the pity and generosity in your character –*
> *but these great and lovely gifts, in a weary world* must *be*
> *tempered with common sense or they will – alas that it is so –*
> *darken counsel and lead away from the straight road.*
>
> *Now, my dear, buck up – be patient – life will open out*

*again for you if only you will have common sense. You have
many precious gifts – and ought to be happy – and useful and
well loved and appreciated for all your gifts. Be brave – you can
be brave and noble – it is the fatal lack of common sense. How I
wish you could buy a pound or two. It's worth all the world!*

I remember Granny well; so do the Jacob sisters, the four
daughters of that Hyde daughter who 'had married a country parson,
due for preferment, and raised up a band of girls.' They knew her for
many years before I was born and have often told me how good she was
to them all, from the day when she married their uncle. It rings true;
without being over-indulgent to me, she was a darling. These things
need to be said, in justice to the memory of Mary Colville-Hyde.

That is not to imply that she may not have made unwise decisions,
and the readers can see that there had indeed been grave stresses in the
life of her young daughter but, in those days, there was no earnest
discussion of child psychology. Surprisingly, and rather touchingly,
there are moments when, in spite of harsh intention, almost in spite of
herself, Mary Butts finds herself writing appreciatively about her
mother.

The Crystal Cabinet is now offered to a new generation of readers –
more interested in the springs of human behaviour, less impressed by
the dictates of convention, more tolerant in judgement. It is an
astonishing work: there are undeniable weaknesses, yet it remains a
powerful evocation of a vanished world and a testament to a vision of
extraordinary intensity. It is time for Mary Butts to come into her own.

CAMILLA BAGG
Bradfield
Berkshire

1
Puddle and Princes

THE first thing that I remember is a puddle of yellow mud. Outside the front door, on the drive, after rain; when the new gravel had been put down and the gardeners had gone over it with a round thing that groaned. (My father said they were fools, because they would not think when to put on and take off the weights that were inside the thing: the thing called the garden-roller that would not move for one, however hard one tried. That memory comes later.) The mud in the shallow puddle was lovely, like something you could eat. It happened when the ivy on the porch and on the walls was smooth and glossy and shiny and dripped. You ought to be able to eat it – like cream or the yellow out of the paint-box; you ought to spoon it up. Perhaps something that isn't food and looks as if it ought to be food will taste all right this time. Nurse was a few steps ahead. Perhaps if it isn't sweet, it is yellow like egg. I had my best green coat on and a bonnet to match with fur round its edge that came off a beaver in the picture book. Dark green. With the gravel it would look like egg and spinach. Pretending (not quite to myself) that it was a real tumble, I splashed full length, and for the quick second, close to the ground where I should not be allowed to stay, my nose in the smooth wet, I put out my tongue. No good, and not so soft. Gritty. So that was mud-taste, the lovely yellow mud that gravel makes. The king – I developed early a child's sense of categories – the king of the muds. Now for Nurse.

I was swung up on to my feet: 'Miss Mary! Can't you see where you're going?' So she hadn't seen I'd pretended to tumble, and I was too young to think that I ought to tell. It was luck; and anyhow I knew now about mud. Disappointed – it always *was* like that – and yellow all down my front, which, when you came to think about it, didn't look nice; my hand tight in hers, we hurried round the high walls, bursting with starlings and covered to the shootings with ivy, to the kitchen door.

'There's your fine coat ruined. What work you do make, to be

1

sure.' Cook was severe: 'We'll have our work cut out, getting that off.' I was the tiniest bit sorry at this. I said the kind of things that grown-up people expect, but I had a question to ask. As we went up to tea in the nursery I ran back to the kitchen: 'Are you really and truly sure that you never cook with mud?'

One other memory goes with this. On the yacht, at Cowes, one summer day. Moored in the harbour, side by side, with all the other yachts. Father and Mother had gone on shore, and the men had gone on in the dinghy to buy things to eat and had not come back. Yesterday they had brought me a pair of new shoes. The dull brown leather shoes with a strap and a boot button, worn before the days of sandals, before the blessed summer nakedness of children today. Days when two kinds of drawers and two kinds of petticoats, a pinafore and serge frock imposed, as I can still remember, a very real strain on one's vitality.

They did not interest me, those shoes, and that morning I was short of interest. They must be made to do something. They must be made boats. I looked over the yacht's side. What with all those yachts lying up, the water in the harbour needed changing. Yesterday there had been a drowned cat, but today nothing so interesting. Newspaper and potato-peelings and orange-skins, and the dirty green too deep to see the bottom; and Nurse sewing and the captain busy and the sun hot and my jar of shells gone all smelly, and the anemone dead, and no going on shore, and then not the kind of shore for Interesting Things, and Father and Mother always going to a dull place called the Royal Yacht Squadron where you were taken dressed-up and it was supposed to be a treat and it wasn't. Even the tea there was dull, and endless grown-ups had to be said 'how do you do?' to. It was always being good and Mother said their names and that they were famous people and you could see she liked it but you didn't; and when would we sail away back to Weymouth and Dartmouth or the place where they spoke French? 'Sherberg', only that had gone wrong for they'd taken you into a shop that was a foreign shop to buy something to remember because it was the first time you had been abroad, and you'd seen in a second what it was. It was a lovely shell-box, pink shells and blue and yellow, all close, with a picture under a glass in the lid and crimson velvet all round, like kings; and later you could pick the shells off and put them in your real collection, not saying you'd found them, that wouldn't be fair, but not saying anything. And Mother hadn't let you buy it. Said you could get those shell-boxes anywhere and they were common when you could see they were beautiful; and made you get a doll because it was

2

different and 'none of the little girls at home will have one like it'. A beastly stiff doll called a brett'n sailor, a doll you couldn't make do anything or pretend anything. A doll you couldn't kill, and who wanted dolls anyhow? A doll they made you show to people, so that he came away feeling less like you than ever. A doll that, when the yachting was done and you got back home to Salterns, you would take out into the wood and torture to death. Punish him for not being that shell-box, put out his eyes and hang him upside down, and then bury him alive like that beastly wax one from Paris dressed up in yellow satin they'd said was Bonnie Prince Charlie. He looked quite different when he'd been buried under a stone and not dug up for weeks. You dug him up and explained because Daddy was there and he laughed: 'We won't tell any one, but, Bokins, what made you bury him alive?' And Daddy had understood that it was the right thing to do because he was so conceited. Besides he had dared say he was a prince and a prince who had been a very special kind of prince, and princes were not like that.

'You are right,' said Daddy, 'princes are *not* like that.'

Now you had come to Cowes it had been promised that you should see princes. Real princes and The Queen. It was getting hotter and hotter, and when you got on shore there was no proper beach. None of the dinghies, pulling in and out like water-beetles among the yachts, was our dinghy. You could make little moons on the white deck, in the soft pitch caulking of the seams. The shoes were lying beside the hatchway. The shoes were going to be boats, with a long stick to poke them about and splash.

The splash happened, two splashes. Then a shipwreck that did not last long enough, as they filled and heeled over and slowly sank, slipping down the green water like very slowly falling down stairs.

Mother was rather nice about it: 'Darling, what did you do it *for?*' Daddy said: 'It's time that child learned more sense.'

Just about that time there were the kings. First of all it was The Old Queen, but you'd been told that you wouldn't see much. Lifted up by Daddy just in time to see a carriage and pair and two wonderfully fast black horses, and a tiny old woman in it, holding up a black parasol. Driving back to Osborne Palace. 'You mustn't call it "palace". It's Osborne House. The Queen likes it to be called that.' I remember the sense of utter waste. 'But it's *like* a palace, isn't it?' – and heard my father's snort and something about 'the worst taste in Europe'. 'Never mind,' said my mother, 'at the garden-party this afternoon you shall see the Prince of Wales and his son, the Duke of York, and Sir Colin Keppel, who helped an Empress to escape.' I liked that man. At tea at the Squadron he had been reasonable about finding cakes that had pink sugar on them – knew that the sugar on cakes had to be pink and that an ice must have a green bit to it for magic.

So, that afternoon, in a garden whose gravel walks and stiff beds seemed very dull after the trees and shadows of Salterns, I saw the late King Edward and his son who is now our King George. Two men, dressed like Daddy, and as old as five could see. And was exceedingly disappointed, but not, and this I greatly resented, for the reasons Mother supposed and explained, out loud, to other people. A miscalculation of values that put even 'seeing kings' in the background. I was looking and heard her say: 'There they are. Those two men are princes and will some day be kings.' I said: 'I didn't think they'd look like that.'

'It's because they're yachting. In London they wear their crowns.' Then later I heard her explain – to the man I liked and who had understood about the cakes:

'Poor child! She thought they would look like the princes in her fairy-books, with swords of sharpness and shoes of swiftness. You should have seen her face fall.' I flushed, and a roundness rose in my throat I should never be able to swallow. Because it wasn't that. It wasn't their clothes. I knew they would be wearing what the other men wore. Only I had been looking for what I could not yet say – that they should look as though made, instantly, to the naked eye, for glory and worship, for the *separateness* of a king. While I was enduring that penance of childhood, its parents' innocent desire that it should have pretty fancies, do pretty tricks. Swallow, in fact, Peter Pan. In a spasm of shame and isolation – the loneliness of a child that feels itself made a fool of because of an emotion it cannot yet express – awareness of *meaning* grew. It was from that time that life ceased to be a matter of pure sensation. I began to be aware of the relations between things.

2
Fir-Cones

EVEN before the princes and the puddle another memory goes back as far as consciousness. Ties with them because at that time there was something in my mind that began to say: 'This thing has turned into that'. Not 'here is one thing and there is that', but that one thing is part of another thing, sets to partners with it; above all, that 'things out of doors' not only came back but went round.

The puddle was in winter, when the Dark began to matter more and more. For I was afraid of it – in the long, uneven corridors of an ancient house, before the days of artificial light. A house lit by patches of moon and fire, the yellow suns of one or two lamps, but principally by candle-stars. Tall wax shafts for planets, their capitals upside down, stuck into silver sockets; or carried in the round, silver-caged bedroom candlesticks like wandering stars. All natural lights they seemed, except the lamps; and fires were made from coal and logs, but best of all from fir-cones, the wooden fruits that came off the pine-trees and belonged specially to Daddy and to the library fire.

There was a law about fir-cones. They must come off the trees called pinasters. The others that came off the Scotch pine weren't big enough to be worth collecting. The others were five kinds – long and closed and pointed and varnished green, very sharp to the palm; long and closed and pointed and varnished brown and a little less sharp. Round and shiny and open in petals, a perfect flower of wood; and these, as my father showed me, turned at once into a flower of fire. Then there were the two others – open, rather soft, often a bloomy purple and apt to be damp, or, open, soft and grey. These needed to be dried, but once dried a bit, they passed away in a single flame, like sheet-lightning, in a breath.

In the spring after the puddle came the first knowing of the pattern on which life is strung. Awareness of the repeating earth, the beginning of all natural religion, its sacrament. A contact that developed quickly into a continual participation.

It was in the kitchen garden, kitchen garden and orchard together, beside the herbaceous walk. It was morning; the sun warmed the ancient, still enclosure, ringed with dark woods and stuck with ancient apple-trees; its paths crossing at wells, all bordered with clipped box hedges about two feet high. I stood in the walk and looked down into a clump of white arabis, just in flower, pushed about by a large black and gold bee. The light ran through me, the scent-releasing air, sap warmed and honey chilled by a quickening that ran cold and hot at once. Something was about like the smell of green, the scent of light; and all about me the talk of every sort of bird, in that place which was a sanctuary. All praise, a 'charm' of sound. So the sun was out again and the arabis, and this was called Spring, and the bees knew it and those birds; and I could not speak, but stood absolutely still. Then, at the same time, I wanted to throw myself down and rub myself against the ground – the earth I was not allowed to sit down on in winter, because the cold got up out of it and hit your inside. But Nurse went away and I ran up to the top of the orchard, to the old croquet-lawn, and lay quickly down and bit the grass, and breathed it in, smelling with the deepest breath I could draw; and rolled over and over nine times like the new moon, and jumped up, shaking off the little bits of moss that had stuck all over me – it was a very bad lawn – and ran down the garden towards the house. Feeling that I had felt something that ought to be felt, known something that ought to be known, done something that ought to be done. And could never be undone. Never lose that smell and that arabis and that bee.

It is by now my sincerest conviction that, of all the crimes possible against childhood, to deprive them of a country upbringing is the most dreadful of all. Especially in infancy when perceptions are awakened; especially at adolescence when values are realized and comparisons are made; especially in childhood when the nature and use of objects are learned and unconsciously related.

You can surround a child in a city with beauty, you can surround it with art, with gaiety and loving wisdom, with adventure even and the purest of the abstract forms. Yet, if you grow him there, you will grow him without the means by which to grasp the reality of these things, their relation to his body and its needs, their relation to being. For one thing, he will take human logic for the whole nature of reality, if he has never seen the sun shine on the just and the unjust.

6

Moreover, you will have deprived him of that food – the mind's counterpart for all the vitamins, essential as air and far harder to analyse – of which Lord Russell spoke when he wrote of a little boy, taken into the country for the first time, on a winter day; and how he flung himself down in a wet and uninspiring lane, with small animal cries of ecstasy: an emotion – I quote from memory – 'profound, primeval, *massive*'; feeding his tiny soul on the soil and the water and the earth-smells.

More and more we are assured that maladjustment to reality, external and internal, is the cause of all our woes. (Without strict definition as in what this reality consists.) But with regard to such primitive contacts the dirtiest cottager is given better material for his picture of the world.

3
Stones

THESE things happened between the time I was three and the time I was six. It was then that I began to know that I possessed things; and then, very sharply, that there were things I did and things I did not want to possess. A process accelerated by the business of the shell-box that I wanted and the doll I did not. (That doll would not die. Battered and hung and buried, he lay about for years. He did it on purpose, and my feeling for him never changed an inch.) Meanwhile, I desired, from the very beginning, books, and things I had found myself, birds' eggs, but with a deeper pleasure, bright pebbles and shells. These tastes persist. Today I cannot touch a lump of crystal, coral or amber, lapis or jade, without the deepest sensual joy. For this, as for all else of its kind, my home was singularly fortunate. Bright stones on the heath-paths were common enough to be found, rare enough to be exciting; and four miles away ran the lion-gold curve of the coast towards Studland, the sea-star and fan and heart-scattered Shell Beach.

There was the day when I found the Star-Stone. Where too I learned the Clean. Out on the heath with Nurse, on the narrow paths, the heather short in winter and black, and the paths of pure white sand and little stones. White paths to my eyes not yet three feet above them, paths between dark wiry heather borders, tinted with the faintest sparkle of gold and rose. The very clean. I trotted along with my button of a nose on the track, sniffing the rain-washed stones, the scent of the furze. Picking up pebbles to go into a cotton bag, swinging it to listen to the clear chink. Even Nurse said that stones weren't dirt.

As they lay on the path or in pockets on the moor, the pebbles were each one alive. Alive, in communities, in the stone-world. So clean that nothing grew on them; nothing stuck to them; and as the rain washed them they shone – the rain, or in a bowl of water or from your spit.

It was there I found it, a pebble the size of a blackbird's egg, one side sliced off to show a cluster of crystals of violet quartz. Nothing would persuade me that I had not discovered a great jewel. It went home to live in the stone drawer, and be king of all the other stones.

8

With another that was rose-pink and had a line of gold in it, called the queen; and they had twelve children, frequently changed, as one *mana* waned and another waxed.

Nor to this day can I go to a place where the earth is made out of any substance so essentially satisfactory without returning with samples – to lie in a bowl or the pool of a garden-stream, or stop a door or hold down papers – deriving from them still communion and delight.

About the time I saw the arabis, I saw something else, and because of this and the arabis began first to sort out existence into subject and object, myself and the world. These were the last of the very young experiences, after them life began to take on coherence and pattern; I knew there would be repeats, and new things that were part of old things; that however new would be the same, however alike, never exactly the same.

A little time before I had had a fright. On the huge Victorian knee-hole desk in the library, beside Daddy's standish you were not to touch, stood a small dim photograph, upright in an iron frame. The photograph of a very old man with a straggling white beard, not short and red like Daddy's, but white and flying, and above it the eyes glared; and it seemed to me that it might be a picture of God.

Till then I had taken 'God' as a matter of course. He was what you said your prayers to. There was only one of Him and He had made everything, but what made it mixed was that there *was* another one called the Lord Jesus; only it was only one, and you asked either of them for things that you wanted and they gave it you if you were good.

Suddenly I was appallingly frightened. If God looked like that, then something awful about a place called Hell which Nurse had talked about, and over which Mother and Daddy had been entirely vague, might be true and might be anywhere. My dead cat the cook had killed in a temper might be there because it had eaten a fantail pigeon. I went about sick with terror at the thought of that face. I did not dare go in to the library; yet, if I was alone in the hall, I had to go and look where the awful face with the glaring eyes and the white beard was standing on my father's desk.

Until the Mercy that keeps its eye on small children forced the question out of me, and my mother's voice fell like the dew from heaven:

'God, darling? No, of course not. Think of the boys you play with at old Miss Osborne's house. That's their grandfather, old Lord Sidney.'

But my father put the photograph away.

In those days I had a hiding-place, under the dining-room table, under the folds of the linen table-cloth that hung to the ground, over another that never showed, that had been a curtain, of blue and silver thread. A cave divided into three by the great carved paws of a lion, again that no one ever saw. For it was not really a lion but a leg, and in the dark I could curl up between the paws and listen, and sometimes at a luncheon-party steal one of the ladies' shoes.

It was from there, one day after lunch, I heard my father say: 'I put that photograph away. The child might think it was God again. I don't want her to be frightened.'

The last of the fear went then, went exquisitely. But the question remained: if God did not look like that, then He must look like something else. Perhaps 'old Lord Sidney' was *like* God.

Then one night I woke up in the nursery at some unknown hour of the night. I do not think Nurse was there. Only that I was told to get up and look. I ran through into the day nursery, knelt on the window-sill and looked out.

There, through the trees and above them and beyond them, beeches and firs, where the green lawn met the black pine-wood, were the stars. I knew what they were called, I knew that they were there, but for the first time I saw them as the host of heaven; and as I knelt on the ledge I saw that they were the same as the arabis, part of the same same; only this time, as well as participating, I adored. And have managed to keep the same eyes that saw them that night – the eyes of the same child. Understanding, without the least difficulty, that this was the answer to my worry about God, establishing in my mind where God was to be looked for, and how things could be called 'like' God.

It was from the same window, a little later, that I saw an adventure, this time on the ground, in daytime, this time among the roots of the same trees.

It was a wet day. I had to stay indoors. It was blowing, a huge sou'wester, except for the Channel seas the only violent thing in nature that I knew. Again I knelt on the window-ledge, watching the storm as it surged up across Poole Harbour from the Purbeck Hills. I could not think of it as anything else but a live thing, as visible as it seemed to Wordsworth that it might be. Not just 'South West Wind, Esq' as Ruskin called it, with our modern instinct to protect children by domesticating the wild, but a true daimon, as the young of each race first see power. Something like the Greek stories my father gave me and sometimes told me, only not in a book. In my home, roaring and straining and making the great boughs creak, which was the tree speaking, being made to speak by the storm. The bough below the hollow in the fork, where was the squirrels' larder. Bough of a beech-tree, round whose green-powdered trunk, in summer, I had seen seven squirrels running, and I had minded that I could not be them, but if you were a human being, you did other things. And even in winter, on warm days, they would come out and go to the larder and help themselves to nuts.

Not though in that rocking wind. I knelt, going with it, trying to get into it, and looked down to the left, on to the banks of the sharply rising pine-wood I since suspect to have been part of an earthwork and made by man. In the magic map a child makes of its home is a place apart from the green wood and the lawn, the orchard or the heath, or indeed any other part of the woods. A place about which, if I had been asked, I might have said: 'There are deads about it.'

High up I knelt and looked, on to the banks bright brown with needles; and there'd be a fine fall of fir-cones after this wind. All but the thickest trunks were swaying a little. All that was long and light tore about in ecstasy. The high branches, and down below the little bushes called arbutus, whose berries looked so all right and were always either teeth-setting or flaccid-sweet, as though they had just gone bad.

There was a little bush, doing a dance by itself, like a live child. Not the careful dances you had to learn, but skip and bounce and do what you like.

Then I saw, at the foot of that bush, a little man digging. He was rather like some story books. Only he was real. About two feet high, exceedingly thin, dressed in green with a rusty red cap, digging like mad at the roots.

'Oh,' I said, 'so you *can* see them.' I was not that kind of (often fabricated) imaginative child. Nor was I asked to assert – my parents would have thought it bad taste – in a theatre, out-loud, that 'I do believe in fairies'. The wind was different, and a goddess called Artemis who shot with the new moon.

I watched, breathless with interest, for some time. Then I saw him look up, catch my eye for an instant and he was gone. There was only the green bush whipping about in the gale.

I debated; and the child, debating pro and contra the reality of what it saw is substantially the same as the woman debating some variant on the same theme. On the whole I was satisfied that I had not been deceived. Yet one must be careful because it would be such fun to be taken in and I had already been told again and again how bad it was to deceive oneself.

I knew it was true. Yes, I did. I had better not tell anyone.

There were not many people to tell. You did not *tell* Daddy. He knew. (I think that I did try to tell Nurse, and that was a warning not to tell anyone else.)

So, holding my tongue, I went back to my pebbles, and in their chink and shine and colour and lick, or the hot smell and the flash that came when you knocked one kind called a fire-stone on a flint, began to learn the meaning of stone. The life, the potency that lives in the kind of earth-stuff that is hard and coloured and cold. Yet is alive and full of secrets, with a sap and a pulse and a being all to itself.

So that now, living in a country with all its bones showing, whose fabric and whole essence is stone, which is dominated and crowned by stones; standing stones on the moors, cairn and castle and 'coty-house', each field transfixed by a phallos; on whose beaches are found jewels, in whose quarries veins of marble and crystal: neither stone nor flesh are without contact one with the other, in extension of the contact made so many years before on the nursery floor.

My home was not one that had been for long in our family. Sometime after the Religious Wars we had left Norfolk, where we had lived since King John's time, and settled nowhere after for long. An eighteenth-century great-uncle had been Bishop of Ely, but from our ancestors we had inherited, not land, but possessions, and the love of them. China and silver, clocks, snuff-boxes, pictures, rings. A rather small, slow-breeding race, red-haired, with excellent bodies and trigger-set nerves. Persistent stock, touched with imagination, not too patient of convention and very angry with fools. Undistinguished since Tudor days, when we made some show, East-country squires, rarely emerging, often soldiers by profession. None too patient of our fellow-men – that trait repeats itself – profoundly sure of ourselves, for reasons best known to ourselves.

For reason of a secret common to our blood. A secret concerned with time and very little with death, with what perhaps medieval philosophers called *aevum*, the link between time and eternity. With which goes an ability to live in two worlds at once, or in time and out of it. Even in a further dimension of time. A secret which might make us devout. Or it might not. Incline us to mysticism, as in the case of my great-grandfather, Tom Butts, an official at the War Office, and one of those eighteenth-century types who combined respect for the Archbishop of Canterbury with the introduction of Swedenborg to the drawing-rooms of Fitzroy Square.

That was as far as we went in spiritual novelty. Quite far enough, whose secret does not ask that of us. Instead, as if to externalize it in works or to return thanks for it, old T.B. made the gesture such a secret asks of a gentleman, not by foisting on the world inferior productions of his own, not merely by his additions to our family collection, but by becoming the friend and the patron of William Blake.

It is Blake who has left us his portrait, the delicate impatient head, the dark eyes' brilliance, the sensitive lips just saving the whole from arrogance. The carriage of a hero – who never did anything we know of as heroic, unless one allows the amassing of those pictures, in water-colour and in tempera, half the best work Blake ever did; twenty years ago on exhibition in their entirety at the Tate Gallery; now scattered, but, when I was born, hanging at Salterns, in the eighteenth-century rooms my father to receive them had added to the house.

When I was fourteen my father died, an old man in his seventies. For various reasons and to meet death-duties, my mother, naturally ignorant how to handle such matters, sold them, inevitably for a part only of their worth.

This part of our story is here out of place, but since this story is, in part at least, the story of an un-making, the undoing in less than half a lifetime of the work of centuries, the first hint of that process may fall as early as it will.

4

The House

SALTERNS lay on the shore of Poole Harbour, the huge estuary, a
hundred miles round; and when, just after the Crimean War, my father
bought it, one of the remotest places in England. A young officer with a
distinguished war record, but an only surviving son just come into his
inheritance, content to leave his profession. I have heard him say that
he bought the place because, in 1861, you could walk down to bathe, in
the open sea, a matter of three miles, in your night-shirt. Half of Poole
Harbour is still one of the most beautiful places in the world. When the
filth, the tram-lines and villas that pass for civilization in this 'lost and
imbecile century' have rotted away, the whole of it will again be one of
the most beautiful places in the world.

When I first began to see, it was still in its perfectness. Yet as I
grew there began to be signs, noted by my father and he spat, by my
mother with equal scorn, of the intolerable, witless change creeping in.
The change that has since achieved itself, turning the north-eastern
side of the Harbour into what it is now. As a matter of geography, the
ancient town and port of Poole, which the Danes stormed and an
Armada ship, which Drayton in his *Poly-Olbion* gave for litter the four
islands, is now linked up with Bournemouth, twelve miles to the east,
by way of what was once the village of Parkstone. Now no longer a
village or a town, but a suburb of two towns, part dormitory, part slum,
part 'residential' district; and the old Upper Parkstone, where once the
clay-workers lived, round Monkey Island, which the gipsies had for
headquarters, is now a waste of workmen's dwellings, centre for an
ugly, unprosperous industrialism, displacing the land of my first
memories, the old, hardy, fragrant, rural world.

Salterns was not a large property, but the largest round about, and
made up for it by including half a dozen different kinds of local
countryside. Its garden, tended as it had been for more than a century,
a Perfectness. Less than a hundred acres, inland towards Bournemouth
on the north-east, open heathland the young firs were beginning to

encroach on. Then, towards the house, a mysterious belt of wood. Several woods meeting on rising ground, ending in a dark half-moon to enclose the garden and the house. Inside this cusp, the orchard and kitchen garden, below these the ancient white stables. Then a belt of shrubbery. Then the House. But the House turned its back on the hill and the woods; its green lawn ran out softly between the points of the moon, between tall beeches, with a garden on each side, and a terrace garden behind it opposite the front door, built out of the foot of the hill. On the other side, between the beeches, the lawn flowed down to fields, studded with oaks and descending easily to the high road; and two hundred yards on the further side of the road, flooding it at the high tides of the equinox, the Harbour ran; across the Harbour, like a child in its womb, lay Brownsea Island with its high bank of woods; and behind Brownsea the green body of the Purbeck Hills, like a naked god laid down asleep.

Place I shall never see again, now they have violated it, now that body has been put to vile use, such uses as men from cities do to such places as these; such uses as its own people do not know how to prevent. Now Salterns is no more than a white house pulled down and built on to, its back broken; split up. And in the fields are several little houses, like the one I am living in, little boxes of rough-cast; and beside each another little box for the car to live in at night. The cars that allow those people to run about the earth, and wherever they go to impoverish it. Driving out or abusing or exploiting something that is not their own; that, unconsciously, they resent – and would do well to fear. For when Nature ceases to be the Mother, the all-nourisher, you are either left without her, or with those aspects of her which are hostile to men who have not made their submission. It is only by obedience and conquest, or by blinding ourselves, that we cease to see how strange she is, the potential terror lying dormant, that the shifting of a stone will evoke. Again, the process is subtle and only dimly are we becoming aware of it – the effect on character, and so ultimately on survival-value, of the huge proportion of persons, now attaining political advantage and what they think is power, who have been born and bred out of touch with the rhythm of natural life. To that one might attribute much of the spiritual sterility of our intelligentsia, boys and girls taught to impose themselves, not what is imposed.

Place I shall never see again. Except from a long way off. From

Purbeck, from the top of Nine Barrow Down it is possible to stand and, on a clear day, see the maggot-knot of dwellings that was once my home. The earth that once had the sea in her lap, a lap full of country sweets.

The House was the kind of house the Dorsetshire gentry lived in, such as had not kept their Tudor manors, or were unable to let loose Palladio and his followers to build them a classic barn, with pillars and plaster and porticoes – strange taste in a county which produces the Purbeck limestone, the most beautiful of all building stones. Sometime in the eighteenth century Salterns had risen modestly, of white plaster and a slate roof. A large porch and large sash-windows, wood-divided into smaller panes; a long stone-flagged hall, and a conservatory stuck on the side that looked out over the hills. The central core, the old morning-room and library, later all one library, probably part of a much older building, with the eighteenth-century additions at each end. A lofty double drawing-room and a dining-room, the first one whole end of the house, and both rising straight up to the lofts under the roof. At right-angles to all this, the servants' hall and kitchen; the new wing, and this three storeys high, built by my father in my infancy, stuck on at the angle of joining.

The rest of the house was its hall, entered by the front door, flagged and wide, airy and shadowy, a delicately drawn staircase rising round three sides of it, lit by tall windows; and at night by a huge iron lantern, with bottle-glass doors, each with a coloured and one with a ruby eye. Victorian – Viennese – Gothic, and much later replaced by a brass candelabrum, hung like a pale gold crown, to burn acetylene candles, at that time an exciting innovation.

In that house a life was lived in some ways so utterly different from life as it is lived today that one despairs of a comparison. Yet, in other aspects, the continuity is unbroken. It was a profoundly English life. In the very last years of the old Queen, very little had been changed since her accession. Indeed, on 22 January 1901, in some ways we might just as well have said: 'Queen Anne is dead.' There was no bathroom and no telephone – not until nearly the end of this book. Apart from a rare visit to London, we went about on foot, in a brougham, on horseback or in a boat. Bicycles were a new game; and I remember a fountain-pen for a strange novelty that no one could get to work. The food was admirable, more limited in variety than today, but fresh as dew and largely home-grown. The maids wore their caps and aprons over scarlet dresses, the coachman our livery colours. Fine quality went along with a careful economy now much more rarely seen; and to my father, who had made a fine art of reticence, the least touch of pretension was the thing that must not happen. This my mother knew was his form of pride, less the quality of that pride than its value as an approach to life. Never were two human beings thinking so differently about the same things. Her desire was to underline and bring out; his to omit, until, through omission itself, something appeared that had classic line and distinction. All I was old enough to know was that what 'came out' of my father was something that carried with it a wholly satisfactory satisfaction. 'Like' the arts, of which I was just beginning to be aware; 'like' one's teeth in an apple, which was not the same as cake or the finest box of sweets. 'Like' the line of a wave against the bows of the yacht. 'Like' the turned words of Latin I sometimes heard on his lips. First intimation of the secret knowledge we shared.

It was the tang of his irony I enjoyed; his way to his way. That others were without it seemed to make their vivid preoccupations and romantic delights or serious enthusiasms somehow unreal. Behind my father's short laugh lay real knowledge; without it, story or observation missed the heart of the matter. I was too young to understand how marriage to a man so much older than herself, her isolation, with only one child in so subtle a place, with so alien a mind, thwarted my mother's youth. Drove her into dreams, who was offered reality under terms at once too strong and too remote. From a gay household of sisters, from moderate poverty and the merry interests of a country-town to the wood and wind-lulled quiet of Salterns, shared with a man who had reached his time for contemplation, the fruits of his understanding, who had never asked to share them, unless, implicitly, with one small child.

Still less, while he lived, did I see the suffering caused by it all, nor realize that one day, when her time came to make up for it, she would go out to dare life armed only with clichés about things as they ought to be, the romantic play-words made into passwords which had once consoled her loneliness.

What we all appreciated was the energy that made her throw herself into the adornment of the House; that the strange accumulation of spoil my father was content to possess, contemplate in some platonic ether of his own, should be seen in their loveliness.

In a neighbourhood stagnating aesthetically, as only the provinces at the end of the Victorian age could stagnate, Salterns was remarkable. With no great house near to challenge comparison, nobody had anything remotely resembling it to look at – a place where there was dark panelling and noble furniture, lovely toys of ivory and tortoiseshell and enamel, mysterious paintings and china from the East and from the early exquisite days of the English potters. Silver and musical instruments and little old pictures of battles on copper, and brass polished to the colour of pale gold, and miniatures and seals and snuffboxes, and thirteen grandfather clocks, and swords.

Apart from the Blakes and one discovery made later, little of any great rarity or value, but beautifully displayed, both for show and use, and intelligently increased.

It would look very wrong today: the rich confusion of an interior by Browning, the moon-flawed vistas of Rossetti – who my father knew in his last days, who was coming to visit us when he died, and who deeply influenced his taste – an out-moded chiaroscuro in comparison, say, with the chaste, choice austerities of Mr T. S. Eliot.

But a good nurse for a child, and the education it gave me had an advantage often denied to the child of present-day enlightenment – that I was allowed to have my own taste. I was allowed to begin on Scott and Dumas and Ingoldsby and enjoy them; I was not expected to admire Donne or Wordsworth; and when Doré's Dante became a favourite picture-book there was no one to explain that it was bad art, that Blake or Botticelli had done it better.

Neither of my parents had ever dreamed of the science of up-bringing so popular today. They applied a rule of thumb handed down the centuries whose chief points were clean hands, civil manners, no tears at minor injuries; not to read books with dirty hands or leave them about on their faces; if you were given letters to post not to look at the addresses, and never, never, under any circumstances to say anything that was not true. In comparison with that God did not mind anything.

Also, and this so long as I was very young, without any nonsense or affectation, that I was, in a sense, a person apart; that I had privileges implying duties and duties that gave privileges; that because of these certain things were forbidden – I might not wear any ornaments or tie up my hair with coloured ribbons, and my clothes were plainer than those of many children who went to the same dancing-class; and every day, for twenty minutes, I had to walk round the room with a book on my head.

Things like these, all related to something I knew that my father held, which made a crime that tied with untruthfulness of the faintest gesture that looked like showing off. Outside these he would say: 'Leave the child alone.'

So for the first ten years I ran free, free of the house, the heath, the woods, the garden, the fields and the yacht, the salt-marshes from which the place took its name. Running alone I learned not only the shape and colour, the likeness and the difference, but something of the inward being of each separate thing. Not only one kind of tree from another, but one tree from another tree; one flower, leaf, fir-cone, apple from its neighbours. One stone from another, sand of the shore from sand of the pits. Clay as against gravel, leaf-mould, garden earth or the green harbour mud. Running water from water in a wood pool, a clay-pit, in a bath, in the marshes, in the sea. Taste of saps, green pine-needle to rose-petal, every bird and each.

I was avid for more and more experiences like these. It was a profound sorrow that near us there were no running streams and, taken to one, I could not bear to leave it; or, conversely, it was too sweet, and I would run away from more pleasure than I could endure.

I longed as well to see enormous green trees, 'like the kind William Rufus was shot under'. Caves, cedars of Lebanon, or wistaria growing all over the wall of a house; snow. Turned over and over again in my mind that in New Zealand there were whole mountains of rose-pink stone; that in China there was a river washing over a bed of jade; that there was a place somewhere in America where fountains of hot water spouted up and black bears came in at the back door. Thinking of the nautilus steering over blue glass seas, of the dreadful rocks of a place called Kerguelen, and a thing called the Aurora Borealis; the awful splendour of the King of the Condors above all birds. Most of all of the Himalayas, standing across the north of the world from the plains of India. There was Mount Everest no man had ever climbed, and behind that was the country called Thibet, where none of the soldiers who came to see my father had been allowed to go. The high places, where there were snow-leopards and turquoises to walk on; and behind that the grey world called the tundras, ice and snow and marsh and magic and mosquitoes and the end of the world.

Gradually, with nothing said about it, like so many bricks provided, my father supplied me with material for a picture of the world. The cycles of antique story-telling into which man's consciousness has passed, that pleased me as they please all children, the first pleasing that never wears out, only deepens and re-quickens, like resource to a well-spring, a hidden source of loveliness and power.

The gardens at Salterns were blessed with fourteen wells. (And to this day, I have very little idea why. For if they ever did, and heaven help us if they did, they no longer supplied the house.) They stood at the crossing of the orchard walks, round and ivied and one with lead lions looking down into it. You found them in the shrubberies: there was one in the wall of the old terrace you could only get at sideways and shove stones in through a hole in the brick, and there was a hollow plop a long time after the stone had been pushed through. There was one with an echo and one in the stable yard, no coping, but a neat hole with a white flagstone over it, and the coachman very hard to persuade to lift it up, and he would never leave you to throw stones into it by yourself. The only hope was when he was busy, after a long drive, washing off the carriage mud. Then the thing to do was to hide behind the bank till he came out with his bucket on the end of a rope and sent it clanking down. Go off and start sluicing with it behind the brougham; then, after several journeys, stay and work with his brush behind in the springs. Then you could scurry out and stand in the wet patch round the open mouth and look down. Water that showed very bright and pure. Out of a clean dark where no frogs bred and where, in summer, because of the stone, no hedgehogs looking for water could fall in and be drowned.

Before I understood it in any way about people, I could not endure to think of animals being hurt. Then came the first understanding of that sorrow. It was on Weymouth sands, and Nurse had left me alone for a little, in my sand-pit, with a book. The book had a story in it about an eagle which someone caught and blinded and put in a cage. Suddenly I found myself crying, seized by an utterly new sensation, of helplessness and agony of mind. And saw my own tears, beads of mud on the dry sand. Something was coming up inside my breast and clawing at my throat. It was a different kind of being unhappy.

I asked God to comfort the eagle, and was then a little comforted. But in the story no one had cared. The beastly people in the book would not let it out of its cage. I could not let it out. When Nurse came back she did not understand in the least. That made it worse. I felt that I and that eagle were alone in a world become suddenly much larger, and full of things happening like that. Alone with being miserable. (I do not think that I tried to tell anyone else.)

With its wells outside, inside the House there were thirteen grandfather clocks. *Spécialité de la maison* and one of my father's favourite toys, their winding and synchronizing and timekeeping a play of his old age, and to his child a great assurance of the friendliness of things.

There were two grand ones that stood face to face as you entered the hall. Of mahogany, one all marquetry, with voices like clear bells; one played a tune at the hours and the quarters, and its face told you the phases of the moon. So did the one in the Blake Room, his song sometimes a second behind the other, from the furthest end of the House a sweet voice answering, and fun, however bad for time, because you heard it twice over.

The one in the library was the greatest friend, an old brass face and a solid tick that went with the tinkle of the fire falling low, the shrill roar of dried fir-cones bursting into flower, the steadier roar of logs, the mutter and cheep of the established fire, its dying sighs. A brother to the one at the top of the back stairs, a farmhouse one with a white face painted with a man with a scythe, reaping.

One stood by itself in a recess by the window on the front stairs, a lean dark clock, exceedingly old and eccentric with age. It had a tune on five notes, but it played it when it liked, breaking out into song at its fancy and for as long as it liked, till we did not wind it any more.

There was another that I remember, a spinster of no particular character in the old morning-room; and another that talked sensibly at the foot of the nursery stair. Not one of them is in our possession now.

When my father died, the clocks ran down. No one seemed to understand the keys, kept in a brass-lined spittoon, with a tortoise for a body, on whose head you trod to make his back stand up. For a little time some were kept going, and when my stepfather arrived, one or two for convenience. But no longer twenty-four times in a day and a night was the long house filled with voices calling the hours. Sometimes followed by a laggard, and my father getting himself out of his battered leather chair to bring it into line with the rest.

5
Fear of Pan

NATURE shows herself to man essentially under two aspects, Loveliness and Power. A description that fits also the primal creation before he has tampered with it. It is also safe to say that without the experience, from the first, of power and loveliness man need hardly take the trouble to be born. Nor can he experience this, at his beginnings, except from its source in the external world; which source again, over large tracts of the earth, he has obliterated in favour of his own works.

There is something both disquieting and pitiful in the sight of a young nature raised principally on streets and on people and on books. A rough specimen of childhood such city-raising sometimes brutalizes and, invariably, through a subtle want of training of the senses, makes under and over intelligent. But a sensitive child grows into a strange creature, often abnormally introspective, curious of others, full of notions not corrected by experience, got at second hand, full of *ideas about* rather than *experience of* life, and bewildered when it does not happen according to his books.

Among educated people there seems to be a deliberate blindness about it. I have heard a mother of distinguished reputation, questioned on her determination to bring up her children in London, explain: 'But here they have the cinema. I think it most important not to take them away from that.'

A case particularly surprising in its results.

But at Salterns, at the dawn of my life, Power and Loveliness walked naked over East Dorset, side by side. Lay down to sleep together like gods on Purbeck, rose out of the dawn-washed sea. Aphrodite and her lover bestowed themselves in a nut – as where the Deity was seen by Juliana of Norwich – a shell, an adder basking, the bracken pricking up its hood, an owl sailing with lamps in its head.

Though the loveliness comes direct, power, as Wordsworth was at such pains to make immortal words explain, is not so easily learned by a child.

22

It seems again a rule, an unalterable fact of experience, that a child comes to know power through the experience of fear. As it happened to Wordsworth and seems to have had a great part in making a poet of him. (And what makes Wordsworth so important to us, that we hang on his lines and thrust our whole beings into their interpretation, but, in part, his interpretation of fear?) He would have had no child spared that; as fear of the Deity was called wisdom's start, so fear elicits the imagination. The imagination that in her most exalted state is one with reason; as he shows again, when he makes poetry and Euclid the two ultimate possessions of man.

A great deal of cant is now being talked about protecting our children from fear. Along, as usual, with a great deal of sense, if parents went sensibly about the troubles that rise in youth from a botched approach to reality. Yet it is normally forgotten that if a child is brought up in an almost religious certainty that everything in the garden is lovely, what will he do when he meets the snake? The slug and the innumerable caterpillars; the blue tit caught by a cat, the badger starved and broken in a trap?

A garden is the best image of the kingdom of heaven man has made, a nursery in the natural and the supernatural order at once. Yet now the nursling is no longer told about Eden for fear of encouraging him in the habits of superstition; has it rubbed into him, in place of the Catechism, that 'every day and in every way Man is getting better and better' – Man, not men; that 'Science so loved the world that it sent down its only child Evolution to take our nature upon it'. That infant must occasionally be puzzled by what he sees actually going on.

Fear he is bound to meet, and without, so far as I can judge, any satisfying explanation for it, once he is outside the securities of a man-fabricated world; fear not as a discipline, an approach, a means to a fuller apprehension, the reward for whose conquest is interior power, but fear likely to become blind fear, because it must always be explained away, never faced, let alone embraced.

Witless Fear. Mindless Fear – there is another name for it – Panic Fear. That old god, waiting in the woods or behind the flower-beds or up on the screes will give them a taste of it, whose feet are not set, like Pheidippides, on a race which makes the thyme-spray a palm and death the victor's crown.

I remember – I grew straight, and the loveliness came first and the fear after, the fear one has to face so that strength should not be sterilized out of loveliness.

I was afraid, when the great gales blew, of one or two trees, creaking and straining, 'with groanings that cannot be uttered'; of a particular fork and a limb striving, and the look the tree had on its face.

Out in the woods, of the whole mad clangour in the tree-tops, their possession by a rocking, shrieking power.

Of quiet in the woods, what would slip out from behind the tree-trunks, trotting on the empty paths.

Of the high cliffs most of all and the awful seas breaking on them, a lift of green water and then roar and ruin, cruel white fingers lifted up the rocks, and a mystery of torn water and myriad bubble clusters. A sight I saw continually from shore and sea.

Of a little breeze, fluttering on stones and waste turf, or round a barrow on the high places of the downs.

Of dark places where a fallen tree had rotted, of a toadstool, a dead rat. Where corruption went on quietly. Of untroddenness and a tangle of savage thorns. Down in a hollow of the outer woods, by a place called Hawk's Larder, where a shrike had stuck up its bits of flesh on a stump. I did not mind that, that was birds; but a few yards off the core of a tree lay rotting, and I called it to myself a place where things went bad.

Of corruption anywhere, a cabbage stalk, an apple on the ground with wasps writhing out of it; a dead bird, the white breast-bone showing foul feathers and worms feeding on it. Of the world you came upon when you suddenly turned over a stone.

That my body, so Nurse said, would be eaten, like the bird's. I felt sick and trotted off on one of my private expeditions to the library to find Daddy and ask if I might be embalmed, till the trouble all came out, and looking at me with his sunk, sea-deep, brilliant eyes he made me say after him the verse that ends: 'yet in my flesh shall I see God'.

Of the Harbour mud, the miles and miles of it, at each low tide the intricate green flats, threaded with slow channels. A crust of green weed, but underneath it the wrong mud, grey and greasy and with all those deads in it. I had seen our dog, struggling to join us when we had put off at low tide in the dinghy from Lilliput Pier. He should have gone back with the carriage, but the coachman could not catch him, and the fat old terrier staggered across the flats and began to sink and howl most miserably. Until John, my best-loved of the crew, backed and stuck out an oar for him, and he held on very cleverly and was somehow got on to the pier again. Still less, in that state, was he allowed to come with me on the yacht's milk-white planks; and we left him, looking after us, whining and most unhappy; and the coachman annoyed for fear of his white breeches, calling him back; and not even Daddy saw that after that awful fright he ought to be comforted, decks or no decks.

The first dog I remember, and my first word of Latin. My father called him 'Why', because he was a present from a sensitive person, and because he turned out to be a cur.

In these ways I was made aware of other forces, patent or lurking, in the ordered loveliness of my home. Forces, as I began to see dimly, man could not master until he knew how to play with them – was it not a pride of seamanship to sail the *Vanity* close in till her bowsprit overhung the Hook, the deadly sandbank at the mouth of Poole Harbour; then put her about and swing off on another tack, while you ran to the stern to look for the bones of the great ship, wrecked there some winters back, now nothing left but her broken back and her ribs, wedged in the golden sand?

On that part of the Dorset coast the cliffs were white, white and mighty, the cliffs of the Isle of Purbeck from Studland to Swanage. The side that ran into Hampshire, our own side, we despised; yellow crumblingness, good to dig in, but which ended in Bournemouth, and that was bad enough for anything. A place where you could not even dig and had to wear your best clothes always, where Daddy went to a club and Mother to shops or to pay awful calls, and in all ways you despised it. The long drive made you feel sick, and you might not talk much, and all the way back in winter, with the wind sighing in the trees, the dark was enormous and there might be wolves. Would Jeans drive fast enough? Would they pull him down off the box? Would Major gallop home or would we have to throw someone out? We could let them have the parcels first. I *knew* Daddy would never throw me away to them. It was only partly a terror, in part one of the Awful Games that children love.

Yet on those dark night-drives you remembered things, like the white cliffs, miles off, you watched in summer from the sea; burning white and blue waves dancing at them and up the floor of the cave called the Parson's Barn. A floor of white pebbles, and the men rowed you in gently; let you scramble out and dash up its beach, and there were rose-red anemones and green sea-lettuce and coral weed, scarlet in the pools, and black flints where the chalk had worn away, out of which you could strike fire.

It would not be like that now – the Other Side, the things that

25

happen when you are not there, had come in and taken possession. I knew well enough the ravening fury of whiteness, pounding in and out of the cave, roaring up to the roof, thundering at the roots of the bones of the earth. All that was going on there all night. The horse's feet went clop-clop, the brakes went on and off at familiar hills. Outside, the fields and the lanes were equally in the power of the winter and the night. Yes, winter and night were two awful powers. Even the wind and the sea were less, were, in some way, under them.

I got that clear. They were the Lords that were the opposite to the things one usually wanted. Then, because a soldier's daughter must not be afraid, because if she meets a thing she is afraid of she must get as near it as she can, and because God is everywhere, I began, when I was about eight or nine, to make myself run about the garden after dark. (Besides, it was the cats' day and I was conscious already of a great sympathy with cats. Not dogs – cats.) I had an excuse – to take the letters down the drive, though the fields, to the pillar-box by the bottom lodge, to catch the early morning post. Hardly over a quarter of a mile and, once out in the fields, fairly safe. But in the pitch-dark drive that led from the house – that was another matter. Especially once I had read *The Hound of the Baskervilles* – a book that quickened an always lively sense of an *immediate* supernatural. Sending me out with dread, bringing me back, white and panting; and making the end of each day preparation for the twenty minutes' endeavour of each night.

6
An Enemy

I HAVE not set foot in Bournemouth for twenty years, and only trust that I shall never do so again. To a small child it was a place where people lived differently, and one did not see how they could be happy in a place where they could be looked at all day long. At Salterns no one could look at you unless you wanted it; there everything was your own. Besides, there was a miserable little stream that ran through the place they called the Gardens, where Mother and Daddy supposed you would like to take your boat and sail it with the other children, while all our nurses sat looking on, crocheting on the round green seats.

'After all,' they said, 'it's a stream, and we haven't got one at home.' 'Not a real stream,' I thought, 'they've had to put steps in it,' and what I meant was that, as an amusement, it was beneath contempt. A stream you had to go to in your best clothes, a stream you mightn't paddle in or even get reasonably wet. (There is a tariff of dampness each child has with its nurse, dampness and holes and clothes to spoil or not to spoil, whose every clause is of vast and sometimes tragic importance.) But in Bournemouth there was only the intolerable: 'You've got to play like a young lady for once.' Because of this I hated the beautifully rigged schooner yacht I was given. All the more as, just emerging from babyhood, I did not see that what lay behind it was my mother's innocent desire to be rid of me while she shopped, and to see me, prettily dressed, playing in a seemly manner with other seemly children, in what was still, at that time, a select watering-place. Children who made 'nice friends', not the ragamuffins I picked up with the moment Nurse had her eye off me. As she rarely had. For until I was seven and sent to my day-school, I saw very little of other children.

But here it was as bad as the dancing-class; and the little boys always got the grand boat away from me. I did not mind that, but I did not know what to say to other children; for directly I found out and we began to play 'I-shove-you-into-the-water' Nurse would come, and

27

they'd say I was no good – little girl with a nurse always and carrots anyhow.

This did me harm, checking contacts, for I was in many ways an obedient child. Daddy would have let me get wet and get used to the other children, but Daddy was at the Club, and Mother was shopping or paying those calls, and there was only Nurse.

It came to an end – was somehow realized as unsatisfactory; and this, to the best of my memory, I owe to *Treasure Island*.

I can remember my father saying:

> *Fifteen men on the dead man's chest –*
> *Yo-ho-ho, and a bottle of rum!*

and I soon got the rest out of him; and the next time I was bidden to take my boat and what my parents in their innocence called 'play' in the gardens at Bournemouth, I had an idea. The yacht, carefully concealed in the carriage, was launched with several small dolls hanging from her yards, touched up with red paint, and bits of them gone and their heads screwed round; and on the deck sat the Worst of the Lot, and by him one of those tiny liqueur bottles that used, I think, to be found at Christmas among the best boxes of chocolate.

With triumph I pushed the boat along, singing to an audience in sailor suits which soon became a chorus:

> *Fifteen men on the dead man's chest –*
> *Yo-ho-ho, and a bottle of rum!*
> *Drink and the devil had done for the rest –*
> *Yo-ho-ho. and a bottle of rum!*

Thus singing and tramping, with the intense concentration of small children, we managed to get some way downsteam; and it was some time before the inevitable hurrying figure came along the path, and the inevitable voice said: 'Miss Mary, that is *not* a proper song for you to sing.' Nor did it matter much, for the next instant I was aware of my father, standing a few yards off, coming to fetch me on his way from the Club. Leaning on his stick, shaking with laughter; and when we got home, he said: 'You don't like it much, do you, unless you can play like that?' I shook my head; and soon after that I was sent to a day-school, where it was supposed I should find children to play with.

So a town came to represent a dull place, where your clothes were always best, and the only hope was that out of the shops there might come something to eat. Only in winter did they take on some quality of magic life, when, wrapped up and excited, one drove away, up strange drives and into strange houses to the children's parties that were given there.

Children's parties – candlelight and lamplight memories of them, lovely and exciting and kind, or sometimes dreadful when, on the drive home, still far too excited to remember anything but tearing about, I would be told that I had not been good.

I remember though, far more clearly, a first Vengeance taken on a society that had failed to please. I remember that I was five because I was told after, very gently, that I was old enough now not to have done that, when, at Mrs Dawson-Damer's, I did not get the present I wanted. Perhaps there was a child too many, or my present had been judged too old. Anyhow a horrid little boy screamed for it and got it, and all that came to me off the tree was a rubber duck that squeaked.

'I don't like this present,' I said, and Mother said: 'Hush, darling', and a vast old lady with a red face, in black satin all sewn with shiny beads, looked distressed. At home I *was* sorry, partly because Mother explained so gently that I should not have said it. Explained well, for I still remember why little ladies must not say things like that.

But next day contempt for that duck returned. Contempt that I saw that Mother, at the bottom of her heart, shared. ('. . . considering how *very* well off Mrs Damer is.' I heard the tail of that sentence to Daddy.)

'I'll show her,' I said, 'what we think of that present'; and, tying a string to its neck, I dragged it out on a walk with Mother, all the way up the wet lanes to my aunts' house. Explaining that we must go the long way round so as to pass her house, 'The Elms', in the hope we might meet. And Mother, pretending to be shocked, laughed delightedly and we were friends; but my grandmother, her mother, was shocked, which showed how much *she* knew, and we left her house feeling that we had both been naughty together, and enjoying ourselves very much.

Yet I remember that it was instantly possible to forgive old Mrs Damer when my Mother explained further how she had never had any children of her own, and so did not know what one would or what one would not like; and it was interesting to make up a bit in one's prayers to tell God one had forgiven her.

It was the instant of writing that restored this – a thread of blue wool lying on the writing-table. Then the quack of a duck outside in the garden by the stream. A thread, a string, a duck, a duck with a collar of blue paint. Then a party, with a large black old lady with a red face. A disappointment, gentle reproaches, a vengeance, and an awfully good joke. Ending in an understanding, my father and my mother's laugh; and what a small rubber duck looked like, dragged for hours on a string through the mud of the Dorsetshire lanes.

7
The Two Romances

It was perhaps my greatest good fortune that, without pretension, without cant, with a sound soldierly contempt for the 'soulful' or the 'artistic', my life was saturated with the arts. With the visual arts as with nature, a foundation of classic and to some extent of modern literature. To my father, old soldier and something of a scholar, the inheritor and the treasurer of Blake, the admirer of Whistler and of Wilde, these values were more than the tastes of a country gentleman – they were the essence of his being. A man whose tragedy – and I suspect my father of some tragedy, perhaps of apprehension, certainly of incompleteness or why did he make no more use of his brilliant gifts? – lay in an inability to express himself. Too virile for dilettantism, he practised none of the things that composed his nature, with its delicacies, its harshness, its candour, irritability, prejudice, and its natural high spirits. A nature which had flowered only in this, in his superiority, unconscious as a noble child's, to meanness, spite, self-seeking, jealousy, snobbery or any of the common pretensions and defences of men. In this he was perfect – *anima naturaliter*. There my mother, with her vigorous, romantic, emotional nature, truly religious, but uncoordinated by the least touch of subtlety or intellectual love, was far from that understanding. It is true that she learned from him; but no one can learn what they cannot learn, and to try is a sure way to error. Nearly sixty at my birth, he was more than thirty years older than she. Incapable of that irony or that experience, her judgements were based on her desires, on the romance she felt she had missed. With the only too familiar result that, long after, left in control of our affairs, she was easy game for any man (not woman) with a tale to tell. My father's charity was grounded in irony and long experience of the world. Hers was not. With the consequence that, of all our inheritance, there is little left but the memories of this book.

31

From the beginning doubtless the shadow of these things fell, but none in any way intelligible to me. At least until his death. Except perhaps one thing that puzzled me at the time, that remained in my mind and has remained. For it is an old belief that incidents whose significance is at once trivial and profound are not recalled fortuitously.

We were walking in the fields, my mother and I. I must have been about twelve, for I remember that my father was beginning to 'fail' a little. The *Vanity* had just been sold, and my mother was glad who hated the sea, and I too young to realize how terribly I was to miss it. It was evening and very hot. I remember trying with my toe the burnt, glassy summer grass. I was full of a book of Kipling's I had just read, and a poem in it that moved me, as later, at the end of adolescence, the mystery of being was revealed by *Les Préludes* of Liszt. A poetic delight to be blushed for on post-war standards, and today it is a little difficult to know what one thinks, but which then seemed all that a poem should be.

Walking down into the hollow where Mother had planted daffodils and pheasant's eye narcissus, to dance in the grass in the spring wind and carry the eye down the lawn and through the fields to the sea, I quoted it:

> *Thy face is far from this our war,*
> *Our call and counter-cry,*
> *I shall not find Thee quick and kind,*
> *Nor know Thee till I die.*
> *Enough for me in dreams to see*

(the internal rhyme intoxicated the half-trained ear)

> *And touch Thy garments' hem:*
> *Thy feet have trod so near to God . . .*

Then my mother broke in: 'Oh, but he means something almost dreadfully high. He calls it "To the True Romance". But that's not what one thinks of as romance, not like the love of Lancelot and Guinevere. It is something we shall only have when we get to Heaven. Perhaps only want . . .'

To the brutal lucidity of youth this seemed one of those disappointing moments when, about poetry and other things, grown-up people had just got it wrong. Whoever supposed that Kipling would bother about Lancelot and Guinevere? Mother seemed to think that those kind of stories were the best stories in the world. Lots of grown-up women seemed to. When the really only interesting thing about King Arthur was the Grail, and Tennyson didn't tell you half enough and that too piously and one suspected with the reallest part left out. (I had not yet struck Malory or the 'high History'. Chiefly taught by a book, not written for children, on the 'matter of Britain', a gift of my father's and mostly unintelligible. A book which must have grounded me well, but its name even, except that it was a learned one and made me feel grand, is lost.)

If Kipling meant anything at all about King Arthur, he meant the Grail, and not like Tennyson. The real Grail, which was the most wonderful thing to think about in the world and Mother had got it wrong.

Very soon after, thinking it over, I saw why. The extraordinary beauty of my stepfather, his high manners and respect for my father, his lovely gaiety and deep admiration for my mother had fallen already across the threshold of Salterns, shadow of a plume dancing, a form at once ardent and lovely, wind-fed and charged with fate.

This I saw and understood with entire simplicity of mind: that Daddy was old: that he must soon die: that here was a perfectly gay and beautiful person we had always known, to love Mother and take care of her and give her a good time, and make up to her for the things she had missed. I was perfectly prosaic about it, so far as I thought of it at all. (Though knowing it was a thing people were supposed not to be simple about, and a little worried by that.) But Daddy would not *want* to go on happening once the fun had gone out of things. And Mother, I could guess, was frightened; her own happiness, sitting, waiting like the sun a little way over the horizon, waiting its turn. Afraid she was going to break a thing called the Seventh Commandment. Or was going to be made to break it without being able to stop. Only it was going to be all right. Daddy and I had come to one of our wordless understandings about it; it was one of the implicit 'knowings' that no one but us could or were meant to understand. He knew and I knew; and of course Mother wasn't going to do anything she shouldn't – adultery, whatever that was. Why, anyone who cared for them could see it working out; and of course Uncle Freddy was awfully handsome; and if his brains wouldn't so much as cover my father's little fingernail, that didn't matter. Yes, it did matter. It would matter later on, like his drinking such a lot of whiskies and soda.

But to drag Lancelot and Guinevere into a poem about something else – that was a thing which reason said did not matter, which something deeper than reason said did matter very much. It might matter later on. When Tony and I grew up. Tony was so very clever. It might be like having no father at all.

Consciously the Blakes had very little influence on me. The picture *The Four and Twenty Elders* did not look in the least like the Book of Revelation. And I had seen a picture of Sir Isaac Newton in a wig, and could not see why Blake should have drawn him naked, sitting on a rock, tracing figures with a compass on a strange green ground. Nebuchadnezzar now – he might have looked like that; but as for *The Good and Evil Angels, Struggling for Possession of a Child*, I only hoped my Guardian Angel didn't. I used to stand, scowling, under the awful picture from Milton of Death and Sin. Beneath it, in a half moon against the wall, stood a marquetry card-table of the period, folded in half, with gilt-bronze feet, and the most beautiful dark green shells, inlaid in perspective on the pale wood. Tables like that and the china that stood on it were made at the same time as those pictures, and it didn't fit.

Indeed there was only one picture that possessed me, and that not fully, until I knew Macbeth.

> *And pity, like a naked new-born babe,*
> *Striding the blast, . . .*

There was the dreadful, sculptured night sky, and Pity, in the hands of a mounted spirit passing at awful speed, leaning from her horses to place the child upon the body of the earth. Upon a woman, lying as it were from horizon to horizon, her hands folded on her breast.

On this I brooded, and on the engraving from the Book of Job; *When the Morning Stars Sang Together*. Until slowly, not the execution but the conception, the kind of seeing that there was in William Blake, in the end affected me both unconsciously and profoundly.

There were plenty of other pictures besides to contrast with his – a Lely of Louise de Querouaille, and one remembered Daddy laughing when a painter came to see the house, and after looking at her said: 'I would sooner have painted those breasts than all the Blakes in Europe.' There was a point to take off from.

There were books also, splendid in tall bookcases with glass doors. And some of them Mother said you ought not to see, and most of them Daddy allowed you to see if your hands were clean and you turned over carefully. Pictures of lovely naked men and women – the end of a conversation between my parents sticks: 'Why shouldn't she look at them? D'you want her to have a dirty mind?'. 'It's just what I don't want her to have.' Then the four blessed words: 'You leave her alone.'

My mother's puritanism, exaggerated, even in her day for a woman in her position, was to be the seed-plot, and later the hot-bed, for tragic misunderstandings. For my father never managed to eradicate it. If he had, it is no exaggeration to say that all our history would have been different; that he did not was probably, in his relation to her, his greatest failure as a man.

One does not know how far he even tried, remembering something of his idleness, his indifference. Also the time-spirit was against him. A Victorian soldier, who should have belonged to one of several other centuries, and who had strong attachments to the eighteenth, he had doubtless his own repressions. It is not likely that he formulated them. Rather he laughed and shrugged. Sometimes he sneered. Besides, the age set stress on what it called 'purity of mind' and it is doubtful if he saw far enough where her exaggerations would lead her. (Also the anti-puritanism of the nineties was itself a hot-house plant. Swinburne and Baudelaire were its oracles, not Blake. Not Herrick or Landor or Swift.) My father had a taste for classic candour, for Burton and de Maupassant, for Brantôme and Rabelais, which my mother believed to be pornography. A belief that led to the appalling sequel to his death.

There was another kind of picture about the house, eighteenth-century landscapes of woods and hills and lakes – probably painted in Italy. Blue woods with a bloom on their foliage, a sense of profundity, a colour-steeped richness that completely fascinated me. So our own woods looked, exultant, with the pulse of summer in them. And there was one of a storm, the glare of the evil and terrible thunderlight, the quenching of the sun, of all radiance, by a white light, supposed once to be the light of hell. Or rather to be the physical expression of a supernatural quality, lying as it were behind the natural world, visible only in a translation; and which that particular state of the weather made visible. Translations which are being made all the time, and the analysis that science makes of the mechanics of the change no explanation of the thing itself, or substitute for our direct experience of it. At least that was what I gathered that it meant, in different words and from an old book of my father's whose very name I have forgotten.

A set of pictures which, in the old courteous phrase, were 'a great grace' to me.

Over music I fell a victim to a stupidity of education; and the reason that to this day I cannot play a dance for my friends or accompany an old song; or, strictly out of earshot, work out a theme of Mozart or Beethoven, I can only trace to my relations' very natural desire that I should be able to do these things.

There were admirable musicians in my mother's family; my father had done much in Bournemouth, in its early days, for its famous symphony orchestra. Backing Wagner; and it was believed that for twenty years he had not spoken to a near neighbour and enthusiastic amateur because he had heard him mention Beethoven with disrespect.

(It was also said that, about the same time, he had seen him ill-treating his horse; and the two together, like the twin snakes on Hermes' stick, had decided my father against him. Brought him to one of his queer, over and under-rational decisions.)

Obstinacies and prejudices they often seemed, and which my mother, carrying on the tradition of wifely obedience, made sacrosanct. Sacrosanct, when she should have teased him out of them, and thus greatly enhanced his opinion of her. Instead, as even a child could see, she spoiled Daddy, and it is often a bore to be spoiled. Partly because she feared him. A fact that bewildered the child who had nothing to fear.

For in all the pattern of our relations I do not remember a time when I did not know that my father and I stood with the same support beneath our feet. Bows of a ship, stone flags or polished wood; strip of turf or heather or garden-path, we walked the same road, had the same precinct about us. Brought it with us, much as Santayana says an Englishman does the weather in his soul. Not arguable or discoverable even with the mind, but shared. We were woven of the same piece; and death, for I knew he would die soon, only an incident. And if he was disappointed that I was not a musician, that 'practising' for me meant picking out the notes of a song and, as I rode my rocking-horse, bawling it out of tune, he lived just long enough to guess at a compensation – that what to him meant musical were, for me, verbal sounds; that the harmonies that ravished his fine ear his child translated into words.

So far these memories have not often brought me past babyhood.

Sense-perceptions crystallizing out, and for background an infinite security, the order and leisure and busy-ness and well-being of a cared-for if solitary child. Yet from my seventh year, seven years before my father's death, I remember myself dimly restless, with a need I knew for a need, to find an instrument for a sense that was working in me – a need, a powerlessness and a power – that had something to do with the names of things.

What things were called, the names that began with a big letter and were called proper; but you could not do what you liked with them as you could with the others, which were called common; and life seemed to be rather like that, with the things that were common and the things that were proper, according to Nurse.

I would not learn to read. I did not like the look of those little long-shaped blocks that were called words; that split up into letters which did not look the same when you made them in a copy-book for Nurse. Books I collected with pride and passion, dusting and arranging them in a bookcase I had been given for my own. I was never tired of being read to; I would turn over pages and look at pictures, re-telling the story to myself. But I would not learn to read. I remember still the curious state of mind, half defiant and half afraid; due to my being, all my life, a bad starter; and there was no kindergarten to help me. A peasant nurse, herself hardly literate, was not the person to help. Nor was the depressing story Mother told of Daddy – how *he* had taught himself to read by the names of people over shops when he was *four*. Daddy, who in so many other ways had been gloriously wicked; who had made his little sister sick, and in some accounts *killed* her, by giving her the cigar ends to smoke the dandies in Hyde Park had thrown away. Who had spent a crown piece he had picked up on ten whole pounds of *damaged* raisins and, eating them all at a sitting, had nearly killed himself. Who had never so much as laughed out loud once when a monkey at the Zoo stole the fob and seals put away in the tail-pocket of *his* father's great-coat. Who – but enough of Daddy; who at this point had the good sense to arrange with my mother that I was not (except on Sundays) to be read aloud to any more until I had learned for myself.

Inside I was almost thankful. Now I was for it. Part of the worry though was fear that I never *should* know how it was done, and so be different all my life from other boys and girls. Even other grown-ups. The one grown-up who had never learned to read. I should never be *sure* which of the little black marks were which. Even printings were different, and everybody's own writing; and there was the awful thing called Black Letter, which was the way they did it in some of Daddy's old books, that he could read – Daddy who could read *everything*, who had a little girl who could read *nothing*. How dreadful it all was, and perhaps he would be so ashamed he would stop loving me – for now I had to, I should find out for certain I couldn't.

I found out one wet morning. I had come in from my walk, and Nurse had gone downstairs to see about lunch. I picked up *The Yellow Fairy Book* nervously and, looking at the pictures of a story I liked, found myself reading it without any difficulty at all. I rushed at Nurse on her return: 'I can read! I can read!' 'And about time too,' was her very proper answer. But Father and Mother, if sceptical at first, were pleased.

The fear was not quite dead. For several days I read only that story, for fear that the magic gift would go away and the little black squares not make words any more if I tried anything else. A little later I risked it. It *was* all right; and soon it became a question how to keep my reading within reasonable bounds.

It was then I began to wonder why I had taken so long, and to understand why my mother used to be annoyed, saying that I was 'slow at the up-take' and telling me I ought to try and be quicker when asked suddenly to do something. Exhortations which, at the time, paralysed me. The first serious maladjustment I can remember, and I still seek for an explanation of it. Circumvented by discipline and by experience, under certain conditions it is still there – a shrinking from a sudden quick turn when the course is supposed to be on the straight; above all, from the start of a new physical activity. A hindrance in temperament, partly overcome, partly made serviceable, but there. Yet once the transit is made, an extraordinary exhilaration comes with it, as if generated by the psychic resistance at the start. Yet again, on looking back at my life, I am appalled, on account of it, of opportunities missed.

But now I had at least done one thing that had to be done, mastered the secret of those little black marks which were the names and the actions and the qualities of everything that went on in the world. Lots of them went in pairs. Pairs that were perfect were called rhymes. Pairs that were not perfect you could not use for rhymes. When you fitted up words to end in real pairs, you made up the thing called poetry.

There was good poetry and bad. Men who made up good poetry were called great poets, and were the most wonderful people in the world. They were also called geniuses – which was not the same thing as came out of the bottle in the *Arabian Nights* – but you could be a genius in other ways than poetry. Here home was reinforced by my mother's elder sister, a deeply intelligent and cultured woman, with a genius for teaching, encouraging, solving the difficulties of small children. She was born, alas, rather too early and into wholly the wrong environment for the high public position and recognition which her gifts – among others her gifts as an organizer – would have brought her in a more intelligent state of society.

She never married, pouring out to this day her unstinted usefulness on a neighbourhood, grown during the course of her long life from a village to the most dreadful of partly industrialized suburb. And I know no more grievous loss to the world than what it has forgone in the narrow scope and under-employment it has offered such women. Nor, in depriving itself of their children, its deeper loss.

But my debt to her surpasses any words that I can ever find, as great a debt as I owe to anyone in this world. It is also, alas, a debt which I cannot pay. For what my inheritance from my father enabled me to do, and to become, for her has little or no interest. In a sense I am his fulfilment, fulfilment of the name he gave me and the race that bred me. And this is not true for her.

Actually, it was from her as much as from any other person that I became aware of the infinite significance, the living mystery of words. Lessons I learned with an ease in extreme contrast to my utter stupidity when conventionally taught a subject with which I felt I had no concern. But at the start my aunt was always there with a new verse or a lovely line or a new story out of the treasury of English words.

Yet even to her I could not tell at first what I had to do in order to feel quite right inside – to learn to do more than get choice words by heart and think about them, but to make up new ones, make them do what I wanted them to do. Choose them for myself, make them go in pairs, say *my* say. Make up the tunes which were just as much tunes as piano-tunes. Only they were word-tunes and I knew, I knew – not how it was done, but that I could do it. The *Lays of Ancient Rome* (this was at the very beginning, before Kipling) were tunes, made up out of little tunes inside, turned into pictures and then mixed-up. 'Lars Porsena', the two words, was an air, sweet with something terrible in it. There was the running-up tune about the boar. First you ran down: 'That slew the great wild boar'. Then you ran up:

The great wild boar that had his den

Amidst the reeds of Cosa's fen,
And wasted fields, and slaughtered men . . .

Then you ran down again: 'Along Albinia's shore'.

Then there was the man who lived in a castle 'O'er the pale waves of Nar'. Nar – what a name for a place, high up and far off and right back, where Awful Things, even if the poem didn't say so, must have happened before even Rome had begun.

But the best bit of all was about the fighting, and how I hoped Daddy in the Crimea had fought like that. There was a coloured print, taken I think from some earlier engraving, *Ensign F. J. Butts on the Heights of Alma*, very crudely done as I remember, but Mother was very proud of it. There he had the regimental colours in one hand and a pistol in the other, which I hoped killed people, but I could never get out of him whether it had ever been like Horatius when

He reeled, and on Herminius
He leaned one breathing-space;
Then, like a wild cat mad with wounds,
Sprang right at Astur's face.
Through teeth, and skull, and helmet,
So fierce a thrust he sped,
The good sword stood a hand-breadth out
Behind the Tuscan's head.

Good word 'Tuscan'. Then silence, and you began again, slowly:

And the great Lord of Luna
Fell at that deadly stroke,
As falls on mount Alvernus
A thunder-smitten oak.

Had Daddy fought like that? Even Mummy seemed doubtful and Aunt Ada not sympathetic about those sort of questions, and when the maids said they were sure 'the Captain wouldn't do such a thing' that was about all you could expect.

Round and round the geometrical, box-bordered beds of the Dutch garden I went, walking deasil, shouting the *Lays*. Shouting inside my head, and sometimes, when I was sure no one could hear, out loud; dizzy as a child likes to make itself, going round and round, waving an old scimitar, its blade wavy and notched to points, I had found in the loft – a treasure.

And the proud Umbrian's gilded arms
Clashed in the bloody dust.

In a slow, rich articulation of syllables, a sense of finality conveyed itself. 'Bloody dust', two short old words, as it were tying up all that had gone before.

Out of the *Lays* there came later, long before I had heard someone say that they were not 'real' poetry – and I don't believe that I ever thought they were, only that they did something that I wanted to me – a verse from 'Battle of Lake Regillus' which took me the first step into the profoundest spiritual adventure.

What, I asked my mother, was:

Those trees in whose dim shadow
The ghastly priest doth reign,
The priest who slew the slayer,
And shall himself be slain:

(Why I did not ask my aunt or my father, I cannot imagine.) My mother, most naturally in pre-Frazer days, did not know. But she always tried hard to think up an answer and, though I could see she was puzzled, said it must be a kind of heathen prophecy about Our Lord. That might have done, but somehow something told me it was not the right answer. The Romans were heathens then. Not their fault, because it was before the New Testament, but prophecies, surely, belonged to the Bible? No, not quite; the Romans had the Sybil's books, only she didn't prophesy about God, only about what to do. Somehow preserves seemed to have got mixed, and even Mother hadn't got it right.

Here entered again the fatal flaw that, afterwards, was to do such infinite harm to our relations. Mother was not only puzzled, she was nearly shocked. Here was an awfully mysterious Interesting Thing, and Mother, instead of being interested, was thinking of words like 'irreverent' and 'not quite nice'. Mother was always hiding behind that. So were lots of grown-ups. I knew – and that was painful because one ought not to feel things like that about one's mother – that she was wrong. She ought to *want* to know. It hurt that she did not want to know – as it was to go on hurting. Throughout all my growth, when, in a child, the candid brutality of the developing intellect knows no mercy.

I was standing at a mysterious door opening. Mother was looking shocked. One of the doors into the Garden of Eden, as I dimly guessed. Looking across a threshold into a garden, where I saw, not trees, as it

41

said in the poem, but the Tree. The Golden Bough growing, the Tree of Knowledge, not yet of good and of evil, but of pure knowledge; and already I saw man, not Heaven, forbidding me its fruit. The Tree that was Yggdrasil, the Hesperidean, the Irminsul. In whose boughs I was to pass as many nights as Odin. With Adonis and Atys and Osiris, the reward of the vigil the key to the understanding of the book called *The Golden Bough*. On that Tree lose my faith; on that Tree die with them as a witness to its resurrection.

All begun with a dirty little yellow copy of somebody's *Penny Poets for the People*, in the nursery at Salterns, more than thirty years ago.

8
Our Children

In theory at least, children are brought up differently today. We hear a great deal about the culture of our picked children; a few advance specimens are just arrriving at manhood on whom the new theories have been tried out and it is just beginning to be possible to estimate their worth.

In my day much of it would have been called plain spoiling (and it is wonderful how, under pressure, even the most advanced parents today, hard put to it, will revert). Part would have been called a recipe for a prig; some dismissed as immoral lunacy. The new ideas on up-bringing seem certainly to suffer from a want of first principles, from a standard of values, or a clear idea as to what education is; what it can do and what it cannot do for a child. Together with a pained indifference to nursery lore.

They assume a whole new series of standards, without much inquiry into their implications. There is extreme tenderness to the child as a person, indifference to it as a unit in the groups which make up our society. There is exceeding kindness to the child's intelligence and to his emotions, ignoring his moral being as completely as a medieval nursery ignored his psychology. Getting out of this by the simple expedient of denying him a moral nature; which means, in effect, denial of the existence of good and evil in the world, or of any need for him to discover his relation to them.

We are beginning now to notice these products of enlightened nurseries and advanced schools, the independent, cocksure children, physically admirable, free with their opinions – and sometimes piously anxious to echo the most knowing of all their parents' knowing friends. Riders roughshod over parental frailties and preferences, and exploiting, as only a growing child knows how to exploit, their tenderness and solicitude.

Conscientious young parents today suffer from a new sort of bad conscience. They *may* have been injured themselves in youth, and are so hypnotized by the literature that has grown out of *The Way of All Flesh* that they suffer from a secret fear that whatever care they take of their children may mask a hidden selfishness; that, if they do anything with regard to them that makes their own life easier, they are doing it at the children's expense.

Unconscientious young parents – but that is another and funnier and more sinister story.

To small children nerves, grown-up nerves, are fun. With no unpleasant consequences to themselves to make them think twice, adult exasperation to a five-year-old is a source of pure joy. A lark. It is only in very rare children that you find the rudiments of compassion. A perception it is hard to arouse, dangerous to overexcite. Nor are they often really cruel – their torments, to which parents today feel it their duty to submit, spring from curiosity and primitive humour and triumphing life.

To the child it is all very stimulating and flattering the fuss that is made of him now. Often healthy when his egotism is not over-nourished; decent when sexual curiosity is satisfied, not excited. Yet it seems, in relation to man and his present world, to rest upon a curious kind of idealism. Rousseau's assumption that man is naturally good, crossed on Darwin's that he is chiefly a beast; brought as it were to the boil, that each fraction of each individual has the right to full expression – in origin a misunderstood left-over from Christian philosophy. Boiled over by the post-Darwin assumption that, thanks to Evolution, every day and in every way we are getting better and better. But, finally, taken off the fire altogether by the popular determinism which denies, with all supernatural sanctions, that man's being is under the control of his will.

With this pot-pourri to guide them, our advanced educationalists are out to give the child as good a time as possible. Amiable intention; as Zadig said to the Angel: 'But . . .'

Another thing they forget is that, given a reasonable chance, a child will look after its own good time. Again, that without knowing exactly how to ask for it, he desires direction for his energies. For his pleasure as much as for his work. That

> *All play and no work*
> *Makes Jack a young Turk*

as I heard an old nurse say, certainly a bored, over-mischievous little beast of Jack or Jill.

In my own early training the vital errors came at adolescence, after my father's death. (Errors he would have been too old, supposing he had understood them, to prevent.) Only a training, the fortune of my lovely, quickening home apart, that would be supposed, on current standards, to lame me for life.

I do not believe that it did. The wounds I did receive came from a deeper level of reality than any theory of education. Instead, I believe that I owe to those earliest years the chief impetus and the proper use of my powers; that such desire and such capacity as I have for truth was balanced and quickened there; that the justice I was set to learn was neither temporal nor arbitrary nor snobbish. (There were efforts to tamper with that standard made later, but they were made too late. It had been set.)

However, the assumptions on which my *first* training was based are hardly those of today. My parents were in authority over me; I curtsied when I spoke to an older person. I really was supposed to look up to my parents; I took it quite happily for granted that what they did was right. Perhaps I had not forgotten the rubber duck, but once I spoke pertly, and partly to show off a new expression about old Mrs Damer's red face, and my father's reproof for impertinence, one of the very few I can remember, withered me up.

There were sins. Lying was the first and worst. Then 'not being brave'. Anyone might feel frightened, but not to try not to be was the second worst thing in the world. Other people had feelings and I was to consider them. Other people had things, and I was not to hurt or paw them or hint that I would like to have them; and Matilda and the Dwarfs was taken for a very real moral lesson indeed. I had things and I was to share them, but never on any account brag about them or show them off.

As to what my fourteen-year-old daughter today calls cheerfully 'Sex', – I never gave the matter an instant's thought. Like any country-child, I knew how animals were born, and supposed vaguely 'we happened' in the same way. When my brother was born I was nine, and Nurse told me the usual mixture of nonsense and hush-hush. On which I reflected, saw that it was nonsense, that the baby must have grown inside Mother just like a colt or a kitten and told Nurse to shut up. Which, after a slight protest – I remember that she looked at me shrewdly – she did. And then again I thought no more about it.

It was far later, long after puberty, that difficulties came, and then largely through revolt against the vicious refinements with which, at that time, the whole subject was treated. But never, I protest, with agonies of thwarted instinct or a false sense of sin. Rather I grew to look on the people who should have helped me as poor afraid creatures, afraid to enjoy themselves, afraid to tell the truth to themselves or to anyone else; realizing that the Victorian age had raised a special series of taboos unknown in any other. That it had not always been like that. That now Mr Shaw and Mr Wells had come to the rescue, the problem did not exist. 'Sex' was there for our delight. Fear or even mystery had 'no more dominion over it'. And with this fresh set of fallacies to guide me, in utter innocence of body and mind, set off on my adventures.

To return now for a moment to the new education. It seems possible to trace its more obvious lunacies not to its semi-scientific theories – they have more or less come trotting along behind, brought in later to fortify an emotion. For there is one thing that seems clear about our age – for the first time in England, at least since the seventeenth century, the foundations of society have been jarred at their base. With one result that people are not now so certain of their right to bring children into the world.

Of this one result has been that a sense of paralysed apology has crept in between parent and child. And along with a brave and tender wish to spare it mistakes that were made in the past, there are the external difficulties. Everyone is much poorer. It looks like another war. They must all be prepared to work for their livings – which is a very different thing from having to work. The prices are not what they were. Nor are the loyalties. The old pride – in the regiment, the ship, the shop, the university – has lost something of the old, uncomplicated satisfaction. So many homes where a family, a race, has grown like a great tree, the treasures of so many generations have been sold. In the onward march of the nations towards the foundations of the New Jerusalem whose distinction is that it will have neither Throne nor Altar nor Lamb. That's the way the money goes! What a world!

Very few children are naturally grateful. No sane parent asks for gratitude from them, which is the flower of love. Their business is to train the child into proper recognition, reasonable give and take, which is the root of family life, as family life is the basis of all human society. A baby has only rights. A child's growth is measured, in one respect, by its growth in duties.

Is it today? Today a child is reasoned with, bribed, coaxed, praised, persuaded, thanked – only there is far less of the unquestioned share in a partnership, which means, by the nature of things, a proportion of dull jobs and services, done in obedience, without question.

It is largely a question of stress. Praise is good and encouragement and recognition. Only there lurks behind it now, whenever the child is being difficult or behaving badly, this strange new fear in its parents' minds, a fear which can be heard, muttering to itself: 'We made this thing. How *do* we know what's best? Are we stifling its emotions? Will it get a complex? Does it understand? What will happen to it if it does not understand? We must make it understand. Will it hate us?'

Unless the parents are concealing sadistic instincts behind all this, or the child is abnormal, it will not. What it will do is to sense the uncertainty of purpose and play up. Play it up for its own heathen ends, and, strangely enough, resent it. It is a way, by losing its confidence, to lose its love. For if, with Pascal, 'nous brûlons du désir de trouver une assiette ferme', how much more is that true of a child?

Here again we see the Advanced Parent, insisting on reason in season and out, often in the secret satisfaction (he can stand it) of being sure of *his* plate, forgetting the child.

In one of the wisest of contemporary books, Mr Duff-Cooper, writing of Talleyrand's boyhood and the education, incredible to us, of the high-born children of the eighteenth century, brought up never as individuals but solely in the interests of their family, shows how the 'modern method reflects greater credit on the parents; but evidence is not yet sufficient to prove that it produces a superior type of individual.'

I was, without doubt, given reasons, and above all explanations, of low order and insufficient quantity. I can recall one that enraged me, when an amiable person, asked about the stars, replied that some people said they were pinpricks to let out the light of heaven; and though I was so little, I was only puzzled at the time; later on I hated her for talking a kind of silly poetry about a Real Thing. This though was an 'explanation', not a train of thought. The real point is that, until they reach the age of six or seven, the reasoning faculty is not in full working order in the brain of any ordinary child. There is a subtle *un-reason*, an inability to catch the connection in the most brilliant baby. Think of *Brave New World*, and the story of the howl that for a generation put an end to one line of psychological research.

But now the young father and mother, their central belief in their own authority somehow sapped, seem often to try and bolster it up by appeals to reason, whether the child is old enough or not. From the cradle it must be made to understand, recognize the arguments why it should do or not do this, that, that or the other thing. One result of which is strained nerves, temper, and tears.

When what Jane wanted was to be told what to do and be made to do it; not be presented with an elaborate choice of alternatives, depending on calculations she cannot yet make, piling up on small shoulders a load of conditional clauses. Nurse knew better: 'It's one thing or the other, and make up your mind, Miss Jane, for then you'll have to stick to it.'

I have seen children even in their early teens made half hysterical when too many elaborate decisions were left to them, while I sat by the fire, reasoning away out of pure conscientiousness, so as to be quite sure the children would follow the plan that pleased them most. To be made aware of fidgets, sighs and a drawl of discontent. Until I plucked up courage to pull up short with what I'd decided myself as best for all. To be surprised at the content, the instant appeasement that followed.

Again, your quick five-year-old learns easily to exploit those arguments it has plenty of use for as a means of getting its own way: 'I don't understand: I won't go on till you've explained.' It has a grand time with that, holding up everyone's convenience for its own, and subsiding into howls should a decision go against it.

'Its own way' – that is the heart of the business. Shaw said somewhere, and all young parents to be were deeply impressed, that the misguided creatures look on a child as a little wild animal to be tamed, when it should be regarded as Evolution's last experiment in eternal life. Generous and loving parents reacted to that. Yet five minutes in a nursery shows that a child's own way, undiluted, would lead it straight into its grave. To which the answer is made: 'Yes, over a minimum of physical things. In all other ways let it express itself to the utmost; on that its character and its happiness depend.' Which is really an assumption that all children are born angels, and its logical conclusion the negation of education in any form.

(That, I believe, has lately been tried, in a school – one has a vision of prostrated homes – where the children beat the masters. A school that closed owing to the nervous breakdown of the teachers, not of the taught.)

Yet the balance could be struck and justice done to parent and child, so long as the parent believed that the ultimate reason for his labour, his authority and his love was the interpretation of an eternal will, on which depends all the glory and vitality of created things.

With that belief in his mind, that the raising of a child meant, as it was said once, that it 'might glorify God and enjoy Him forever' – *then* it was possible to take a realistic view of the creature under his care and what it was best to do with him. Parents no longer believe this. As to the beliefs, however aimiable and enlightened, on which he is trying to work today, what ultimate authority do they give him for trying to interfere?

All he can do, logically, is to see to the child's health; see to it, so far as he can, that he is not unhappy, a negative task. On his own beliefs what further *raison d'être* has he? His business is again to *spare* the child to the utmost; since, finally, all he has to offer it is pleasure as a means of escape from 'the pains of this ghastly world'. He is no longer the guardian and the companion of an immortal soul; neither father nor mother have received a commission from any supernatural world.

So we have this curious spectacle of our rather wistfully apologetic parents, picking often non-existent stones out of their children's paths and piously walking on them themselves. Or forcing on them elaborate descriptions of the mechanics, the variations, even the aberrations of sex to satisfy a curiosity that has not been aroused. Answering – I have heard this – the question 'What is God who lives in the house called Church?' with 'Hush, darling, you mustn't talk about that.'

If at Salterns there had been no enchanted gardens, no woods or dim dangerous marshes or bright stones, if there had been no art there or lovely things of silver and ivory and wood, I should still owe it one supreme thing, that it partly taught me and at very least allowed me to interpret life in terms of 'la primauté du spirituel'. That all these things were made by God. All was to be referred to God. All was or was not according to the mind of God. All made easy for a child to understand in terms of life and play, growth and adventure and courage.

I sometimes shiver when I watch children being brought up without a vestige of this, comparing at least the formal school training of other children and wondering what on earth it is all about; facing a father and mother, as embarrassed as their grandparents when asked where babies came from. This kind of dialogue:

'People needed to think there was a God who made everything, and so they built churches.'

'For God to live in?'

'Well, where they could meet and think about him.'

'Didn't God make it?'

'We don't believe that now.'

'Who did make it?'

Here the father interposes saying it is now more a question of 'what' did.

'Things, very slowly, made themselves.' Pause.

'What started things making themselves?' Then one is back at the new theophany 'that Science so loved the world that it sent down its only son Evolution to take our nature upon it. . .'

Along with the segregation of men in cities and for the last three generations the breeding of him there, this widely diffused atheism seems to be a new thing in human life. Coming as it has, at a moment of extraordinarily increased power over the mechanism of nature, its results baffle calculation. Yet one thing seems fairly clear, that at few times has so much rubbish been believed, not by the half-educated but by the highly-educated. The class we have named the Intelligentsia. That rarely has it been possible to sell, to the best fanciers of ideas, the most obviously ill-bred pup. 'Fancier of ideas' – that perhaps is the trouble. For ideas are not to be fancied, but examined for their relative truth.

Rubbish, often *faisandé* rubbish, not only chattered about and played with, but printed, published, paid for, made effective.

Bosh – a newly devised, semi-scientific bosh. Or, most painful of all, a semi-mystical bosh, with a vacuum for nucleus on which mysticism rests. This is what has happened to the townsfolk. The countryman has his own way of staring through these things. The countryman – God help him though if these people get at him, teach him, as they are trying, to distrust his ancient loyalties, his primitive sense of reality. Bring him, as they say on the radio, 'into touch with modern thought'. By which they mean their handbook scientific hypotheses and dish-wash of literary culture. Always at third hand, never the immediate contact as when a flint is struck with steel.

Yet, after all, it *is* the intelligentsia who have the tradition of European culture to hand on. Only we are afflicted today with a generation that has 'theorized itself silly' and in so doing betrayed its trust. Or, as Monica Curtis said: 'The intellectuals feel it was really they who landed us all in the soup, because they none of them knew what they wanted, and at the bottom of their hearts they believe it is quite time someone slapped them and sent them to bed.' Did not know what they wanted; have no standard for their values; there is the heart of it. Even the people who know what is wrong, a Jean Cocteau, a

Wyndham Lewis, slaves to their own neuroses, maimed by some subtle psychic castration, waste their years in denunciation, personal squabbles and sterile, brilliant distortions; in spites and suspicions and futile *amourettes*, when they might, as it was once said of Dr Johnson, be tuning-in Europe to their spirits.

Behind it all, outdistanced, outmoded, half-discredited – as Voltaire in 1778 by the Paris wits: 'Voltaire est bigot, il est déiste' – stand the two figures, once prophet, now one part G.O.M. to one part Aunt Sally, Mr Wells and Mr Shaw. Two men who, in their day, for all they have done in parergon, have helped pull down the intellectual structure of Europe, as much as Rousseau and Voltaire. And in a minor degree, the exquisite genius of Lytton Strachey – the *feminine* genius, as Wyndham Lewis sees – contributed to this. Not consciously, and with compensating beauties of pure style the other two never achieved, saved by something like the innocence of genius writing about persons such as Gordon whom ultimately he did not understand. Saved also by its generosity, making, for instance, his praise of Newman more penetrating and more lovely than many of his professional admirers when he writes of the hours 'glistening with the fresh laurels of spiritual victory, the crown of an apostolic life'.

No, it is not so much Strachey we have to blame here as the deadly club of his imitators. We all know them now, the pert young men, scurrying like earwigs under the feet of their betters, and charting the thin places in the sole. Books like Plomer's *Cecil Rhodes*, ephemeral as pastry, for the reason that they never come to grips with their subject at all; and spreading far and wide the notion that human greatness is all a matter of luck, of showmanship, of a conditioned reflex: isn't there. Depends on cunning: depends on economics, self-hypnosis, cash, homosexuality, impotence: does not exist. Or, as is so painfully apparent in a number of cases, was the result of an obsolete belief in the existence of a Deity, as creator and sustainer of the world. Which is absurd; and now that such belief has been fortunately exploded, we shall presumably have to do without that sort of greatness again. Though not one of them in a thousand could tell you the reasons why.

To such uses we are putting our superb opportunity – greater in some ways than man has ever had before. Perhaps never before have great bodies of men, all over the earth, had so fair a chance, so many good, plain, tangible means of establishing their lives on the double basis of reason and spiritual intuition, of experiment and authority. The eternal question of his food-supply so far as production goes is

51

solved. Transport and communication more solved perhaps than they need to be. It is difficult, for instance, to see what end is served that an ageing *amoureuse* in Spain should be able to ring up her fancy-man in New York daily; for him, breakfasting with a more attractive stimulant, to growl and spit into the instrument, yell 'static' and ring off.

Still, for one use or another, we can do it. The use is up to us. These things and with them one half of the human race permitted the full use of its powers; and, for the first time, the records of the past open to us.

All these goods, or neutral but powerful things, we have gained, and the prophets were a help. To be left now without such prophets as we had; or such prophets in their dotage and more than half discredited. And one has not heard that a second edition of *Landslide* has been called for; such men as Charles Williams have their hundred readers. And – well – we know the people who have their hundred thousand readers today.

To have got so far, and then seem to be spoiling it all. It might be less disheartening if the accumulating evidence of ancient history, and of the pre-histories, now becoming something more like history, did not suggest that, by natural law, the process is inevitable. One out of many repetitions, long lost, now resurrected by the archaeologist to tell us that this is the story of all high civilizations. The decline after Rome, until lately, we could dismiss; the factors now are not the same. But suppose we become more certain, with every decade's digging, that, under one set of terms or another, this is what *must* happen to the natural man? It is no good saying that Spengler was one of those appalling Germans who are born nuts. His facts remain; and his 'audacious attempt at a synthesis', so far as I know, unanswered except by assertions based on faith and on faith alone.

Faith in what? That is the point. Faith in the ancient philosophy, the work of Christendom on the Greek and the Roman mind, which says that there is a deliverance for man from the blind processes of natural law? Not a bit of it. Faith in this new Deity, Evolution, and in man now become his own deity, held with an uncritical tenacity which may do some credit to the hearts of our intelligentsia, but none to their heads.

The intelligentsia – not the scientists. They as a rule keep their months shut and get on with their work; and in England at least, if a recent questionnaire is accurate in its results, a majority of them are theists if no more. No, not the scientists, but our publicists. (Some few of whom are actually men of science.) The bright band of the

Whalxylites, the Gerald Heards and Julian Huxleys, the company of Father Knox's *Broadcast Minds*. Men whose message to mankind, like the old taxi-windows, falls naturally under two heads. One, that every day and in every way we are doing more what Evolution tells us, and our children, from half a century to a millenium or so ahead, will be grateful to us. Or, (and this is more up to date) that every order of knowledge, from the new physics to the new psychology, assures us that it is our fate to know less and less about more and more. Or, as Mr Heard says, we have escaped 'into inescapable ignorance'.

Omitting the corollary – that if you prove by means of the human mind that the human mind can know nothing, and since you have only arrived at that conclusion by a process of mind, thought, all you have proved is that you cannot prove anything at all.

So matters stand very much as they did before, and, as Aurelian MacGoggin said, 'We must all worry along somehow for the good of humanity' with the help of such Newtons and Beethovens, such Bacons and Pasteurs, such Platos and Rembrandts, such saints, soldiers, architects and scientists as illusion cares to send. Remembering that if there is no proof that their work has any significance, there is no proof that it has not.

Unless perhaps, one day, we cared to look up some of the old proofs.

The mark of the depth of the gulf between the world of my childhood and the world of my maturity is that these questions, which go down to the foundations of our attitude to life, cut at the roots of Yggdrasil, the World-Ash, the roots where the Worm gnaws, were never asked at Salterns. Because it was believed that they had been answered, in the past, once and for all.

What is our difficulty in writing about the past? When we have gathered together the clothes and the toys, the beliefs and the disbeliefs; the states of the weather, trade, agriculture, the arts, the diseases, the disasters and the dreams – what is it then that we have to do which is impossible or almost impossible for us? Get the temper that went with those, the ambience in which they moved. Not what they did – and that is hard enough – but how. In what humour, with what half-realized values behind? These debates are facile, but it is not easy to get to the heart of them. It began in the nursey with *The Chaplet of Pearls* , where you knew that for all that was put in there was so much left out. A colour, an ambience that made the sixteenth century different from the one one was living in.

Genius may solve the question by leaving it out. The Three Musketeers live in all time or none, and much of Scott. Or by divination, and this hardly ever, though there are passages in the ill-named and forgotten *Ladies Whose Bright Eyes*, so natural, proper and inevitable as almost to make one shiver; if they were not so happy, cry out 'these are not natural'. The usual earlier solution was to pitch our fathers' values neck and crop into the past, and uphold them there through thick and thin. This, with great attention to correct detail, was responsible for such highly popular confections as *Ben Hur* and *The Sign of the Cross*. Confections that nauseate once that particular bit of present is well over; and in an attempt to bring them up to date we have the delight of seeing the Empress, Poppaea Sabina Augusta, played by a Hollywood trull.

However, it is a good fortune of this generation – one of the things we may be fairly said to have got out of it – that the gulf the war opened behind us has given us the simultaneous possession of two worlds at once. We – it must have been the same for the people who lived through the Terror and the Protectorate – have lived in two ages. (It is the most wistful of all speculations what life would have been like if there had been no war, if one age had passed tranquilly into the next; how blessed it would seem, how full of possibilities of achievement. How many – and this is the worst of all – dead or maimed in body and spirit would now be at the height of their ripened powers. How much more money there would be to spend, how many lovely things preserved.)

Let that be. The common complaint now is that the world of one's youth was too comfortable a world, that with its security went bigotry, snobbery, pettiness. Partly true, but those were errors already questioned. It did not need that war to have mended what was amiss.

Changes were coming – my father's decline and death, my own adolescence, marked a pivotal time. Among other signs, a shadow fell, not only over my home but over our circle of provincial life. A subtle shadow. A shadow competing with an added brilliance when, to receive my stepfather, our whole life was reordered. It was in my father's piety that I trusted and in my aunt's. (An adored schoolmistress who was a scholar alienated me, for it was her learning that I wanted, not her faith.) It was far later that I understood anything

54

of my mother's belief. At my father's death I felt what I could not express, that in his scepticism and his irony was a piety deeper than any I had had explained to me. And on his death two wrongs were done his memory. Both in good faith, but whose result on his child was a slowly awakened horror of blind faith; which was to lead me through a desert round about the Sphinx, to wrest an answer from it.

Yet at Salterns I learned, as easily as I breathed, prayer and praise, and the superb Liturgy which is the matchless inheritance of the English child. Who minded learning a poem called a psalm, with the curious name 'In convertendo'? So that when anything really bad went wrong you could say to God: 'Turn our captivity . . . as the rivers in the south'. Or the mysterious signature: 'Hearken, O daughter, and consider, incline thine ear: forget also thine own people, and thy father's house'. Or the splendid spur: 'Good luck have thou with thine honour: ride on . . . and thy right hand shall teach thee terrible things'.

Or points of nature, related and driven in: '. . . a tabernacle for the sun: which cometh forth as a bridegroom out of his chamber, and rejoiceth as a giant to run his course'.

Or of confidence restored: 'O praise the Lord . . . ye that excel in strength . . . ye servants of his that do his pleasure'. Down to the old 'stumping' song, so useful about the house: 'The sun to rule the day: for his mercy endureth for ever; The moon and the stars . . . the night; for his mercy endureth for ever . . . Sehon king of the Amorites: for his mercy endureth for ever; And Og the king of Basan . . .'

9
Brother Aubrey

THERE was a beautiful mystery at Salterns. On the library wall, at right angles to the ancient chimney-piece with coats of arms below, and above dim mirrors in black carvings and a shelf full of pipes and feathers and tobacco jars, there hung a picture. A picture with a curtain drawn across it of faded red silk on tinkling rings. It was never drawn, but I knew they tinkled, for once, when my father was out, Mother had drawn it back for me; and once or twice I had dared to do it for myself. A curtain that was never drawn until my father was dying; and then one day he ordered it to be drawn back, and the face of his dead son smiled down at him. A very bad picture, in pastels, of a young man on a boat, in a striped pork-pie cap, with the most brilliant and sensitive eyes I have ever seen. Delicate from his birth, he had made a man of himself out at sea; and at twenty-two the sea had taken him back. Upset him in a squall off the Hook, and a week later killed him of pneumonia, caught from exposure sitting astride the keel. That was the end of Cecil Aubrey Tilbrook Butts, the 'Brother Aubrey' whose name was never to be spoken in my father's presence – so my mother said, so I was afraid to do it though I longed to – the boy whose death was the ultimate cause of my existence. For my father and his first wife had gone sailing round the Mediterranean to forget – the 'late Mrs Butts' he had married as a very young man, just after the Crimean War. At Constantinople she had gone shopping in the bazaar, and on her way back had fallen dead on the quay. And in the cemetery at Péra Daddy had ordered what, from a dim shiny photograph in a Gothic oak frame, looked like a young pyramid over her. So, returning a widower, childless and singularly without kin, it had seemed to him that our name would be written in water at last. Hence, a year later, his marriage to my mother, and a year after that my birth.

It gave me early a dim acquaintance with death, the anguish of his loss. Not unbeautifully. It was there, and I was not to chatter or be curious about it, but my mother often spoke of it, who had known him well. Also of the words that greeted my own birth, when she asked him if he were angry that she had given him a girl: 'I have had two sons' (one died in infancy) 'and I lost them both. God knows.'

Also, all about the garden and the house the dead boy had left delicate signatures. In the wide corridor that led to the new wing, still called 'Brother Aubrey's Room'. A shadowy place, only lit by the rising stairs beyond, and a lancet window filled with painted glass he had copied from a design of Blake's. The glow of orange and sapphire stained the polished boards, and there was a deep cupboard, its doors painted sea colour and slashed with peacocks' feathers. Homage to Whistler, as, later, my own brother in his turn was to do homage to the ballet.

Inside the cupboard were put away his maps, his charts of the coast and of Poole Harbour, his books on boat building. Sea-tack and fishing-tackle, paint-boxes and sketch-books; his violin. He had some talent as a water-colourist; delicate impressions, swift and clean, hung in piety up and down the house, of the endless moods of the vast estuary on which his life was spent. One I remember – a fishing-boat, riding in furiously on the flood tide, her bows violently (and incorrectly) foreshortened, but conveying with a minimum of statement the sensation of insatiable speed. Power of wind and water, mast and sail, the body and wings of a ship, all in agreement with their element, four speeds made one, the bows of her leaping out of the frame.

Homage to Turner and to Whistler, faint image of the vital impulses of past days. Where are they now? Sold as so much rubbish when the house was sold – after the war, a white elephant in a ruined neighbourhood. I could not blame them for that; all the same, at that moment, some possession fell upon my people. A possession as of a cause that abandons itself, and I was abroad, and, despite promises, even my own things, my books and furniture, my father's gifts, my childhood possessions, not even these were spared. They vanished, with even the box that held his letters to me; letters from his Club, mysteriously called 'The Rag', a wonderful house in London near a palace, where there was a room lined with books, and part of the books were doors, and those books weren't books. They wouldn't pull out and he laughed. They were letters printed, so as to be easy for me to read. I appreciated the trouble, but I really wouldn't have minded, who for years tried to ruin my own in attempts to imitate his exquisite hand.

Nothing left for the ghost of his dead first-born – nothing left for him to haunt. Except these memories. A death which, for a time, was so faithfully remembered. Though memories can be like Fenrir's chain, made not of Thor's iron, but 'from the noise made by the footfall of cats – the roots of stones'.

The garden too was full of him. One place we called his and there we played until I was too old to see ghosts – the summer-house-by-the-sea.

The Victorian era was the time for summer-houses. Not the small stone temples of the previous century, but their 'Gothic' descendants. We had three. The black-and-white summer-house, hidden in the shrubbery in the woods, from where the green under-tree tunnel called the Lavender Walk ran parallel with the orchard to the house. It was round and flagged, a fantasy, and decorated inside with white wooden stars, made out of the painted timbers taken from a ship.

The summer-house-on-the-hill, a long way off on the heath, made of stone, with a real fireplace; and built, so the joke went, for Brother Aubrey to practise in, where even Daddy, half a mile away, could not hear him play out of tune. A place christened later 'The Butts' Arms', when it had a more romantic history; from whose eaves, one summer night, a wryneck flew out and caught in my mother's hair.

The third, the summer-house-by-the-sea, was Brother Aubrey's summer-house, built on a high bank at the edge of the wood, looking out to the harbour across fields. A place where the sun poured in and the harbour-stream poured past, an eye set in the face of a dark wood out of a world of light. From there I first watched, night after night, the sun set behind Purbeck, fitting itself into a cup in the hills. Watched it from Aubrey's tree. For in front of the summer-house, on the high bank, a huge pinaster sprang, six foot of trunk and then parted into the shape of a lyre; and Aubrey had left it so that you could scramble up into the cleft and sit there, with a cushion in the tree's arms. There was a board too for your back, so that you could never fall through into the field beneath but give yourself up wholly to the wood-scents, to the breeze and the light and the rook-cook of pigeons inside in the wood. The tree in which he used to sit and watch the tides and paint. And hopes always of an adder, sunning itself at the foot of the bank, so near but quite safe.

The tree might still be growing there. It was a great tree. Only it is not. One of the trees cut down when, at the end of the war, our timber was sold.

It was one of the first to go, and with its crash went the shriek of its dryad. The dryad Brother Aubrey had known, departing with the others that he had known and I knew; fleeting away across the grass, across the world of light, across the harbour-stream, to Purbeck, which is sanctuary.

It was because of him that we had a church of our own, a chapel built by my father, inland, on the very edge of our heath, beside the lane that ran through the village of Lilliput, in memory of his son. Also to serve the growing district round the harbour-side, some miles away from the parish church, the Victorian Gothic of St Peter's, Parkstone.

As such buildings went in those days, it was enterprising. Perfectly hideous without, of pale brick, inside there were oil paintings round the walls, small replicas, I believe, of the popular German religious painting of the last century, and the inevitable Holman Hunt. The Sanctuary was not without decency, even mystery; and after my father's death my mother added a rood-screen, which, if it has since been given the gold-leaf which at the time it lacked, in its clear greens and scarlet would pass for decent post-Pre-Raphaelite work, unpretentious and gay.

A brass tablet to my stepbrother; then one to my father, and on it a text so utterly inadequate as comment on such a man as to rouse my sharpening wits to criticism. The troubled speechless criticism of a child, which, following on what was done a few weeks after his death, was to rouse me to the opposition particular in its vehemence to my own generation. A hostility the war was to temper seven times, which only later experience was to re-fuse with understanding. Reconciliation, and on both sides something approaching forgiveness.

10
Aunt Monica

ALL this is too far ahead. By my eighth and ninth year babyhood was over, and my father not yet failing. Also I had begun my first five great adventures with and out of books. First there were the *Lays*, then a story called 'Soria Moria Castle'. A poem called 'Arethusa' and two whole books, *The Heroes of Asgard* and *The Three Musketeers*. These were my first possessions, or rather the things by which I was possessed, the stuff my imagination seized on with which to build.

Also, when I was about seven, I was sent to a day-school kept by two old ladies in the Parkstone woods. A school which has since become justly famous and where, to my great benefit, I remained until my father's death. For in many respects I got from it the best that a school can give; desire for knowledge intelligently encouraged, kindness and experience of the common run of the world. All those solid gifts which make thanks half a life-time later sound thin and graceless; for which at the time there are no thanks given. Yet the neurotic child I might have become – later, after years of unwise handling and painful growth, almost became – something of the kindly good sense of Sandecotes prevented in me.

When I first went there it was no more than the Old House, the red Victorian-Tudor mansion, with its stone quoinings and wide hall, its shallow wide main staircase with glossy boards. All set, dark green, warm and perfumed in deep pine-woods, among which grew a particular low bush, with glossy leaves and wax-petalled flowers with gold crowns in their centres and hairy, sticky stems. Some garden-escape, but those acres of countryside were laid out in fairy-book trees in the heart of an open heath. (True greenwood lay round Salterns and along that part of the harbour's edge, fields and pasture, studded with oak and elm. Backed in against a rising land of dark pines, red-carpeted, and in parts as steep as a cliff.)

Especially behind Salterns itself, up Bryant's wood; and from its top, across Donkey's Common, ran a track, all furze and mushrooms, down Sandy Lane, then up through another wood. In all not more than a mile to the school gates; and I often rode over on my pony – which made the other girls jealous and accounted for much young unhappiness. Or else Nurse went with me or the old coachman's wife whom I did not like. She was a dirty old woman with an angry mind, who had in her some quality that made me wince. Perhaps it was her physical dirt – only not that alone. Something perhaps like an ignorance too deep for any goodwill to plumb.

Until, after a year or so, I attained the glorious liberty of being allowed to go by myself. Then, a year or so after that, my mother did an unwise thing, insisting that the short way to school was too lonely for me to run through alone. I do not know why. Perhaps there had been some scandal about tramps – but the result was that a child, carrying a heavy satchel, had to walk another mile each way; and what was far worse, through the potteries, where the clay-pit lads sometimes shouted after one. A thing one dared not tell, for fear of having the coachman's wife again, and my other wild runnings cut short. Again, what was almost instilled into me, by prohibitions and by hints that I did not understand, was a fear of woods.

Quiet in the woods is a very real magic, a tangible daimon to a child, as a German painter showed once. (It was a merciful thing that picture was waiting to be painted. It might have found its way into the nursery at Salterns and precipitated a life-terror.) Worst of all was that over these grown-up alarms – in which by that time my father had no share – hung a faint flavour of sex. I did not know what I knew, except that about it all there was something I must not have explained to me. It was silly. It was grown-ups saying: 'You mustn't' and talking among themselves. About something dreadful, or rather there was supposed to be a something dreadful – of whose nature you were utterly and entirely innocent. Yet to know that there is a something about which you are not to know, which if you were to meet would be awfulness itself, is to have the very strings of fear pulled in your heart.

Was it possible that there was a dreadfulness, apart from magic, in the pine-woods? And for that all that you had to say was a prayer. I knew there was none for me. The danger, as I sensed it, lay in minds, at home. Only anyhow it wasn't there.

Thus there was almost a separation made between the woods and a child. Almost, not quite. For it was over this exactly that I discovered, finally, without any shadow of doubt, that prayers were answered: that Our Lady, who was the same as Artemis, whom I asked God if He minded me saying my prayers to, and He didn't, told me with unspeakable comfort that I was not to mind. They would not harm me. I was never to lose them. It was All Right.

On thinking it over it seems possible that my mother at this time may have had some special reason for her intermittent attempts to make me feel that there was something particularly different about being a girl. Some local scandal possibly over roughs from Poole, or even nearer home. Only the process worried me. A girl as distinct from a young gentlewoman. A far more difficult difference, with something strange and even dreadful attached. A thing somehow connected, ever so vaguely, with a thing I never liked to tell anyone, with a tramp I had seen, in a copse near Parkstone, relieving himself. Somehow I knew it was more than ordinary modesty – common sense told me that poor men must do that as much as anyone else, and it couldn't be wrong to do it out of doors if you hadn't anywhere else. It was – it was – something in the look he gave me in the second before I ran away. Yet I felt if only it could be explained and *said,* it wouldn't be so bad. Once you were allowed to understand things a wonderful change came over them, and there were some things Mother used to explain very well. Like the bishop when you were a baby who came to stay the night, and you were afraid you had to kneel down to him all the time. Only somehow not those things. Not her or anyone else. With this went a further conviction that all this business of being a man or a woman, whatever it was, wasn't a nasty mystery. It wasn't with animals. So why with us? Sensing, that in my mother's attitude (not in my aunt's simple reticence and comparatively lucid explanations) was a mixture of fascination complicated by shame.

Still, it is more than possible that at this time there may have been a reason. And this a very dreadful one. The thing that happened – I did not understand it then – I do not understand it now. No one has ever understood it. A thing that here serves chiefly to illustrate the little effect the most appalling tragedy has on a young child, how out of any situation its instincts will extract the factors likely to be useful to it.

It was the death by drowning of my prettiest aunt. Still little more than a girl, and I was eight, that January, on the day the old Queen died, three months before my brother was born.

My grandmother and my aunts, my mother's mother and her sisters, lived in Parkstone, in a large comfortable house of peculiar architectural dreadfulness. Glorious in situation, built on a sandy hill, its front door filled with coloured glass and reached by a flight of balustraded steps. But from each of its comfortable, shabby, sun-steeped rooms you looked out on to a scene of extraordinary splendour, at the utmost expanse of Poole Harbour and the Purbeck Hills. From the far west, behind Poole, where Lytchett Clump humped itself on the horizon, to the mudflats of Holes Bay, to the masts and grey roofs of the port, to the silver dimness where the Wareham river began its scour. Slowly the eye would travel south round the earth. Grange Hill, where Purbeck divides, and a huge down-spoke slides down the horizon to Flower's Barrow above Worbarrow and the western sea. Above Grange, King's Barrow, among the bare undulations the one pointed crest. Round to the hub of the downs, to where Corfe Castle stands on its hill, with its towers.

Steadily on – Brenscombe Hill rising to Nine Barrow Down; Nine Barrow Down decreasing on to Ballard, to Old Harry Rocks and the eastern sea.

This on the horizon. At the foot of the hills lay the great heath, and alongside it the Harbour's most mysterious reaches, Arne and Ower and Scudder and the black hook of Goathorn thrust out into the flats among the little islands behind Brownsea – Long Island and Green Island and Snake-and-Rabbit Island.

A country no man, not Hardy even, has found full words for; adoration keeps its lovers silent, adoration and awe for which only some ceremonial utterance that has never been found is fit.

Call it then:

> *A savage place! as holy and enchanted*
> *As e'er beneath a waning moon was haunted . . .*

That is as much as man has said, and yet there is much more that never has been told about that land, that probably will never be told.

Between them and the harbour ship-road, fed at low tide by little lanes of water running out between the green flats, and marked by tarred barrels stuck on poles, each with a cormorant for crest, lies Brownsea Island. A bank of dark woods two miles long, and at the harbour mouth where the great tides pull in and out, through a neck of water no man, it was said, had ever swum across, stood its little Italianate pink village and its castle. The first place to make castles real. It was a magic place to go to. Also a curse hung about it, no one who owned it lived to enjoy it long. A curse one had the supreme satisfaction of seeing worked out for oneself, in the series of owners who visited or had visited Salterns, who had died off in one way or another, and the castle again changed hands.

This was how the earth showed itself, airy and vast, from my grandmother's windows. Finer than any view from Salterns. For Salterns lay low, rising gently out of the marshes. From there the island and the hills lay low down on the horizon, but from her house one saw them as from an opposite hill.

Between one house and the other I ran, as my father aged, my interests and affections crystallizing more and more about my eldest aunt, Ada.

Her apart, there was my grandmother, tiny, exquisite, a little antique goddess of awful propriety, whose iron will, sweetly masked, was exerted in a tyranny over her unmarried daughters that very early I understood and began to resent.

My mother was the daughter she had liked least; her one grandchild, so far as her principles allowed her, she indulged. She lived to an immense age, still treating these middle-aged, accomplished, gifted, travelled women as if they were children. One of the old breed who gave the Victorian age its bad name, but I should imagine rare. And a supreme example of the power-sense triumphing over religion and morality, even over convenience. Her desire was to live, a mateless queen-bee, surrounded by her workers, her unmated children; the one she liked least left to carry on the race. Children of a gifted priest, a son of the Oxford Movement, who had died young.

After Aunt Ada, there remained Aunt Irlam, Aunt Monica and Aunt Agnes. The first on her way to become a painter of distinction. Particularly I remember one life-size canvas, hung in the Academy, away back in the eighties 'on the line', and I believe one of the pictures of the year: *The Young Violinist*. Aunt Agnes, just grown-up, in a dress of copper velvet and a sash of copper silk, her red curls strung with sunlight, the wood of her instrument glowing, her blue eyes bright with music. Brilliant beginning – which an ever-increasing deafness caught up. As though Fate was playing again my grandmother's cards.

It was my Aunt Agnes who approved of me least, a noisy child an admirable musician had no hopes of; a young woman whose withdrawn purity the coming tragedy was to freeze to crystal, who had already little taste for a child's hot and alien blood.

My Aunt Monica was all but her twin and her inseparable companion – inseparable, who were to be so dreadfully separated. Yet I can only tell this story from what I have been told, and still less from my own small, self-absorbed memories of it.

It was the day of the old Queen's death, grey, raw and damp. I was to go to the pantomime in Bournemouth, and had run up from Salterns to their house – called Milnthorpe from the north-country valley from which they came – to lunch there, and go on by train with *my* aunt.

There I was received lovingly with bad news. There would be no pantomime because the Queen was dead. I ran off with a child's stormy disappointment – why did the old Queen, who everyone said loved her people, die like that and stop their having fun? Into the sewing-room, where Nanna Rae, their old nurse who had been my mother's nurse, sat, waiting for lunch. Aunt Ada would be sure to think of some other amusing thing to do. Aunt Agnes came in and turned over some music. No need to hurry lunch now for the train, but it was late. Soon I understood that we were waiting for Aunt Monica, who had gone out on her bicycle and had not come back.

Then we had lunch, and though the others made light of it, I could see my grandmother was anxious and annoyed. The early afternoon passed. On such a day it would soon be dark. It was arranged that I had better go home. I stood on the top of the steps, saying goodbye, my aunt beside me, when we saw a working-man coming slowly up the long flight. Coming slowly, his face a colour I was soon to see on a number of faces, a kind of dirty clay-white.

Some one told me to run back to Nanna Rae's room. I waited there. Some one cried harshly and called her away. I heard another voice crying in the house. One of the maids came in and sat with me. A young girl. I remember with contempt her little, self-satisfied smile, meant possibly to reassure me. 'It can't be anything serious, Miss, or I should be wanted.' Then my aunt came in, composed and deadly white. 'We are to go home now, darling. We are driving in a cab. I have to tell your mother. Aunt Monica has had – a bad accident. She – is very badly hurt. Come with me quickly.' Then, half to herself: 'She has – oh, it is too horrible – it is unbelievable – she is drowned. I must go now. Bad news travels so fast – but what news to tell Mary now!' Meaning, which I did not yet understand, that in three months my brother would be born.

I went very quietly to say goodbye. In the dining-room my grandmother was sitting, the pink apples in her still bright old cheeks gone a strange, deadly mauve. My Aunt Agnes was giving her brandy, moving very swiftly and saying over and over again: 'It can't be true. It can't be true.'

We drove home in the grinding old station cab, through the village lighting up. Along the harbour high-road, past the marshes, their pools and dykes dead silver at high tide, under the dead sky.

Past the peninsula thrust out between two marshes, high with elm trees in whose heart, among the rooks, old Mrs Dawson-Damer still lived, who had given me the duck. Past *the* Salterns, our own marsh, in whose heart was a place where horses were sucked in and swallowed up. Up our own dark lane, the old outside drive; past the lodge and up the inside drive with its twenty feet of clipped hedges and its trees towering above. To the front door and the porch, its ivy oiled and dripping, into the shadows of the hall and on into the drawing-room, where we found Mother alone in the dark by the fire, lying heavily in a great carved chair.

I was sent away. I had not said a word. A little after I was sent for again, and my aunt was giving my mother wine. My father, I think, had not yet come back from the Club. Later on I remember the sharp hooves of the brougham and the clang of his tread on the iron lattice in the flags.

Before I went to bed I sat with a book in the library, while my father and my mother talked in low voices. It simply did not seem to have happened. That was all. One read these things in books and people suffered agonies. One ought to feel like that. I must. It was the proper thing to do. This was a shock. That was what it was called. All the servants were talking about shock. When you'd had a shock (in books) you often didn't feel it at the time and came over bad afterwards. (There was something special though that they were expecting to happen to Mother.) The great thing was to get over it quickly. Like the woman in the rather silly 'Warrior Dead': 'She must weep or she will die.'

Was I doing it right? I didn't feel anything in particular, only a feeling of being sorry for Aunt Agnes so horrible I didn't like to look at it. 'Please, God, let me get over my feelings quickly.' Only what are you to do when you are not having the feelings? When the only one you have, and you don't like to acknowledge it, is curiosity?

'But, Freddy – but, Freddy, *how* did it happen? What does it mean?'

'Mary, you must not torment yourself. It will all be settled at the inquest.'

'Inquest, I don't know what that means. Oh, how horrid! Must there be one? What will they say? Oh, she was such a darling. She didn't – she didn't – Freddy, you know she didn't . . .'

'Be quiet, Mary. Of course she didn't. Now you go to bed. You still there? You get your mother's bedroom candle and light her up and cut along too.'

It wasn't quite my bedtime, but grown-ups were not be argued with that night. A nasty small girl posed her way through her prayers about shock and Aunt Monica being in heaven, and wanted to cry but no tears came, and next day there were lots of interesting things to do. But again what she was ashamed to acknowledge and feared to indulge was curiosity.

Curiosity which in the days that followed perished for lack of encouragement. In some ways I was a biddable child. Such curiosities were a sin against good breeding, and I did not want to disappoint my parents in that. Also next day I had it very firmly rubbed into me that the less my mother was troubled with idle talk the better. Mother who was not well, who was strangely inactive; and even more strangely seemed to know the time when she would expect to be well again. People as a rule didn't seem to, and I only hoped she was right. And could see that she was not to be bothered. As for my aunts, when I saw the look of anguish on their faces, again some dim instinct of delicacy forbade me.

Until, three months later, it passed out of my mind with the enchantment of my brother's birth. With one exception, a hint of facts and a conclusion on which I meditated, the morsel of serviceableness which was all I extracted from a deadly situation, as a strong child will.

The maids put me on to it. (The verdict at the inquest was an open one.) Saying out loud that my grandmother had made her life too sad for her: that it was well known. 'Whether she'd done it herself or not, it was the old lady made her life not worth living to her. Always checking and sending for her home and treating her like a child. And her shaping for an old maid. Glad to be out of it I reckon she was. The Mistress knows it; and if the Captain's old enough to be her father, she's her fine house and her child and another on the way . . .'

So that was it, was it? I'd been right when I'd half thought that all that was the matter with Mother was that she was going to have a baby. Pleased with myself I ran off into the child's private life, already teeming with pastimes and senses, plays and imaginations, hard at work, in the first exquisite days of that employment, making up its picture of the world.

I remember, too, that for a little time longer I tried to cultivate fine feelings, one day greatly annoying Nurse by refusing to go through the woods by the pool in which my aunt's body had been found. 'I can't go there. I couldn't see such a dreadful place' – while all the time I was longing to do so quite as much as Nurse.

Finally the taboo hardened, as such things do, into something more. Into, so far as my side of the family was concerned, something like a positive oblivion. And now my mother's memory of the affair is dim; and on the other side, from that day to this, I have never dared discuss it with my aunts.

Yet a very real mystery surrounds Aunt Monica's death. The open verdict may have been given to spare her family's feelings. There was, as I was actually told some years later, some talk of tramps, of signs of violent movement at one point of the iron-spoked fence (very difficult to climb) which enclosed Witt's Wood with its ponds. If it had happened today, what an exercise in detection, how with Austin Freeman and Dorothy Sayers and Wills Crofts to guide us, my brother and I – heaven forgive us – would have turned detective. But then, even Sherlock Holmes was still appearing in monthly parts.

So, from that day to this, it has never been found out why a young woman, vivid, gifted, gay, divinely, as the whole world knew, innocent, a bird maybe in a cage, but hardly in a prison, and not only deeply loved, but essential to her sister, should have been found, her bicycle, I believe, abandoned among the bushes a few yards off, drowned in four feet of water in a woodland pool.

Except the conviction, the maids' loose talk apart, that etched itself on my young brain that, somehow, some of the blame lay with my grandmother. Aunt Monica, people said, had wanted to do things. And had not done them. Had wanted to learn things. And had not been allowed – well – to learn them *properly*. (She had a most lovely contralto voice.) Had only been allowed to learn things in the way young ladies were allowed to learn things. Which was like only half-learning them. It was different for boys. I did not want to be a boy, but I wanted to learn the things boys learned. In the way boys learned. Properly.

Already at the beginning of this century, *en province*, I knew that it was not easy for a gently raised child to do this.

I must – it was my Angel told me this or perhaps even Artemis, or even Apollo, her brother – they must let me learn what I needed to know. Then do what I needed to do. That meant writing. At that time writing poetry. I was going to be a poet. The kind of poet whose books people will not read until after he is dead, and then they are very, very sorry. (The first half has come so true that one only hopes that the other will follow.) Never for one instant did I think that I was ever going to be anything else. Poetry, as I knew already, was the alpha and omega of all writing. I would make up poems about the birds and the sea and the harbour. And my own feelings, especially when I was miserable. And about the gods and the goddesses and about God.

Then, on a sudden intuition, it flashed into my mind that Aunt Monica's death was going to help. If she had died somehow because they would not let her do the things she needed to do – they might be afraid the same thing would happen to me. (Though I could not imagine how I could come to be found floating in a pond. No, it would have to be the sea.) But suppose they said I wasn't to, and I reminded them, they'd be *bound* to be afraid.

No conception of the reality of the tragedy touched me; and at the bottom of my heart I knew that all I could do was to be honest about my own insensibility. Nor that it would be wrong on my part to make its dreadfulness serviceable for my own life. If I could.

As I believe it was. At least, from that time on, my aunt seemed even more unwearying in the pains she took to develop my mind and to nourish it. On my father's death and my mother's remarriage a period of illiteracy descended on Salterns. It became more fashionable, under my mother's sure touch, far more beautiful; but no more fascinating catalogues and great packages of books arrived, some splendid, some worn with antiquity. These ceased, and with them a life, and with a life an age, and with an age a spirit. There was more life about the place, and less.

Only my aunt continued to read with me the English classics, teaching me the use of such of my father's books as were allowed to remain with us.

11
Heroes

WITT'S FARM, its woods and its ponds – I have no doubt they are villa residences now and trust they are damp – lay in a tongue of green valley behind the potteries running up into the heath, a pine-wood on each side. The potteries stood between Salterns and my grandmother's house – a coarse industry, drain-pipes and bricks – and on one side of them acres of workings, pale clay-pits; and behind these, nearest to the woods, abandoned pits, half-filled with Chinese-blue water, and queer grey cliffs oozing and dripping; and everywhere a tangle of brambles and savage thickets. Also a rare place for birds.

Places where I was not supposed to go. Certainly not alone and Nurse wouldn't. Not even after blackberries. Not after birds. A dangerous place, she said. With its dove pearl and white and raw yellows, to me a very curious place. If I had known it, pure Edgar Allan Poe country, altogether different from the innocent gold sand-pits from which the potteries were fed. Pits that lay exactly the other side of Salterns, only much nearer and there was much less of them. The first not a hundred yards from the iron gate in the wood, due east of the house, a short-cut to the village of Lilliput with its single shop.

Pure gold sand; honey and lion and nasturtium and primrose – a soft fall as I found out once by accident, falling from the overhung lip of a short cliff.

The workmen too were different. All the roughest of men, throw-outs from Poole and the hideous wilds of Upper Parkstone and Monkey Island, men whom the land did not seem to want, or the ancient town or the sea. But kind in the sand-pits and unkind in the clay-pits; clean in one and dirty in the other. So went the nursery-rune. Civil in the sand and rude in the clay was certainly true. A first brush with industry, in that part of the country and at that time, a despised job and a despised race. Servants had 'characters', maids and gardeners and grooms. Characters were very important. But these men, I was told, didn't need characters; and indeed to Viney, the farmer near us and his men, the

70

pottery men were a lower caste. A sign of failure – badness of heart or clumsiness of hand closing the skilled jobs to them.

Along the highest and the furthest of the pottery pits ran Witt's Woods, and under a yellow and white cliff a pool of the same lacquered jade-blue. A little way off, as if to stress the kinship with Poe, stood a solitary house. On a peninsula, thrust out into the pits, whose base was in the woods, the workings hacked out on the three sides of it. No more than a cottage, but its walls were cracked like the House of Usher; and what had been its garden dreadfully strangled by the tide of thorns which seemed to have crept up out of abandoned workings below.

A time came when fresh diggings cut it off altogether and, as a peninsula become an island, it stood alone. But earlier it was easier to reach and, before it was condemned as unsafe and nailed up, Nurse used to be dragged there because I wanted to explore.

It was there I learned the meaning of desolation, the evil kind that comes when man has been and gone, when he has been driven out.

I would have it that there was a story about the house. Nurse said very sensibly that there was not, and couldn't I see with my own eyes that a man and his family had lived there until they cut his garden away to his door? I couldn't. That wasn't what I was looking for, but under a good deal of silliness went a touch of that pure fear by which one learns. Fear of what happens when Nature's face is cut open – that there a wound is left, a wound as dreadful as any you could imagine in the body.

It was the same, in a tiny way, gardening. You came upon worms, although worms were Useful Things. And turning over stones there were roots that had gone white and bad things with too many legs.

But suppose, instead of two or three, you did it for hundreds of feet? It would be worse – I could see it was worse – and was persuaded that at the bottom of the blue pit lived a worm that was worse than any snake. It was not a noble terror that I was learning there, but a fear of evil, smooth and treacherous like the clay's satin grease.

Yet this also was *part* – of a line I was to learn later and repeat with awe, expanding it as my knowledge grew: 'which glorious brightness a great terror bred.'

Nor was it that I thought of it as a stage set for my young aunt's death. The two experiences were not in the same order, lying about, unrelated in the still half-empty storehouse of a child's mind.

Witt's Woods fringed the pale land of the potteries, the wounds in the earth's body which, when they closed, were scarred and scabbed over only with savage growths.

Witt's Woods that stood out in my mind for a part of the same thing, for its trees were mean, its ponds shallow and stagnant, not fed by any stream.

Yet in autumn when most of the outdoor fun was over, when only the toadstools were left, there grew in Witt's Woods near the railing, hard to get at, easy to see, the tiger of the fungus world, the magnificent, drunk-making, not death-giving, fly-agaric.

They grew there in that happy family grouping of which toadstools have the gift. Burning white, burning scarlet, white trunk with its pure frill, scarlet dome stuck with clots of white dust.

Every year they grew in the same place. I remember my mother saying: 'How wicked they look growing there.'

So much for my tenth year, in which my aunt was to die and my brother to be born; and, however little I recognized the processes, birth and death were to lift me over a threshold of experience into consciousness – not only of events but of continuity.

That is the point, I think, when what happens becomes part of a pattern, its variations and its intricacies part of a design, and the measure of the mind's growth the apprehension of this.

Until a further point is reached – and not always reached. What is this pattern a pattern *of*? Children are not always satisfied with the regulation replies – even with the present one that says the pattern is no pattern at all. Yet out of their understandings poets are made, and law-givers and heroes and some suicides. And some perfectly quiet people, in a garden or a kitchen or at sea.

While this was happening and just before and just after, there were two things in the world that I knew now to be the Best Things, and one was being out of doors and the other was books. The first growing slowly into a special sense, an awareness of the year in and out, as of the long and intricate measure of a dance. And with this, in some way an illustration of it, went a game – a shaping, making, planning, imagining game, which had in it an obscure element of ritual, the whole complex of play, dropped and picked up year in year out, that centred round the Stump.

That must be described by itself for, in a sense, until I reached my teens, it was the sum of all that mattered, the instrument I had somehow discovered to play my own tunes.

Again, at the same time as I read the *Lays*, I came upon the two other members of my first trinity, *The Heroes of Asgard* and *The Three Musketeers*.

I remember with exquisite sharpness that day's bliss when a mistress began that book at school. Told us small children about the Cow and the Ice and the Hero whose gold hair had come up out of the salt the Cow had licked. First his hair and then his head and then the whole of him, and how the City of Asgard was built, and Bifröst the Rainbow Bridge set over it; and how the World-Ash grew, Yggdrasil, and what lived in it and on it and at its roots. Heaven give that woman Paradise for the world she opened to one small child – a child who for some reason did not dare ask but managed to track down the blue-grey book to its place on the shelf in the Mistresses' Room, wait till school was over, lag behind and, kneeling on the floor, with a stubby pencil write down its name. I ran off home with it to Daddy and he grinned: '*The Heroes*, what's that?' But I must have asked for it with such intensity that, by what looked like magic, it came back with him in the brougham, and I read it and read it and read it. With never-failing interest and never-failing satisfaction. Because it was about the beginnings of things; because it was a way of telling what was true; because of the days of the week; because it satisfied in the same way as bits of the Bible in the Old Testament satisfied.

Children have a wise and blessed sense that things which grown-up people tell them are not true, are still, as the Negro preacher said of the Scriptures, 'quite true enough to be going on with'.

It may not be too much to say that with that book I relived in part what must have been the spiritual experience of our ancestors. Heaven alone knows what inheritance from my mother's north-country and my father's east-country blood moved in me. I only knew that I was stirred in the secret roots of being even more and in another way than by the first stories of the classical sagas I was learning at the same time. No battle of Gods and Giants nor story of Kronos swallowing his children satisfied in comparison with the building of Asgard. With Fenrir and the Norns even the Graeae met their match. With Bifröst, the Rainbow Bridge that Heimdall shall ride up on the Last Day, when it shall break at the sound of his horn, and an end come to the Gods and the world.

Twilight of the Gods – I dreamed over that bitter eschatology, knowing that we were guarded by our Salvation, yet quite clear that without it that was what men must think, and the Snake go on gnawing for ever at the roots of Yggdrasil, even with Baldur risen again and innocence restored. If there wasn't God, that would *have* to be true about life.

Then, as always happened, as had happened with the *Lays*, one thing in particular about those Gods entered my mind and remained there, charged with a significance beyond the rest. A significance made up of present, future and past. For a child's life is all present, which, very rarely, is seen by it changed into its eternal present, or what I was taught to call Eternal Life. There its past and its future are shown to it, as it were in a further state; and when these moments and the saga-moments corresponded one with the other one caught oneself saying with awe: 'Some day I shall know more about that.' Or, perhaps more rarely: 'I have always known about that.' Once or twice: 'That thing and my life are part of one another.'

It was when Odin went to Mimir's well and there gave his right eye for wisdom and, before he received the gift, stayed nine days and nine nights in the arms of a tree. There the author had the genius to give the words of the Edda, at the same time bringing to the ear the hard rhymeless monotone that was the measure of that speech:

> *I knew that I hung*
> *On a wind-rocked tree*
> *Nine long nights*
> *With a spear wounded*
> *And to Odin offered*
> *Myself to Myself.*

(Curious to think of a seven-year-old child urgently repeating this.) As a thing that was somehow alive, without pretension or self-consciousness or fear. Pointing again to the ancient belief in an essential personality, passing through the stages of growth as though they were no more than illustrations of its essential nature, or shadows confusing its reality, the pure being, the same at six months or sixty years.

The thing that had happened to All-Father, Odin, was a mystery. Part of an everlasting pattern, to be thought over in little snatches of recognition with which went a very secret reassurance and peace and, as one after the other one learned the myths of one's race, a feeling that these stories were the most real of all stories. Also that trees were repeated in them. There was Dodona and the warm wood Bari I always pictured to myself as full of broom in flower. It was that perhaps which put the magic into the broom-spray the Plantagenets stuck in their caps. Then there was Odin's tree – only there it was not the tree that mattered but the God. (I had not yet heard about the Irminsul.) The Tree that mattered always was Yggdrasil, and that mattered like the not yet understood Tree which had the priest, and which again I had · not yet learned was called The Golden Bough.

One wonders if anthropology has penetrated yet into the modern nursery; if someone has in preparation a children's edition of Frazer. If anyone had told me then about the Irminsul. I should, without any thought of disrespect to Odin, have gone out at once and made myself a fetish-tree.

Suppose I had been told more and more in order to have more and more explained away. (The actual notes to *The Heroes*, written at the time of Max Müller and the sun-god craze, try to do that. But they, while they made me rather unhappy, supplied so many new facts that one saw at once that the only thing to do was to leave the 'explainings' alone.) It wasn't just looking at a rainbow made them know about Bifröst, nor Yggdrasil having been invented by analogy with anything else on earth or heaven.

Yet the elements of science were not wholly wanting in my training, principally because of my father and my mother's insistence that I should make good use of my eyes. I can see my mother smiling as she rubbed in the lovely fable that in the training of English children has meant so much, *Eyes and No Eyes*. The story of two boys who were sent out by their parents for a walk on a windy day. One returned, kicking his heels, saying that it was all so dull; the other bursting in, all excitement. He had (I forget the details, but it went like this) found a nest (and only taken *two* of the eggs and *not* frightened the hen). Found a rare plant, met a cuckoo plagued by other birds. One thing after another – but the point was they had both been for exactly the *same* walk! At home too there were prizes for observation, a whole half-crown for learning the names of all the flowers in the herbaceous border. Again, my reports must be accurate; what I saw must be how I saw it and where I saw it; and what I thought I had seen must be checked when I got back in my books.

Little Girl from her Dad –

For being so good
When her throat was so bad.

I remember, my throat still bound up in flannel, convalescent over the nursery fire, and my father coming in and the verse was written on the title-page of the first of three green books, which you do not see nowadays, but which would be hard for the young naturalist to find better. *Our Country Birds – Flowers – Butterflies and Moths.* Each with endless plates in all the colours, clear descriptions and a little easy science.

So with these books and others, even in a family that had no such interest, I did not come off so badly. As often, it was later, when the time came for definite teaching, for theory and the satisfaction of the whole rational being, that the hard times came. When, struggling with one's own growth, one had to fight in ignorance, and with all youth's fierceness and innocence, blindness and determination, find the knowledge that would sustain the growth. Allow one to rise to the full capacity of one's gifts. Knowing as a bear-cub hunts for honey or a young dog worries a bone that unless one's mind was fed, one would grow up disproportionate, full of holes and patches, with ulcers even; that reason and a mind starved for the knowledge they craved would drive me in upon myself, make me in the end a nuisance to myself and to those round me. And as I grew I saw that I might do more than grow up – I might grow old. And become (I had already seen one or two) what people called a 'peculiar' woman, a crank of some kind. And I did not want to be that. And I did not want to be driven in on myself or out of my proper shape, but to grow out into what one knew for the open weather of the spirit and its clear skies.

I was sure of this, sure as if an angel, in a tiny *annonce faite à Marie*, had told me that God never left any one without the knowledge they asked; with this came an equal certainty that in the world it was particularly hard for women to get these things. Lots of women in history had, and what had been done once could be done again. Besides, as I learned when I reached my teens, women were even beginning to make a fuss about it. Had I once in all my childhood and all my girlhood met one person with a complete understanding? But no – that is not fair. For my girlhood, even after my father's death, my mother and my aunt were sufficient. Rather it was later, in the transit from girlhood. But instead, with the rest of my kind, I met the war. And after the war, found myself, with what was left of us, on the further side of that gulf, angry with the fires of hell and unspeakable sacrifices the generation before me understood as little as it had shared.

If even then I had found it? As I did, but in patches. Profited as I could, with one or two older men, and with Roger Fry profoundly. Only by then I was persuaded that however I needed to learn there were few persons I had cause to trust. It is curious – we were wounded all over again, most of my friends and I, once the war *was* over, from the fact that so few parental arms were opened to the wild young things it had spared. Many of us and I among them had behaved badly enough, bravely enough. Were all half-dead for want of being cared for, for want of the understanding we were too wary, too disillusioned, too tired to *ask* for, ever.

If it had been offered – but how many parents out of ten thousand, with tact, with quietness, with love-in-reserve said: 'This was our coming-of-age gift to you all. If you've been bad, you've been brave. If you've been tiresome, you're tired out. Whatever you have done – and some of you have done so supremely well – it is you who have suffered most. Whatever we have done and suffered, we cannot have suffered what has been done to you. Come home for a little to be cared for, and let us see if we can find a way to save such children as we have left.' How many of them said that? I once made a representative collection of the sort of things they *did* say – to the children whose not infrequent response was to die or go to the dogs. 'Mary of Roses . . . all young things.'

All this is a long way from *The Heroes of Asgard* out in the woods at Salterns or over the nursery fire. Only once, when the war was on, alone in a Hampstead studio on an air-raid night; the planes droning overhead, the thump of the big gun on the Heath each time it fired giving the earth a twitch, the shrapnel whistling in the sky and pattering on the road, while the moon held the mid-vault, I remembered the saga-words and thought that we were all up that Tree.

If *The Heroes of Asgard* opened a heavenly path to walk in with the 'angels of the mind', it fought for favour with another book, *The Three Musketeers*. There was a beautiful edition in the house, finely translated and with pictures. Head pieces and colophons, whole pages and delicious insets in the text by an engraver named Maurice Leloir. Not the kind of book production we are taught to admire now, and Leloir a pupil of Meissonier, with his realism and his costume-accuracy; but again a path to Paradise for the imagination of one small child. Not a pleasure that walked in the high places – a good thing to counteract too much of that – but with its feet well down on the earth, among glorious men and their adventures, Hermes and Heracles at home. That is why, I think, in every country *The Three Musketeers* is one of the most popular books ever written. In a great historic setting, pretty well true, full of high persons out of the past very fairly described, there move through it four examples of manhood 'roaring with the love of life'.

Flung down on the page with something that is more than poster-brilliance, the four friends, in common with the men of Dickens or Shakespeare or Homer, have something more than a three-dimensional quality, something of immortal as well as mortal life. I fell in love with them all except Porthos – he is no little maid's fancy, a coxcomb less lovable than Nick Bottom, and his gorgeous unrefinement, at that age, shocked. (Though I laughed at the scene with the procuress, which Mother did not like at all.)

Otherwise I was excited, 'thrown into delicious agitation by the glorious bodies of men', as girls were soon to be by Lewis Waller, and now fall for the latest movie-boy. But it was (with Robert Louis Stevenson) to Athos that I gave my heart. I might flirt with the others, rather alarmed by d'Artagnan, not quite envying the Duchesse de Chevreuse her Aramis, but it was to Athos I gave myself in abandonment of hero-worship and the dawning instinct of sex; and since little girls must play these games, I might have found an unworthier object. He rouses at least a deeper and more generous emotion, even a subtler, than is possible with Douglas Fairbanks.

For an admiration made almost into a ritual, my painter aunt was kind enough to copy the picture of him returning from the first duel with the Cardinal's Guard. In colour, on a gilt panel, it was the very centre-piece of the room given me once my brother arrived to fill the nursery. There I read the book and re-read it, telling it to myself in relation to Athos only; married him, and as Comtesse de la Fère did all I knew to make up for his unfortunate experience with Milady. I remember one night a dream from which I woke up weeping, because he had seen the vaccination marks on my shoulder and thought they were some other kind of branding, and would not believe what I said – because there was no vaccination in his day, only smallpox. At which I had the grace to grin to myself and fall asleep. Dear Athos – I still feel gentleness at the name, gratitude, love. He made very real the lessons of fine breeding and unpettiness: 'the horse might perhaps have been bought for less, but while d'Artagnan was arguing with the dealer, Athos was counting the money out upon the table'. That made you remember Daddy's lessons, even after he was dead. I made him also a friend to be talked to out alone in the woods. A friend to be comforted, not only for his high mysterious griefs, but because again he appeared to me sometimes as part of a pattern, with the Bluebird Prince (not Maeterlinck's, but out of Andrew Lang). With other heroes and, strangely enough, with Hector whom Achilles killed, dragging him at his chariot round the walls of Troy. A story my father had told me when I was very little. Almost the first story that I remember, which extraordinarily impressed me.

Athos was one in the series with these, only he was 'coming down' history. Nearly to our own time. Lots of things in the House had been made when he was alive. And the next question, the later dream was – when should I meet him alive, the Wounded Prince?

As I did. But that is not part of this book.

12
The Stump

IT was in a hedge in the middle of the fields, and when I found it there, by the pond, Mother called it The Stump. It had once been the bole of an oak, and by some grace of nature had been worn, smooth and unrotted, into the model of a small mountain. Perfect and complete, with *everything*, cover and cliffs, pools and an open valley, all rising to a central peak; over all of which an infinite variety of stories could be played out.

Finding it, I instantly desired to possess it more than anything else on earth, nor shall I ever forget the satisfaction of that morning when the gardener carried it up on his shoulder and put it down in the black-and-white summer-house for me to do what I liked with it.

They left me alone with it. It was long before Tony was born and it was wholly mine. Yet I remember one thing about its early days that illustrates the strange resentments of children, when my mother suggested, in all innocence, that I should arrange my soldiers on it and call it the Rock of Gibraltar. I tried it once and found that it would not do. Besides I had an infinity of other plans for it. Still, the effort pleased her, and she asked me, she asked me fairly, if she might show it to a visitor. That meant getting out the tin men again. I did and the visitor was duly impressed; and then I dismantled the arrangement to start a real one of my own. Poor Mother said again that she was sorry I hadn't liked the idea, that she thought it was a success; and afterwards she referred to it as 'the way the child did the Rock at Gib'. I never forgave her. For it had nothing to do with that place, or, and this was important, with any place that was *in this world* at all. Or with soldiers. It was a magic island, one of the Isles of Greece, but a magic one. Imbros or Lemnos or a name like that. Mother had got it wrong. She hadn't seen what one was trying to do. I had been polite to her and her visitor about the place called Gib, but the Stump didn't like it and I hadn't meant it. Nor did I attempt to explain. For the nature of the Stump was that of a mystery to be guarded, the whole business concealed by the natural silence of a child.

For months I would not touch it. Then, suddenly, it would become vital again, and I would awake in the morning with the exquisite thought that it was there, waiting for me; and from the time I was six until I must have been not far off sixteen, transported from summer-house to nursery and out of doors again, it was the thing on which I worked out my 'imaginations', the one thing not even my brother was allowed to share.

Until the day came when I made what somehow I knew to be its final arrangement and, knowing it was the last, never touched it again. Made this last time, before I went away to my school in Scotland, in Brother Aubrey's summer-house, the summer-house-by-the-sea.

When it was finished I looked upon what I had made as a set piece and called it 'The Island of the Sirens'. An island indeed it had often been before but never with such completeness, as a spectacle, a piece of theatre, a work of art.

Then I ran back to the house and called my mother to look at it; and – from that day to this I have never discovered the reason why – instead of the admiration she had often given and which this time I believed I had earned, she was shocked: 'No, this time I don't like it,' she said. 'It's very cleverly done, too cleverly, but there is something unwholesome about it.' And I, remembering nearly ten years before her gaffe about Gibraltar, was bitterly hurt. Also by that time I was an adolescent girl, and in the temper to meditate on such criticism. What on earth did Mother mean? This time I had taken a very critical visitor who I was secretly afraid of, Mrs Watkins who lived at Lilliput House, and she had admired it greatly and I thought sincerely. And Mrs Watkins didn't like Mother – that was well known. Besides you could see it in her cool, critical, bright French eyes. Two women who could *never* like each other. Now she had praised me and my mother had not, and it had taken weeks to do – oh dear, oh dear – what *had* Mother mean?

Only by then I knew that the Stump had done its work; and so that no one, not even the brother I so much loved, should have the handling of it, I asked the gardener, the same gardener who had carried it up from the fields so long ago, if I could have it burned.

Grown-up people say that children like to pretend that the things they love are alive. This is nonsense – they *are* alive, and animism a natural possession of childhood. Alive, not with a copy of their own life, but with the life, the *mana*, proper to the thing itself. The virtue Chaucer knew about. It is not an understanding they will talk about, and over which they resent interference, on a sound instinct that this communion with a beloved object, this awareness of its vitality, is a power that belongs to them, that grown-up people generally have lost. Lost through being grown-ups and saying this thing is alive and this thing is dead, great sillies! Yet this can exist quite happily in the child's mind with admiration and obedience.

Blessed are the grown-up people who have not lost it – a reminder of the conditions under which we enter the Kingdom of Heaven.

Thus the Stump to me was a live thing. Alive with personality, the character proper to a large, worn, wise lump of old oak. As, among other things at Salterns, in *their* proper way, were several of the trees. On one of them I looked, not with awe only, but with that not craven fear which Wordsworth insisted is part of the making of a man. The tree was a mighty pinaster, which towered apart from his peers off the high-banked tunnel of the Lavender Walk. Looking up through shrubs from the root-barred path below you could just see his enormous sides, gripped and clothed by a robe of ivy almost to his wild crest. The ivy down there in the shade was leafless, ivy roots stitched with brown threads and woven like ropes. But high up it was a glory of covering, polished leaves reflecting the light, in magical contrast with the great tree-crest, blue and unreflecting, a plume of boughs raised in some mystery of tree-contemplation against the 'unattainable blue' of the sky.

You had to go some way off to see him properly. To the moss-paved croquet lawn above the orchard; there, from the top bank on to the woods, an opening into dark trees that in Brother Aubrey's time had made a wonderful setting for a pastoral play, you could see his full height, lord over his tree-squadron, but in a manner different from the other commanders in the woods. Not patriarch or shepherd, like the oaks of the greenwood, nor like the birches, maiden-queens. Nor like the larches, a peculiar people, standing in a demi-lune, by themselves on the far orchard side. Nor dull, handsome strangers like the ornamental pines Victorian gardening had set about the place. Nor that awful bore, the huge macrocarpa, standing by itself on the turf-bank where the lawn joined the fields. Nor like the hundred others of his kind about the woods; though, with the stone-pine, the pinaster divides the magic of the firs. In his glistening dress he was a lord apart. Uplifted in more than his own contemplation, in dreadful power. Uplifted in glory in his fadeless dress, a thing to fear and adore: 'which glorious brightness a great terror bred'.

There was an hour when his beauty became almost too great to be endured, in summer, in the high blue weather, or at sunset when the heavens were charged with horizon light. There, from the old lawn, where at dusk the hedgehogs would be out, running squeaking with their babies, hard brown prickles and soft white prickles; then, before the shadows had fallen, clothed in ten thousand light-points from the sun's last rays his wild crest was lifted to receive. And with light something further and nameless out of the sky; who, in a few hours, the moon would clothe equally.

He had no name. When the woodman came, he died. By the time they came, so much was dead. I had never dared give him a name. For one thing, I was sure he had one, and I not allowed to know it. Only, now and then, when the 'mind's angels' were active, I saw he was a tree, come somehow to growth and power in a Dorsetshire garden. But sprung from the gold fir-cone, seed for the tree for the Bird of Paradise to alight on, and perch and soar and sing:

> One of the awful burning cherubim,
> With heaven-assaulting gaze, she pierced the dim
> Azure, and 'Holy, holy, holy' was her hymn.

> . . . I rest not till I gain
> The gates of an whole pearl, the golden floor:
> Then in the tree of which I am most fain
> I light, where of all bliss is endless store:
> Then sing beside my shining mate for evermore.

A poem, one of the few authentic poems of our time, *poetic* thought examined to its depth and fitted to its proper expression; and on reading it my mind returned instantly to that tree. What did the woodcutter do with it, the stuff of its living being sawn into planks? Better to believe that the stitches of its ivy-robe had made it useless, and that the Phoenix-harbourer returned quickly to its fire.

One wonders what present-day parents make of Wordsworth's expressed dislike of a child untempered by some such contact with what is fearful in nature. In its strict sense, awe-full. For it is a fear, and if the child were to say anything about it, they would think it their business to try and dispel it, explain that the tree was only a vegetable being strangled by another vegetable, expatiating on the mythology of trees as a result of the wish-fulfilment and the false analogy. One has heard them at it. And observed wise children shutting up, certain that whatever a tree is, it is something more than what grown-up people have to say about it. Real terrors, with no imagination about them, only panic, are another matter. For that they must protect themselves in what Father and Mother have to say as best they can, now they are no longer encouraged to ask Heaven to help them.

This I was spared, allowed to keep the animism proper to little children, over which they are so secret and so sure; the knowledge in them that may harden and deepen, imagination allying itself with reason; which was what Wordsworth meant when he said that poetry and Euclid were the two final possessions of man. In that way saints are made, artists and gardeners, all the people who can say: 'Tout est dangereux, tout est nécessaire'; who, incidentally, find that life is everything but one thing, terrible or exquisite, deadly or magnificent, any number of pairs of opposites in subtle alliance, but never for one instant dull, which means insignificant.

Of this animism glorious fear is only a part. There was no fear about the Stump or the little stones, who came out of their drawer now and found their proper setting. One's business with the Stump was really to make worlds, and those endless games were images of the whole of everything one could think about, and express in terms of a mountain which was an island, and a magic island, which lived in the Greek sea.

Hence my still remembered anger at having a wrong conception imposed upon it by well-meaning grown-ups from without. Not that they ever interfered. Even Nurse was singularly long-suffering. For it was a wet game, necessitating pools of water on the Stump and in things round it; and children can make a little water go a long way. I only remember one protest and no water to be used for a week, and that was after a flood. I suspect it kept me quiet; even that some of my arrangements may have charmed; even that in some ways I was a difficult child to stop.

The sensual delight in grouping, shaping and arranging, the utmost expression of sight and touch, the long joys of finding things to go on it out of the garden, I feel to this day. The drawn-out and repeated bliss of filling the pool under the crag. (The crag at the top that carried a pole, that became a gallows – which I wanted to change into a cross and was not allowed to because of reverence.) The pool was a few inches beneath, smooth and dark, and at its deepest, two inches deep. Two inches of dark crystal water, whose floor you paved with glass beads and the smallest and brightest of the stones. This was when the stones out of the drawer were 'sent back'. That is, they stopped being persons and became again plain stones. You told them this, very distinctly in a low voice, over and over again, and it was important. A magic. It usually meant – this was when I was very little – that the *mana* of some bead or button had replaced them. Only stones, by their nature, were better than button or bead, because they had made themselves. However I allowed them to bathe in the pool and adorn it, so that in my mind it still shines bright with its pavement of crystal and glass.

Then round it and about it, and sometimes if the money-box allowed (for what with bathing so much their hair came off and, bald, they were no use or could only do for devils or pirates or the crew of Odysseus' ship) were the dolls. The only dolls I ever liked, or admitted, so far as I can remember, into my play. At the stationers and toy-shop in Parkstone, little china dolls, about two and a half inches long, naked, their limbs jointed on brass wires, painted with black boots, but with long hair, in several shades, right down to their feet. Silly little faces, but it was the hair that did it. Utterly refusing to clothe them, except for an occasional silk wisp, they did very well. I hated their black feet, but that could not be helped. But while stone and shell or even bead and button took on vitality and character, not human but their own, the dolls remained nameless and quite dead. *They* were symbols, properties, part of the landscape. Very awful they looked, hung up by their necks, their hair flying, on the crag, from the gallows-tree. Part of a play I have forgotten, a memory that just escapes me – unless it had to do with the men on the Dead Man's Chest – the reason why I should have hung them there.

Below the pool there was an open space, almost the shape of a large open shell. There on cushions of flower petals and fine moss they would lie about and sing – Sirens this time. Odysseus heard their singing. And Odysseus, who was to land among them, Homer or no Homer, had his own difficulties. For the Stump – it was one of its charms – was balanced on a narrow base, and its oak walls overhung in cliffs and promontories, an island for under-rock sailing, best of all when at one late period it rested on a looking-glass sea.

Actually the only possible landing-place was in front, at the mouth of an immense cave. Polyphemus – one remembers this because it was one of the definite theme-stories, not like many of the early games, image-making without definition or coherence – Polyphemus' cave (and he had a war with the Sirens) was the only place where the Hero could land. Up a cliff, by a plasticine ladder, to its mouth. A ladder which was always breaking, so that once inside all he could do was stay in the cave, and from the edge of the rocks above the Sirens would lie in rows on their tummies, looking down on him, and sing. So that he had to listen though he could not get at them – which I thought very funny indeed. For again, the great cave had no exit except by another ladder. Though once I scalped some of them, so that they could join the crew as his sailors, and with their hair twisted a rope and let it down for him to climb up.

'What *are* they doing?' I remember my father asking.

'Singing to the men in the cave underneath. They can't get up and they can't get down. They've got plasticine off the ladder in their ears, but they can't help hearing a bit. Anyhow, Polyphemus will be back soon. It's his cave.'

There was Daddy, roaring with laughter. It *was* a good joke, their getting caught between the Sirens and the Wicked Shepherd. Then I remember his suggestion: 'What about Polyphemus' eye?' And then it was that I had my revenge on the 'brett'n' doll. For he was still living, undestroyed, and could be made to do for Polyphemus. I scratched out his real eyes and made a proper hole in his forehead with a lighted match, and my father called me a 'bloodthirsty little beast'.

Then there were other sequences before the final production of the Sirens, when, as I remember, they had the Island to themselves, one group reclining on a large pearl-shell, blue nacre shot with silver and rose, and others bathing in its gold fellow reversed. Another dim saga played round the figure of the Ivory Maid, a horrid little celluloid figurine given me at my own request by Colonel Everett. The oldest of the grown-up friends, it grieves me that I never showed him the gratitude and the affection he had earned. A debt I did not understand I owed until it was too late to pay it.

Colonel Everett of the Black Watch, who had fought in Egypt. Who is long dead, he and his sharp-tongued sister; who lived in the house next to ours along the Harbour edge; who let me try on his feather-bonnet; who gave me costly presents, much too good for a child, only spoiled by being exceedingly ugly, awfully expensive and dreadful to look at. There was one, a work-basket of the finest straw, lined with plump pea-green satin and fitted with every sort of coloured silk – for a child who could with difficulty thread a darning-needle and poke it through a linen button, with both ends of the cotton tied tightly together and only too often finished with a bead to make sure that the cotton would not pull through.

Mercifully I was not expected to do much needle-threading. For my mother was a celebrated embroidress, and used to tell me about her own youth, forced by Nanna Rae into the hours of plain-sewing she detested. So that, when her turn came, she had mercy on her child.

Beloved Colonel Everett, who kept – and again I did not know it until it was too late to let him know my pleasure in it – that simplicity of mind that is sometimes the property of old men of action, which, through a common innocence, makes them friends with children. Colonel Everett, whose courage I now realize; who, tortured by a malignant affection of the hip-joint, disciplined his fine old body into constant activity. Going about the country with his lame stride, taking me with him, and listening with endless patience to my first efforts in story-telling – embroideries, I think, out of episodes from the *Arabian Nights*. And, as we learned later, the lines carved on his fine old face were less of years than of the intensest physical suffering. Yet still he rode and swam, and on one occasion carried a small child who had walked too far. A man who loved my mother and when, widowed, she chose another man, tried, I know, to warn her. Nor did his sister, very properly, ever forgive us; and soon after they left Heathside, the small low house, set in a wood, with a wild garden, and I never saw him again. Until I was grown-up, and he almost too old to remember me. I in my first plumage and he, no longer able to do his soldier's business and hold death at arm's length, lying now with it staring him in the face and only the long years of pain to show. One thinks of him now, riding in Paradise, or at war with rebel angels at the head of his men, with only a tiny limp to remind him of the mortal years.

But I loved their home – chiefly for its trees. They grew on a rough lawn in front of the house, turf so rough that it was purple with orchids in spring. A set of ilexes, enormous and of great age; and one so huge that it split into three and had to be propped up.

We had no ilexes at Salterns, and I revered these, with their red stringy bark and leaves glittering with a myriad points of light, like a tree bearing crystals.

It was Colonel Everett who gave me, as it were, a measure, a standard, by which to appreciate the other old man of my childhood, my cousin, Henry Butts.

13
Cousin Henry

DESMOND MACCARTHY says somewhere that he should like to write a novel in which the chief characters were an elderly soldier and a maiden aunt. Chief characters, and what is more, life-bearers, setting the pace of the book's action. In it the two stock comics of the 'Intelligentsia School' should bring the forces of D. H. Lawrence into the light. Illustrate them. Exactly.

Again, it would be easy to dismiss Cousin Henry as the Newcome touch brought up to date, and be done with it. Only he was more than that – the retired Indian civilian, who had once ruled Oudh. To return after forty years to half an acre in a Sussex village at the gates of a great historic estate, now in the hands of the first of a new peerage. To find himself to his amusement arbiter of that village, its self-elected squire.

Actually I have seldom been near any man who gave one the same instant impression of what it is possible to call an innocent light. Indeed to be near him was to be 'like' warm, 'like' gold. The cousinship was distant, and I have heard it said that he had in him a strain of Russian blood. That, if true, might account for the fact that with all his simplicity – or rather because of it – there was something subtle about him. Again, the family legend said that, the youngest of several brothers, he had passed for the fool of the family; leaving Cambridge for the East soon after the Mutiny, to spend a life of adventure and administration whose aim was solely to bring the gifts of the West to the East, and there adjust them so as to form a harmonious and advancing society. To protect the poor; to see to it, as he said once, that there should be more corn and fewer cobras. Telling the story how, in early days, before he knew his people, he had offered so many annas a head for such poisonous snakes brought to the Residency. How they had begun to arrive, and lay about the verandah, first in strings; then in baskets, in boxes, in barrels; by bullock-cart; and more than once part of an elephant-load.

Until it occured to him, and a little detective work showed, that every cultivator in his province was keeping a cobra-farm.

Letters came for him too. From his young Rajah, who, an orphan, he had watched over from babyhood; and over two uncles, waiting their chance to poison the child and his guardian and each other. Letters in gold ink, on vellum; letters in all kinds of strange English – his daughter once showed me a collection – which he would not have shown, for the same reasons that my father would not show anything that so much as implied the congratulation of themselves by themselves.

Their dislike of any such ostentation was probably what united the cousins. For, apart from this, neither had the least touch of each other's quality. My father's impatience, his cynical and subtle intelligence were alien to his kinsman. Not incomprehensible, to whose charity all things had their due proportion in the mixing of this world. Certainly a man returned from the East with some of its detachment. A tranquillity which seemed to reinforce his charity, mixed with something that a child could feel to be mysticism. And, like all true mysticism, coupled in double harness with his commonsense. That my father walked in that country – in his fashion – he may have recognized. Indeed it would be pleasant to believe that knowing this was what brought him to Salterns. For when they were together the two men disagreed. Certainly on politics, for my father was a Tory of the fierce old school, based on a loathing of the commonness of the common, the vulgarity of the vulgar man. (Onomatopoeia is not usually possible with abstract nouns. Yet, letter by letter, syllable by syllable, that word conveys the concept for which it is the counter. V.U.L.G.A.R.) A quality which my father could hardly be said to endure at all. Indeed it was from Cousin Henry that I first heard of a belief in humanity. Strange in a man of his kind, he was a Liberal, not through any particular party optimism, but out of affection for men. Commissioner in an Oriental country, it was out of no pretence that he claimed that his life's work was to teach them to do without him. He meant it. He meant it because, all politics apart, he could not but believe that all men's eventual business was to enjoy 'the glorious liberty of the sons of God'. In his unassuming way he had done his best about that, and Heaven must see to the rest. Meanwhile, his lordship was trying to turn the village stream, which ran gay and sparkling down the village street, into a neat cement drain.

The village did not want it. Cousin Henry did not want it. His lordship did not get it. He also wanted to buy my cousin's acre of orchard and garden, its tiny house and lawn and trees, for a lodge at his own park gate. He raised his offer and raised his offer, while Cousin Henry remained quietly there.

So, as the Naboth of his village and, as much as he had ever been in India, Protector of the Poor, Cousin Henry went on his way. Upright on his grey horse, the wind of the Sussex oaks under which Queen Elizabeth had shot her arrows into the heart of a deer, lifting his pure white hair; and, smiling down at his friends and at his people, there distilled from him again one's baby-thought – 'like' warm, 'like' gold. A fineness, like 'a perfectly well-bred child' as my mother said once. Who, I think, was puzzled by him, who did not really like him. Or, perhaps he was one of those men who ride out to their lives' work out of Paradise, and against whom its gates are never quite shut.

14

The Wasted Land

SCHOOL was never wholly a success. It was nearly so the first time, the second time failing through sheer unregarded unsuitability. Also, at that time and in that world, little was known and less cared about the education of girls. Nor had my first training been such as to fit me for contact with my kind; like the education of William Beckford 'as weak in teaching the art of getting on with others as it was strong culturally'. And I was still an only child when, at about seven years, I began to go to Sandecotes, my day-school in the woods.

It is now justly celebrated, extending the elements of human culture to a district – a district as distinct from a neighbourhood – now the dreadful juncture of Poole industrialism and the suburban extension of Bournemouth. A place which has lost centre, character, distinction, hierarchy. Places so mixed take on a new character – *corruptio optimi* – almost as if some new and vile form of marine life had crept out of the Harbour mud and spawned and spread itself on land.

Gone are the ancient woods, pine and beech; for the delicate drifting lanes, lined with trees, twelve miles of high road, clanging with trams, run from Bournemouth to Poole. High roads and side roads, or desolate, weed-grown, leading-to-nowhere roads for development, lined or part lined or petering out into wilderness with villas, detached and semi-detached, in every style from Edward VII to George V Tudor-Gothic. The Sandbanks, in my childhood a pale sand and couch-grass wilderness, honeycombed with rabbits; and the tallest dune, High House Manger, a two hundred foot slide on a tea-tray into the soft, pure, drift at its foot, now levelled down for a planting of bungalows, in winter derelict; their blind windows silting up with the ceaseless spin of the sand.

Of which piteous change this book is a record. As dreadful an example as exists of the ruin we are bringing on our land, the defilement of the beloved.

It began when I was young. Its moderate beginnings threw my parents into despair. A work that has since been completed, all along the northern bank of Poole Harbour; and now a garage and a cinema overlook the graves of the village people, my father and my step-brother's graves.

We do not live there now. Where Salterns once stood in its tranquillity there are two houses; one, I believe, a boarding-house; and where the fields ran down to the Harbour, a number of people live, in the little red and white houses along a road that was once our drive. Of the garden and the orchard in the woods, of the woods themselves and the silver path over the moor to church, I have not dared ask.

Ever since I can remember the shadow of this defilement and this desolation rose on my life, lengthening with it. Until, some time about the end of the war, there came a point I suddenly recognized as spiritual saturation. The thing had *won*. It could not be stopped. There was more of this new than there was of the old thing left. The growing and defiling and *dis-organizing* had had their way, until there was only its way to have.

Not long after the war my mother sold Salterns. Since then I have been there twice, to Parkstone where my most dear aunt still lives. Not in my grandmother's house, but in one of the others, cut out of the woods of an old estate, but decently hidden away – and then she had pity on me and would not let me see any more.

In my childhood the world of Trollope and of Cranford, the country house and the village; and along the Harbour uplands, from the part called Salterns to the part called Lilliput, little houses of the gentry. *Nichée de gentilshommes*, and so on in descending ranks; now one planless stretch where the slum and the suburb are interwoven, rising nowhere above the suburb or the slum.

As Dawson, our great modern historian, says: 'There is the new Jerusalem of the social reformer, which is all suburb,' but this, from the Wareham river even past the tiny Bourne – as far now as the Stour at Christchurch – not even that excuse. No garden-city designers touched it, as superb a site for a garden-city as was ever given to man. Only greed, the vulgar tastes of the speculative builder, the most casual economic chances all operating together have changed one of the flowers in England's cap into a place where no person of decent sensibility would now willingly live.

This is not an unreasoned complaint. Man has a right to find delectable places and live in them; only not to destroy them in the process; showing himself no more than a nursery brat, only now bent on destroying more than his toys.

Part of a process we see everywhere. Part too of a spiritual process, the natural corruption in man's heart externalizing itself after him. To the external horror at least we are awakening. And, by Heaven's grace (it is our one temporal hope), since such building is too poor to last, this leprosy on the face of our land will rot away. Leaving no lasting scar. 'Green earth forgets,' said Trevelyan, thinking of battles and the absence of school-masters. Even under Fleet Street the Fleet is running yet. And the earth is strong.

Something of what was happening to the land was made clear to me at school. There were children there (most unwisely) I was not supposed to know. Sometimes I wanted to know them and then, to do me justice, I did. Sometimes I did not want to know them, not for the shadow of a second because they were poorer, but because there was something like a different sort of difference about them.

And here began a complicated muddle, a readjustment the war solved by cutting the knot, but a tangle of values in which my generation was involved; in which the new generation seems to be at a loss.

Then, in the country at least, the line was very sharply but clearly drawn between the people you could be friendly with and the people you could not. A division in which wealth made little difference; birth and profession set the standard, tempered by a certain allowance for exceptions. A sense of general values it is not so easy, it seems, to acquire. If you look today, without prejudice, at what happens, now that the old rules of thumb are abolished and every one knows every one else, it seems to work out in practice that people are forced to know every one who wants to know them. The anti-snobbery, so necessary once and so inevitable, has now gone so far as almost to paralyse choice.

Already, by that time, my school had become essentially divided: to train little ladies whose parents were beginning to try out the new idea of real education; daughters of the professional world, who had actually accepted the idea; and, especially among the day-girls, daughters of local tradesmen, anxious for their children to be civilized as well as taught.

93

Taught we were, sensibly and sometimes with imagination, just a little before the time when girls' schools began to make a fetish of athletics, and the fashion had come in, at least in the south, to treat them exactly as if they were boys.

A world to which I could not abandon myself, as I have never been able to. A world in which I frequently got lost. Only once, far later, for a few months – or was it really only for a few hours and then to a specially ostracized minority during the war? (Did I ever believe in absolute pacifism? Not a bit.)

The first part of the war I spent working for the L.C.C. among the derelict homes of East London. Youth takes the injustice of nature hardly. This was a desperate attempt to find something to do the basis of which activity was just. I remember walking back from its office, office of the National Council for Civil Liberties, under a high, ghostly winter sky, out of which, every other night, there dropped bombs. Explosions of human rage, valour and skill and science, but in what we had to do I found some peace in the sense of historic continuity. Certain things we were keeping going which, under whatever necessary modifications, were the same in war as in peace. We had spent the day, as we spent all our days, in the effort to keep operative the fundamental laws of society. For one, that the principles of our justice were still applicable, and men did not necessarily become monsters because they were of foreign blood. A discipline the state of war encourages men to forget.

We worked under a terrific handicap, a moral handicap of the most unpleasant kind. We sometimes did foolish things – one regrets to think that Tepitcherin made use of us as one condescending to the use of a contemptible bourgeois tool. Yet to a nation driven past reflection we did perhaps stammer a reminder that, in no matter what crisis, society is based upon certain liberties and certain contracts between the individual and the state, which the state no less than the individual ignores to its peril.

As I walked, trying to understand this, filled with this as with some pure intelligible security, I heard the first wraths of the guns at the Thames' mouth below Tilbury. The wraths so soon to be answered by shrapnel screaming down the air, the whine of planes overhead; and I walked on, schooling myself not to hurry, remembering the words of the Latin instrument 'habeus corpus', and the like: and believed that in our thankless task, by our perpetual appeals to Parliament on behalf of the helpless, we were also a public service. And was comforted. Caught up in what one understood, if only for an instant, was high civic duty, in our appeal to the ancient sanctions hated by a people at war, yet, if once lost, the meaning has gone out of victory.

I felt myself part of the body of the state. It had never happened to me before; humbly I gave myself to it, perhaps all the more sincerely because I could already guess that so far as the application went it would not last. The Council would be ineffective, not only on account of the appalling difficulties that beset it or because the Police might forbid it, but because the power that might make it effective was not yet generated enough on earth. It would fail, proximately as well as absolutely and more than it need, because there was something its members did not know. Coles and Postgates in their brilliant young immaturity. Something between the extremes of its membership, from the Cambridge don to the man who was looking up the war's progress in the Book of the Prophet Daniel. Something that I did not yet know, but I should; something that I carried about within me, as yet unhatched; the egg whose hatching would be my own life's significance.

All this made me work very hard, energizing all youth's fierce sympathy with the undermost underdog. For I had not yet got my society straight, who had received the war for measuring-rod.

So much for the young woman. So the child was hardly the kind out of which successful schoolgirls are made.

It never even occurred to me that it should, at a time when girls' schools were only just acquiring tradition; or that there was anything much worth thinking about in this business of House and Form and Class and Side. There were loyalties I knew, to family and friends, to a regiment; and vaguely but deeply to a culture, a tradition. But School only meant a place where you went to learn things in order later on that you might do the things that mattered. There were people in it who were nice, and people in it who were nasty; bits that were exciting and bits that were stupid and bits that were horrible. In the same way there were mistresses who were dull or who were interesting; mistresses who showed you things and mistresses who made you hate the name of learning: mistresses you could learn from and mistresses you couldn't and mistresses you wouldn't. Fraulein – this was at the very start – was fair game, and she had green teeth which made you think of something sickening out of a Russian fairy story, only you couldn't quite remember it. Miss de Chaumont – this was later – was a great lady, and you did, unreluctantly, as she bid. Miss Hill was a darling and a great scholar. I have still not come to the end of what I owe her. Miss Gray saw through you and forgave you, and you forgave her for doing it; knowing that in her clear dark eyes there was most uncommon wisdom.

Widsom – yet not for you. Not *your* wisdom. You were only a little girl. Perhaps when you were older. (Indeed in my childhood I had only three persons who were wise *for* me – my father, my aunt and Miss Hill. Not a bad allowance, if the first and the last had not been taken away so soon.)

Imaginative children have a great need for persons who will help them to wisdom. Their own wisdom. Which means taking them seriously. For the imaginative child is usually lonely, and is crying out all the time for assurance that when it has seen something the others have not seen, enjoyed something the others have not enjoyed, wanted something incomprehensible to the rest, those perceptions in it are not a delusion but a grace.

This is what the other children will not do. Because they can't; and anyhow, as they must, they are protecting themselves against what may be a superior intelligence by denying it. So the child, unless it possesses some special power, either to please or to enforce its will, is driven to explore an inner world. Where it may get lost. Or in the dark wood it may come upon its own double and fear it. Or fall in love with it. Out of which distrust may come; or over-esteem or contempt for its peers, of which the least symptom is priggishness. As for me, after my father died, both of these last things happened to me.

His death was the hardly-conscious opening of sorrow and the beginning of adolescence. One began to feel ahead. Know what one wanted, what one had to do. And that one would have to do it entirely by oneself.

It was four years since the bright March morning when I ran downstairs to a hushed, happy household and my aunt told me that my brother was born. I was taken into my mother's room, and they said she was very ill, but her bright eyes didn't look it. And in the room next door there was lying in a cot as perfect a baby as the world had ever seen. It slept, then for a moment opened eyes of the unspeakable translucency of the new-born, bubble of jelly into which it is hardly inaccurate to say that, in northern babies, the colour of the sea and the sky are distilled. Leaning over it, I loved it. A love I almost watched. A love I knew was there, had come in suddenly but, as it were, full-grown. That would never go away, standing beside me there, quickening in the quiet of the old low-ceilinged bedroom. Nor did it come into my mind to ask what might happen to it.

Any more than I had the least suspicion that my mother would hardly think it necessary for me to love her son like that.

Though I did notice that my father was not greatly moved, I accepted that as only reasonable. To a man who knew he would be dead long before the boy even began to grow up, Tony had come too late.

15

Intellectualis Amor

IT should be clear by now that my mother did not like me. At least by the time I was out of babyhood. I was not the kind of person nature intended her to like. A thing she could not admit, yet a state of feeling which took matters into its own hands after my brother's birth. What I have to try to show also is that her hardly-conscious rejection of one child and sudden flowering of devotion towards another was not a thing by itself. A sign, an expression, one of the terms of a series of integration and disintegration in which the whole fortunes of our family were bound up.

Yet, by now, remembering the picture of the Good and Evil Angel, it is possible to think of her as no more than the pawn, pushed about between the players, the good and the evil genius of our race. Walking about the gardens and the woods of Salterns, two figures in masks. One does not quite believe it:

> *Nullum numen habes si sit prudentia: nos te*
> *Nos facimus, Fortuna, deam.*

Perhaps in the thread of life, in Heimarmenê, the fine strand running through existence, stringing spirits and their activities like pierced stones, strung her on the evil strand.

Or, in bitterer moments, one's mind turns to the thought of some infernal spider, spinning from its belly a web, on which eventually, sucked dry and quivering, hung my house, an empty shell.

Four years later my father died – as if a strong, small, gold sun had set. Gone as we so often saw it go, set into the cup of the hills behind Arne, a gold disk, a wafer in its paten, a Grail-image.

So it was at his end, a short illness and then finish – or so it seemed to me. To my elders, doubtless, a drearier business. For a year or more he had been failing, and the *Vanity* had been sold and he had gone to the Club less, and sat more and more in the battered leather chair opposite the library fire. A revolving bookcase beside him, and on the right of the fire the door into the cupboard that was almost a room. Set deep into the ancient wall, country gear and fir-cone baskets on its floor, but above that, shelves. Shelves for all that were most precious among my father's books. Treasure that had something to do with the treasure in Daddy's mind and *that* treasure I knew I shared. And knowing I shared it was a secret with Daddy; our not saying anything about it, our just knowing we had it almost like Orpheus not having to look back.

And one day I should also share the knowledge that lived in the cupboard and came out of those books.

Books I did not often see, who, with washed hands, had the run of the great stately shelves. Little old books, squat and thick, with little pictures, or bound only in yellow paper instead of a proper back. Old books in French, a whole lot by a man named Brantôme, who knew Mary Queen of Scots. Or one alarming poetry book by a man called Ronsard, and Daddy had once made me spell out a poem about a lady sitting by the fire who remembered: 'Ronsard me célébrait du temps que j'étais belle.' He said that when you were old that was the best sort of memory you could possibly have, and I didn't understand in the least. Then he told me that the man Ronsard had taught Mary Queen of Scots how to write poetry and she did it 'pretty well for a Queen'.

Then there were books by a man whose name began with the English, but went off badly into French, Guy de Maupassant, who wrote stories 'not for you till you're grown-up'. And there were books and books and books, all bound in black and gold, with marvellous pictures, which were the real *Arabian Nights*. Only I heard Mother say: 'Freddy, you are *not* to let the child look at that.'

I didn't hear his answer, because it was wrong to listen, even by accident, but afterwards she made me promise, even if I found one lying about, and I promised, though I wanted to look at those pictures most dreadfully.

Mother knew about the cupboard too, with a difference that again I did not understand, but accepted as a child accepts what its mother says; without its altering in the least what I knew about Daddy. One day she spoke to me about it. I was not to look at the books in the cupboard. It was full of dreadful books. Books, she went on to explain, that only men read, and she wished indeed that my father would not read them. But I was always to remember that men were different. They could know about things and keep a pure mind, that if a woman knew about them her mind became – 'dirty' was the word used, and that was very wrong; and anyhow men hated women if they knew about 'those things'. Also it seemed that even God would have to try specially hard to forgive Daddy for reading some of the books that were in there.

What 'those things' were I had not the faintest idea. Nor, odd as it seems, much curiosity. If they were really bad, as Mother said, and it did not occur to me to disbelieve her, then I did not want to know about them. It must be as she said, a difference between men and women. At the same time, another and, as I dimly understood, a deeper part of my mind did not so much as rally to my father's defence as know he did not need me.

Perhaps towards the end of his life he did go a little 'gaga'. Probably there were books in that cupboard the booksellers in their catalogue marked as 'curious'. And what if there were, one smiles and says today? But this much I remember; there were *Moll Flanders* and Burton and *Les Liaisons Dangereuses*, Balzac and Stendhal and Baudelaire . . .

These I remember because I saw them, these and others. And because of what happened after, what my mother did once he was dead. The act which drew me painfully up out of childhood into the unsteady maturity of one who has watched, and even taken an innocent part in a dreadful thing.

I did not know why, but even then it seemed to me that my mother had made a bogy of that cupboard. Perhaps she thought that my father kept them in there because he *was* ashamed of them, when his reasons were obviously those of convenience, safety – for some of them were of great value – my youth, and possibly the curiosity that must have tinged her own horror. He had never troubled to show her, and now it was too late. Only a short time left now to sit before the fire and read his classics; and I ran off, puzzled. 'On my honour', rather proud of being taken into my mother's confidence; and since she had told me to be scandalized, scandalized, in the abstract, I was. Only behind this – I remember so well – was another feeling. A feeling I called 'the hollow feeling', and am blessed and cursed with to this day. A feeling which tells me, besides the façade of proper feeling and the expected emotion, that 'it is all my eye'. That what is true is something quite different, not necessarily the very opposite of the side one is asked to applaud, but something implying deeper values, something imperative and pitiless and ironic. That is the hollow feeling. And a voice saying: 'It's the Bunk.' No help, no compromise. Only it is impossible to revere the Bunk any more.

It was exactly that feeling which possessed me over the matter of my father's books. Already I had begun to make excuses for my mother. Make them, but not admit that I was making them. Trying to stuff the hollow feeling, because Mother *could* not be wrong. (If she was wrong, how could one know what was right? It was wrong even to think that one's mother could be wrong.) Staving off my punishment.

For behind these was the question of loyalty. Not only to my father, but again to the family-apprehended values whose understanding was his particular gift to me. To the mystery of the arts that made our two minds blessed. *Dei – intellectualis amor*. I did not question my mother. Only I could not but notice in her exaltation of disapproval an undercurrent of excitement equally strong.

It still makes me ashamed that I came as near as I did to disloyalty. I was in a period of young priggishness, and another part of me was alive to the fact that it was the proper time for my father to die. Die and get it over. So that Mother could marry again the gay beautiful man who adored her from afar. It happened like that in books. I could feel time tuning up for a new movement in our symphony, the first bars opening to the air of gratified desire. Later on I read Blake, who said that meant beauty. Anyhow I knew that Daddy and I would not meet again until we had entered the thing called eternity, which seemed to mean that, standing still, you could see all ways round you at once. Then and not before, not while we were both alive, should I be able to show him what I had made of the life he had quickened in me. Otherwise that bit was over. It was Mother's turn now.

We were sent away to Studland, my brother and I, with his nurse. The young gay nurse with the beautiful voice, who had come to us out of Oxfordshire, a game-keeper's daughter, and had taken him from the month. Studland that lies on the coast outside the Harbour mouth, under the curve of the downs. Nine Barrow Down to Ballard Down, to Old Harry Rocks whose wife, a tooth of white chalk, had melted into the sea one night when I was a baby, in a great storm. Set in a crescent of moon-coloured beach, pure sand, hard for riding, and picked out with rose and gold, crocus and pearl shells. High up the beaches the sand is winnowed soft, blown into banks to the edge of the great heath that flows along, mile after mile, far inland at Purbeck's feet. A kingdom of its own, hollows where the adders sun and whip across, set with jade and sapphire pits from old clay-workings; rising to wind-stirred ridges, tipped with furze the wind has moulded, like the topiary work in old gardens gone mad. A place where you may come upon wild apple-trees, and small woods always in the form of a grove, a ceremonial planting in the heart of no man's land. Find the rarest birds in England – an arm of the sea where the tide races as fast as a galloping horse. Whose tower (in our part of Dorset) is King's Barrow, whose altar the Agglestone, which some say means the Holy Stone. Whose sanctuary, not far from Ower where the gulls breed, is Goathorn, the black peninsula thrust out into the quiet reaches behind Brownsea. Whose god is the Goat.

August is the coronation of the Heath. When it puts on its Tyrian dress, ling-embroidered with bell-heather in relief, lacings and panels of sapphire-rose. There, lying out under the burning sky, you hear, rising round you, mile upon mile, the bee-thunder. Like an earth-pulse, the drum of nature rubbed lightly, with the whistle of wind and the surf-break for pipe and strings.

Millions of bees, gold fur and gold transparencies, digging, thrusting, shaking, staggering, soaring off; and the heather-honey burns with dark sweetness, and near Arne there is a farm where they make mead.

'A savage place! as holy and enchanted . . .' But on a spring day, walking up the eight miles from Goathorn to Corfe – Corfe where the heath meets the chalk and the turf, the greenwood and the hedges laced with star of Bethlehem – intolerably sweet.

A place that takes the sap out of your blood as it drinks your sweat – to feed itself. Restoring to you an essence distilled out of itself, which like certain maladies remain in your blood forever, a source of secret and dangerous power.

A place so far man has not been able to defile.

I had begun to run there, timidly. Especially at first to the Agglestone, standing two miles behind Studland, by a track through bogs. A rock the shape of an hour-glass. First the mound on which it stands. Then the stone. Roughly, a cone on its point, its apex stuck in the earth, its ragged sides spreading out, the work of nature, not of man. (Unless indeed it *was* man who placed it *in situ*.) Of reddish sandstone, not easy to climb, supposed debris from a glacier, only I believe the strata are all wrong. Or else glaciers did not come that way. Or if they did, behaved differently.

Anyhow, there it is, and there is nothing in that part of England like it. As I have said, some scholars say its name means the Holy Stone. Some do not. Others derive it from something else and others have given it up. 'The rock that the Devil threw at Corfe Castle' is the country version; and as usual, the Devil must have been a poor shot to miss it by ten miles. 'To be sure, but he was up in the moon when he did it' I heard it amended once; and when I was young there was at least one ceremony connected with it – that a young man might do well once in his life to jump off it and wish as he jumped. Brother Aubrey had. Also a friend (I think) of his, and *he* had broken his leg. I longed to do it. Many times I tramped out to it, and once, at the end of a wet summer, got off the path and, caught in a bog-patch, was horribly frightened at the gulping blackness that plucked off my shoes and sucked at my shins; and it was the blackthorn stick my stepfather had given me, called the Paddle, with a little piece of squared steel for a ferule, that, stuck into firm earth, got me out. Red and upright in the ground, it looked as if it was alive and a friend.

I never got to the top of the Agglestone. An affection of the knee-cap, probably hereditary and whose treatment in those days was very little understood, nor indeed did my family realize how serious it was, made me even more timid than I was by nature. So I stood at its foot, thinking of Brother Aubrey, scrambled up a few feet, but lacked the nerve to fight my way to the top.

I do not think that I tried that time at Studland. I had the baby now, and the heather scratched his fat legs and he said there were snakes in it that bit, and we kept to the lanes and 'the long and wonderful beaches', making for our mother a 'treasure' of rare shells.

Until, in the middle of one hot afternoon, my aunt came, and it was all over. A hot train, a white frock for seemliness, a hot cab and then home, and, in spite of a stuffy black dress, funerals were interesting; and my mother in her black veil very lovely by the grave-side, holding Tony by the hand. 'Your hair isn't mourning, can't you dye it?' he said; and when we got back it was Cousin Henry who poured me out a glass of champagne and walked me three times round the old lawn above the orchard 'to get the feel of it out of our mouths'.

Mother was a widow. And she wouldn't be one long.

16
Quiet in the Woods

LATE Summer settled upon Salterns. The impedimenta of illness and old age were cleared away, the battered old chair, the brass spittoon, the pipe-lighters – a local wisecrack ran: 'The Captain'll spend a hundred pounds a year to save the use of a match.' My Cousin Graham who had come to the funeral went away. Cousin Henry went away. (Cousin Graham was not such a good man as Cousin Henry but he loved Daddy more.) 'Me Uncle' he would say and they went off on adventures together one was not allowed to share. He did not like me much, but I liked him, because wherever he went he brought the sea with him. The sea had worked its pattern in innumerable fine lines all over his face, made little arrows – packs of them round his eyes. His eyes were sea-colour and he moved as a sailor moves, cat-light and very neat, and his ears had holes in them, not like Mother's for diamonds, but for the little gold rings sailors wore.

I was not supposed to care much for Cousin Graham and my mother was very careful to explain how little he liked me, but I can never remember a time when I did not like what he brought with him, which was nothing more or less than all the activities of the sea.

He was a well-known yachtsman, loving it with the sturdy love that kept his boat in commission all the year round; and it was that knowledge and that love he and my father shared. You saw it when you saw them together. It had a male tang to it, at once adventurous and sure. So that it didn't so really matter if Cousin Graham didn't go to church, and there was something funny about his not being married, and something even funnier about Cousin Mary, his sister. You were not allowed to know, and Mother said things about wild Graham blood; but, until I saw my stepfather's, he had the most beautiful hands that I had ever seen.

My father went – and the clocks stopped striking. The garden parched, the drought creating a vegetable dust, hot and aromatic, and in the woods the red pine-needles were slippery as glass.

Quiet in the woods – in the bracken, in a lair I had made, where from the high bank the wood looked down upon the orchard and the great straight herbaceous walk, driven through it like a Roman road. One of my mother's loveliest works.

Quiet in the woods, quieter than in the House at night. Where every night I thought I heard my father's quick old step coming up the stairs and across the board that creaked to his room.

Quiet in the woods, the place where there was quiet, for the child who knew by now that she had become a less-wanted child.

Quiet in the woods, in the bracken's arms, who had now no arms but a baby's that were quite her own.

Quiet in the woods, but just behind you a tall daimon standing beside a tree.

'Daddy's gone, I have got to do things by myself now.'

'Your father is dead. How are you going to carry on? You will forget what it means. There will be a fire and your memory will burn with it.'

Quiet in the woods, and I thought of my father's wisdom as buried in a box, under a tree. Like in the old song – a gold box with a silver pin. Some day I should be grown up and I should dig up the box and turn the pin.

'The trees will be gone. All the high trees will be cut down by then. You will not be able to find where it is buried. The box of your father's secret knowledge, which you have inherited. When you come of an age to use it, it will be lost and you with it. That is not the sort of thing men cherish. There is your house and the world, and one is the image of the other. Do you think you have it in you to make a third image?'

So said the evil Hero. Until I sat up in the bracken and answered him, clasping my knees. Something like this: 'He didn't give it me at this time or that. He made it into me. So that it can't be lost – dug up or not dug up. It is in me, and all your magic can't stop it. It will come out of me when I'm up to it.'

'If you take it like that,' said the Hero, 'there is no more to be said. Only look out. There are people not likely to be pleased at a treasure they do not share. We shall meet again. I was your father's shadow or his name would be written in larger letters than you . . .'

It was then I understood He would return indeed, in all sorts of places. To work out his desolation. His name I did not know: his address was the place called the Dark Tower in the Waste Land: that he was the opposite of those who carry the Sanc-Grail. Something was coming to this wood, and the delphinium-walled flower walk, my mother's best work. In the ritual it would be called the Waste Land; and my father had died without the spear-touch: I knew too much and not enough.

Quiet in the wood. He had gone away, the evil Hero, and our lives dragged under the heat. Quiet in the woods. Wait now for the great gales of the equinox to roar away the brittle leaves, with its sheets of pure sky-water lay the dust. Then out of the cooled soil the toadstools would spring up, the purple and orange and scarlet, and the mustard-coloured one like a sponge that the book said was good to eat. When the last of them was tired of growing, the kind with maroon tops and cream gills grown slug-eaten and small and grey, then Winter would be near – Winter when the dead-men's-fingers grow out of rotten wood. But it was fun, standing at the Winter Door, which is one of the Four Doors of the Year, fun to get up in the lifting dark and walk through the woods in the purest of pure light, on Sunday mornings to church.

Then there would be another quiet in the woods; and though He would come back, there were all the Gods and Goddesses; there was God Himself. Between us we ought to be able to keep one bad Hero in his place. Only, what *was* his place?

From the flower-walk I heard my mother calling me.

17
Murder in the Woods

WHAT follows I still hate to remember, and my participation is still my shame. Shame and anger, as though a trick had been played on me. Which there was. Yet, as I learned slowly to see, my mother was also a victim. Victim of the shameful pruderies of her training, a peculiar impurity forced on the women of her generation – heaven pity them! – as purity itself. It is a trick that takes great natural purity and a strong intelligence to see through. Purity and strong intelligence, not natural intelligence only – she had plenty of that – but a trained one.

In looking back, all my years, I think that I have seen more quiet unostentatious harm, destruction of the deadly, not too noticeable sort, done to young women whose naturally powerful minds have been left untaught. Left empty. Left like a powerful car with a lunatic at the wheel. Left to fill themselves with any kind of rubbish, any form of discontent. To burden or perplex, or even more often make them atrociously vain. Invariably to land them in mischief. Lovely instruments with the edge taken off them, put to no use at all. Or to mischievous or even abominable use.

Only character can save them – and not always very pleasant character. Character which often cannot develop without the forbidden use of their natural wits.

This is not so frequent now. Perhaps the chief, perhaps the only reason for one of my sex to thank God they have been born today. A state of things to which my mother was as finished a victim – the victim so perfect as not to know what has been done to it.

A week after my father died, my mother said to me:

'I am going to burn those dreadful books of your father's. We will do it together, up on the asphalt tennis-court. It doesn't matter that they're very valuable. That even makes it more important.' Then adding what even to a child sounded incredible: 'I feel that I am washing Daddy's hands clean.'

It did not make much impression on me at the time. It was with the years that its meaning deepened and I understood what had been done to us all. Until, on a night in my middle-twenties, in my sleep I saw the fire again and the smoke, stinking with paraffin, rising in the perfumed woods. On the old tennis-court, made of asphalt many years before for Brother Aubrey to play on and never used since. It had heaved and split and cracked, pine-needles drifted in its shallows, and after rain there were warm pools for paddling in. Set in the pine woods, at one end grew a large sycamore, and under it there was a long seat, moss-patined and set on stones. The sycamore was one of the magic innocent trees, whose dryad in spring dropped green keys down your back. I used to sit and read there, watched the bushes that sprang up in the broken shallows and the roots that each year heaved and split the paving, and knew, every bit as much as in Kipling, that this was a 'letting in the Jungle'.

In my sleep I was there again, and it was a long time since I had thought of what had happened there. The place I should never see again, and the scorched, grimed, stinking things that sprawled there, face downward. Which had been so gently handled. Which not to handle gently was one of the worst things one was told not to do. In that sleep I saw something I cannot remember, and heard something that seemed to be of extreme significance and which I cannot recall; and I woke up, tears pouring down my face, crying out to my mother: 'You have murdered beauty!' and in the night the full shock of realization came to me.

I believe Cousin Graham protested, but I helped her to do it. Little square old books, the noble pages of Burton in their gold and black, their delicate engravings of fabulous princesses. French memoirs, with their portraits of Ninon and the Dubarry and the great Pompadour. It hurt. However careful I was not to look, it was like a killing of something that ought not to be killed. That it was silly to destroy like this. One of them had fallen open at a thrilling picture of a duel.

My Cousin Graham shrugged his shoulders. Heaven knows what he thought. Heaven knows what the gardeners made of it, and Edwardian ladies feared 'what the servants will say'. But the little hospital nurse, who had stayed on, as my mother's health after the strain of nursing needed care, was not impressed.

As a bonfire it was a disappointment. I think my mother thought they would shoot up in flames, made combustible by their contents, and it would be like a sacrifice in the Bible. It was not at all like that. Stench and smoke – and she did not know what to do and sent for paraffin, and there followed, as I remember, a slow charring that went on for a long time. Lit something that began to burn in me, who had not the heart to go near it, but ran away from that pyre smouldering in the woods.

As she lit it, a cloud went over the sun and, in a few drops pattering, there fell out of the sky the first rain in weeks.

It was the little nurse who blew on my fire. We had gone to stay at Shaftesbury, the most ancient town on the high downs. We stayed at the inn, and the food was different – fun, and it was harvest-time in a world burnt to gold dust.

The little nurse and I went for a walk in the lanes, and I talked about the poetry I was beginning to swallow in huge draughts. She was sympathetic and interested – the real interest one learned to recognize so quickly, which was so rare. We leaned on a gate and watched the sunset, and somehow the question of the burning arose and she said: 'Your mother did not quite understand. Of course they were not all immoral books. Some of them were great French classics. I've seen them in other houses where I've nursed, and heard my patients speak of them.' I don't remember what I said. I probably tried to defend her. Only I knew instantly that what she said was absolutely true. (Also that, with perfect respect, she did not like my mother.) Understanding too that she was sorry for me, even anxious about me, who understood my position far more clearly than I was to do for many years.

For me at that moment, she had made my mind clear to me and I thanked her. But she had made my cowardice clear also.

Two other memories remain of that Shaftesbury visit. A drive we took to Fonthill, to see what was left of Beckford's Palace of Art. One of those fantasies that 'the cussedness of things turns somehow always into a palace of toys'; and 'Beckford's Folly', probably the best name for it. Not quite – 'Beckford's Escape'? Yes, but there is something more. Even to a child who knew precious little about it there remained a memory of that afternoon. A memory, a sensation that clings even to the names of such places, whether one has ever seen them or not. The Palazzo del Té at Mantua, Ludwig of Bavaria's reveries in stucco and gilt and stone. That palace where 'no impatient courtiers ever paced the l'Oeil de Boeuf, no dukes disputed precedence with royal bastards in the bedchamber.' Places full of echoes and overtones, 'creux néant musical'. Hollow air with a trembling in it, in houses built to house a desire more poignant than can be stated even in the utmost intricacies, the utmost splendours of marble and glass and stone. Panel or tapestry or porcelain, mirror or fountain, but through their utmost combination, leaving in the shifting transparencies of light its ghost behind. Dream of a Gonzaga or a Beckford or a Bavarian king. His version still hung over Fonthill with its ghost of a tower. For I remember a tower, and remember too that I was told that it had long fallen.

Also, for contrast, his great-great-nephew (I think), old Mr Beckford, was our next neighbour but one, churchwarden and yachtsman and my father's friend. Quite the dullest old gentleman I can remember, and his son the dullest young man and his yacht the dullest steam-yacht, in which he used to puff solemnly up and down Channel, from Cowes to Weymouth for the regattas and back again. No one at home even pretended that he was not dull, yet some of the lovely things in his ugly house he had inherited from the Beckford collection; and as Mother once said: 'He doesn't understand, or even quite like to think how he could have had such a man for an ancestor.'

The little nurse crosses my memory again. I had inherited some money under my father's will which my mother did not want me to have. One day, driving near Shaftesbury, she cried out that it was not fair. Not fair to my brother. Neither was it fair to her that my father had left us both wards in Chancery.

I did not understand in the least. It had not occurred to me that by his birth I had lost a considerable inheritance – to question that a son came first. Yet it did not seem unreasonable that my father would want me to have something for my own. Mother had got for her life more than either of us, and Tony, of course, would have what she had. I was a little hurt, wondering if I was selfish to be hurt. I talked it over with the little nurse who said: 'Don't talk of giving that money back to your mother. You'll need it when you are grown-up.'

But my mother's cry of anger rang so loud that I was frightened of it.

18
Shelley

IT was about this time that a new perception wakened, an ugly unquiet feeling that there was something wrong about in the place in which we lived – a wrong that was going to get worse and that Salterns was a place cut off. There was my home, the sea on one hand, and on the other the counties of Dorsetshire and Hampshire stretched away. Green lands, across the great heath and Purbeck and the world that began on the further side of Lytchett Clump. There lived our oldest friends in by far the most interesting houses, the most lovely, the most real world.

Only it was hard to reach. Half a day's driving, or else the brougham put into the train at Parkstone Station and put to at the other end. It was quicker, if they lived near the coast, to go by sea. Sail in the *Vanity* along the terrible Dorset coast, Kimmeridge Ledges and the Mupes, Swyre Head and Dancing Ledge and Worbarrow Tout – silver and violet bastions shimmering, and only the racing aquamarine fret at their feet to remind you that they were not made of dreams but were the awful strength of England, sailing the oceans like a ship.

Only Mother was never happy on board the yacht; or only when in exquisite clothes, exquisitely worn, she stepped on shore, or out of the carriage up to some ancient door. And on the drive home we would play our best game, which was remembering as many as possible of the old and beautiful things we had seen, talking them over and discussing their arrangement.

If we had been paying calls nearer home, even in the great brick-red Bournemouth houses, the game changed and we collected horrors. The pictures of stags and mourning or enamoured ladies, the flowered wallpapers and gilt clocks under glass shades, the 'Victorian horrors' not yet à la mode again. The gilt costliness, the 'modern' as opposed to the 'antique', 'good' taste from 'bad'. For with her natural sensibility, my mother had learned a very great deal of this from my father.

So that by the middle of her life she had become a woman capable of creating the loveliest interiors; without any great originality, adapting old and new, one style with another, indoors and out, for the making of that most perfect instrument for social or for solitary life, the English country-house.

Only, between the Green World and us, between Salterns set in wood and marsh and sea and those houses on the further side, each in their appropriate dress, there was a barrier rising. Risen already on the crest of the low hills to the north of us, the butcher-coloured scum of little houses, cutting us off from the world inland. And with the scum, like straws in the foul bright bubbles left by the Harbour tide, the things that go with it – the tram-lines, and raw spaces and little shops.

The things that disappear when it rises – first the trees, and with the trees, copse and bird and rabbit, furze and broom thicket; toadstools in autumn, birds' nests in spring; little paths and brown children and free things to eat, blackberries and mushrooms and sometimes plovers' eggs.

When the people who go with those things go away, other people come. People who do not know the things we knew and do the things we did. (Or so it was assumed. Parkstone may have been filled suddenly with the stuff of philosopher kings, but I do not think so.)

Actually, a sociologist would have noticed a flood of petty-bourgeois, urban culture, flooding the tranquillity of English rural life. A perfect specimen. And from Salterns, a perfect opportunity for detached survey. Only there was no such spectator. My father would have been nearest to it, and he had contented himself with dying before the foul thing actually touched his land. Leaving behind two passionate children. Nor any hope of an organized force with which to meet and stem the riders of that sea.

The tragedy of our time in microcosm, and 'Too late' written up wherever a rag of field or wood, or solitary ancient tree remains, like a reef cut off and soon to be submerged.

Only from the bridge above Parkstone Station the eyes can still travel across the Harbour unhindered, to the eternal line of Purbeck and to Corfe with its towers.

It was about this time that I first began to read Shelley. Since babyhood almost I had heard 'Arethusa' tumbling through my mind, but it was about the time of my father's death that I appropriated his copy – the four red volumes of the Centenary edition – and read them, first in his memory, and then until they possessed me utterly. As in any number of young and ardent minds, working out something in this way:

The world isn't like what people tell you. There are ugly things about, like wolves running, and the Psalms are quite right. There are bad people (not at home, of course, but just outside). There is the awfully handsome son of the corn-chandler, who dresses up like a gentleman, in checks and riding breeches, only not quite, and makes love to girls and doesn't marry them and makes them specially miserable, and you're not to admire him because he's not a gentleman. It's a pity, and I should if it wasn't for those girls, for his head is like a Greek statue. Only you can see he is bad.

Also you feel sad inside, not quite knowing why. That's feeling the world. And the girls at school don't like you much. At least the ones you want to don't. Things are pretty miserable really. Even Mother mayn't be going to be happy when she marries Uncle Freddy.

Only there is a world where things are different, the world Shelley knew. The heavenly world, only not the parson's heaven, more like the 'many mansions' Our Lord said heaven meant.

Only to know about it is truly a great adventure, and you have to dare things. As Shelley did.

That was why, just before he died and we went to Studland, Daddy asked Mother for *The House of Pomegranates* he had given me, and she found him reading 'The Fisherman and His Soul' and he was crying. I knew why. It was because it speaks there of 'the magic and mystery of beautiful things' which is eternal, only it doesn't go with being old. My father cried because he had been faithful to it, and it didn't matter that Oscar Wilde had done something very bad. He belonged to that world, and of course God has forgiven him.

Again, it was later and I was a young girl and came upon an illustration that impressed me profoundly. I was at the Bournemouth Theatre, with my mother, and there sat in front of us, in the stalls, a coarse-built, thickset man with a red dissipated face. He was flirting with a woman, an Edwardian beauty and a friend of my mother's, and she frowned and afterwards said:

'I wish she wouldn't. She'll get more than she bargained for. He has a dreadful reputation.' I knew I should hate to be looked at like that. 'Who is he?' I asked. She told me the name. 'Yes, he's a descendant of that poet you're always reading. The last of his name.'

Was he? I knew he could not be in the direct line, but descended of Shelley? That dewlapped squire with his bull neck, that air of the prize animal, the farm beast with a rosette stuck on him and a ticket. (He wore a large buttonhole.) He would hate his ancestor, and he was what life was like. When the lights went up his bold eyes ran over my points and I turned my head, feeling naked, feeling ashamed. Ashamed too that, once he could not see me, I could not take my eyes off him. For although he was beastly, he had power.

The old cry of the gnostics began its repeat: 'This world is as bad as you please, but if only you can get beyond the moon . . .' Beyond the moon you could fly on Shelley's wings, wings he lends so generously to girl and boy. Captured at the same time intellectually by the superb, silly rationalism which says that the common run of men have only to see virtue to recognize it. Be persuaded by it, be instantly content to live by it forever.

What had that man made of his ancestor's teachings? I could guess. In some way my opening womanhood knew he was the enemy; and, by contrast, Shelley's experiments appeared the noblest conceivable expression of human life and love.

It was said of him lately that his primary error as a philosopher, which error somehow translated itself into his poetry, was a belief that because a custom had been accepted down the ages by presumably sane men it must then have something wrong with it.

Youth, engaged in each generation's spring-cleaning of its inheritance, finds this sort of thing attractive. Especially in my day with a Shaw about. It does not matter unless the essential poise of the character is disturbed. Which can be done by an unsympathetic, above all by an ignorant home. And in my generation our equilibrium was thrown out again and with appalling, destructive violence by the war.

All the same –

> *Ah, did you once see Shelley plain,*
> *And did he stop and speak to you . . .*

Is it possible to retell what that meant nearly thirty years ago? Take you for one of his dawn-rides, christen you in that stellar dew only he could distil. A ride on a comet's back, a dip where the stars swarm like gold bees. All things made of earth and the fleshly elements purified by those of fire, crystal, spray, the light of the moon, and the rainbow for a ladder between earth and heaven. The constant presence and comfort of the archetypes of which our world is the sensual image, and of heroes and heroines crowned with more than common victory – ἐν τούτῳ νίκη – and Hellas the beginning and the end and the significance of it all.

And among all heroes and heroines there remained but two; only

Prometheus and Asia. (Very odd it seemed before I learned scansion that she should be called after the largest and least Greek and most mysterious part of the earth.)

Until it seemed that in the hero Prometheus the meaning of human life was to be found – Prometheus, the rebel, the fire-bearer; who told people they might do the things they had not been allowed to do – that was why he was called Saviour. Sure too that Shelley had found the lost solution of Aeschylus, whose Prometheus never made his peace with Zeus.

How had one to live to be worthy of his salvation? Had not Shelley told us? Surely, surely he had:

> *To suffer woes which Hope thinks infinite;*
> *To forgive wrongs darker than death or night;*
> *To defy Power, which seems omnipotent;*
> *To love, and bear; to hope till Hope creates*
> *From its own wreck the thing it contemplates;*
> *Neither to change, nor flatter, nor repent;*
> *This, like thy glory, Titan, is to be*
> *Good, great and joyous, beautiful and free;*

What more could you want? A hint of philosophic difficulties over Demogorgon crossed the mind. Not quite what an ancient Greek would have thought of, though of Jane Harrison and her *Themis* I had not yet heard. And women – their business was to be 'Free and sincere'. 'Good and kind'. Then they were not just people who didn't matter so much as men, who mustn't be allowed to learn things. (Which was what Mother really meant when she told you how men laughed at Bluestockings behind their backs.)

'Love and man's unconquerable mind.' Youth that so longs for one short passionate key to everything – and still those years seem blessed when I knew that in those five words I had found it. Blessed, though the faith of my fathers went, as a tale grown stale with telling and actually never adequately told at all. History – who could be so blind or so base as not to see it? – was the story of man. Man, lighting his own and his children's children at Prometheus' torch. Until all men walked in the same light as Percy Bysshe Shelley. And he? Oh that was easy. There were as yet in man infinite unrealized powers. When the common man was Shelley's equal, he had become one of the spirits of which man has hardly yet dared dream.

Meanwhile there was simply everything Shelley had written to read. In that one learned especially what happens to Fire-Bearers in this wicked world, and what they must expect and what they must endure. And if one were to meet heavy weather (as one would) there was 'Hellas' to remember – Hellas

> *Built below the tide of war,*
> *Based on the crystalline sea*
> *Of thought . . .*

And if you wanted to know how to carry on, not being a Greek captive maid, there was the lovely, little sober gnomê:

> *Revenge, and Wrong, bring forth their kind:*
> *The foul cubs like their parents are;*
> *Their den is in the guilty mind,*
> *And Conscience feeds them with despair.*
>
> *In sacred Athens, near the fane*
> *Of Wisdom, Pity's altar stood;*
> *Serve not the Unknown God in vain;*

On these hung *all* the Law – surely, surely they did. Stupid people muttered that he hadn't been kind to Harriet – probably she'd asked for it; and if it *was* irritating for Mary to have 'Epipsychidion' written to someone else, hadn't he answered her, saying that if you divided true love you didn't make it less?

Also what about the people who said he was all stars and moon-light, and no dark earth and no red blood?

> *I met Murder on the way –*
> *He had a mask like Castlereagh;*
> *Very smooth he looked, yet grim;*
> *Seven bloodhounds followed him:*

(By reason of which my notions of English foreign policy of the period remained, for the next twenty years, hopelessly wrong.) But at that time there was 'Peter Bell' making fun of poor pious old Wordsworth; and 'The Masque of Anarchy', which might have been written for the raw rough men who worked our clay-pits.

'I am poet, atheist and aristocrat' he had written in a hotel book of himself. 'Atheist' checked me. Was he? Every line he wrote seemed to a child to contradict it. He wasn't. It was his swank. Yet I was disappointed with my aunt, who loved him, this side of idolatory, as much as I did, when she said that, if he had lived, he would have become a Christian. Indignant, and somehow – not comforted, but interested. For however unsure I was becoming of my father's faith, I could not understand how it was possible to doubt the existence, or indeed the continual presence of God.

God forgave Shelley. God in Shelley had summed himself up. Had born Hellas again for us, without which there could be no good life for men.

Indeed, there was one night, some years after the end of this book. Again it was in London, in the last lap of the war, when the air-raids were screaming out of the high winter sky. I was alone in a Hampstead studio, my first home by myself, and the high fragile roof was made of glass, and the gun on the Heath shook the earth and the engines droned overhead, and suddenly panic came over me. I dared not go out through the dripping shrapnel, and the infernal things were zooming nearer and nearer overhead; and instantly the danger of it all and the horror were made clear to me, and I ran to try and hide myself in a little outbuilding, a dark hole full of wood, where the roof was low, and no airy brittle roof rose above me in shadows.

I can only try and tell what happened as I tried not to crouch there. Which was a clear, thrilling, quiet voice repeating: 'Love and man's unconquerable mind. Love and man's unconquerable mind'; and I was suddenly charged with knowledge that, somehow, it mattered that I should command myself; that, in some unrealizable way, I had it in me to give or take away the life from those words.

Repeating them, I went back; and inside the studio and the racket overhead there was a quiet into which I entered where both fear and death were swallowed up.

Last of all, that no perfection might be wanting, Shelley had made a joke. In the proper tradition, parody of a satire-play. And 'Swellfoot the Tyrant' the kind of poetry you wrote about England, George IV as against Prometheus. (A lesson in subversiveness that later was to make me miss a lot of fun.)

Oddly enough it was here that I met my only doubts. This was supposed to be history when Daddy was being born. Not ancient Greece, and something had gone wrong with it.

Queen, Queen Caroline –

Washed her face with turpentine,
Combed her hair with the leg of a chair

So Nurse had sung when I came in untidy for lunch. Besides, there was what Daddy had said when I asked him:

'The King said she'd been unfaithful, so they had her up and tried her. She had a very clever lawyer, but when the lords of England had a look at her, they said it wasn't possible for a woman like that to have had the chance – '

'Hush, Freddy, that's not a proper story for the child.' All the same, it stuck; and I had to suspect my idol of twisting history to make it sound grander than it was.

Yet, on looking back, in spite of childish credulities and uncritical adoration, in spite of trying (and this unsuccessfully) to believe that the millenium would come when the throat of the last king was strangled by the entrails of the last priest; in spite of attempts, the fluff of one's hatching still as pure on one as thistledown, to translate a spirit's practice into a system of conduct for a post-war world, I cannot regret the adoration of those years.

'Did he stop and speak to you?' He did; and the common meanness of mankind of less effect where such voices are heard.

19

Odd Man Out

MY brother grew from exquisite babyhood to tiny boyhood. My mother's second marriage followed a year after my father's death.

Followed in as natural a sequence as music – but not to the same air as when my father held Salterns. Not another movement of the same symphony even; that music I was not to hear again until a long way down my corridor in time I was to listen to Figaro and to the Fifth Symphony.

The musical intelligence I should have inherited from both sides of my family was beginning to translate itself more and more into pleasure at verbal sound. I cannot remember a time when I was not enraptured or tortured by words. Always there have been words which, sometimes for their sound alone, sometimes for their sound and sense, I would not use. From a loathing of their grossness or sickliness, their weight or want of weight. Their inexactitude, their feeling of acidity or insipidity. Their action, not only on the intelligence but on the nerves, was instant. Instant and constant, as my joy at other combinations, and also at what was nothing more or less than our old friend *le mot juste*.

'*That* is the proper way to say it' I remember trying to explain, almost a baby, while Daddy grunted approval and no one else had the least idea what I meant; and I was called 'funny' or 'precocious', and had no idea what *that* meant. Then one day my aunt, I think, told me that in Homer words were called 'winged' and I shivered with pleasure; and the word went into the collection, precious as the stones or the buttons or the games with the Stump, the game that I played by myself in my head, and called 'real' words. Words that went up and down, in secret favour, that rose and sank or elaborated themselves into phrases. Reading brought new combinations; then one day, out at sea, when I was about seven, came the discovery that I could put some of a new set into a pattern and say them out loud.

They were the names, out of Morris's *British Birds*, of all the gulls, and I said them to Nurse, on deck, one summer morning, cruising down Channel towards Weymouth. A blue day, and the wind just filled the mainsheet, and the boom creaked and the bowsprit rose lightly to meet the waves on the race off Old Harry Rocks.

Sailing close in, the Purbeck cliffs blazed their fierce white. Everything wore white, except the flint-black mouth of the Parson's Barn; blue to the feet of white and blue over it, and in the blue a rose on fire. Sea and sails and spray, sky and turf and cliff, and, floating across the blue span, swinging low behind the mainsheet or falling off the cliff tops like spray on wings and everywhere mewing like cats, went the gulls. Gulls whose names I had just found sweet to the taste of the mind – gannet and black-backed and herring gull, tern and skua and kittiwake, puffin and guillemot and Ross's Rosy Gull. The last I had never seen except in a dream, and tried hard not to count; but now, in plain eight-eight couplets, I had made up their names into a verse. Of which I can only remember two lines:

> *And the kittiwake and the Ivory gull*
> *Picked the eyes of a dead man's skull.*

Nurse was impressed. Which impressed me. It was then suggested that it would be nice practice for my writing if I were to put it down; and I remember sucking a pencil and wondering what the names looked like spelt to the *Vanity's* slow pitch and swing.

Then, for a long time, I did not try again.

In my inmost heart I was troubled by it, troubled by a something that I could feel hatching in me. There were words. I could make words do things. But words could do things to me. Words would make me use them. Only of my own will I was afraid to begin, because once I had begun they would not let me stop.

Or, and that was worse, I should not be able to do what they said. That would be a new pain, not being able to find what you must.

Prose was not so bad. It didn't drive you as hard as tunes. And what they made you write in school mostly didn't matter at all.

This last was only too true, rarely did the work set seem worth troubling about. When it did, I believe I occasionally astonished my teachers, who otherwise reported with weary truth that seldom had they a child of such reasonable abilities who did so little work.

That was what every report said; my father's real anger on one occasion made no difference. I did not know why. When the right lesson came along it was as though a lock had been fitted with its key. Otherwise, smudged exercise books and endless day-dreaming, bad marks and a dubious reputation. And I, sensitive and in some ways biddable, did not care. Or rather I did care, but I was helpless. In a way I was always learning. In my home, and there in my father's day the standard of culture was so far higher than our neighbours as to make me, in certain ways, incalculably in advance. But as for the regular acquiring of a scheduled set of information – I had far too many other things to do; until the day came when Miss Hill took me in hand.

By that time my father was in his last year, and soon I was to leave her chosen, enthralling, intelligible teaching for, in every sense of the word, a harder school. It was the crucial moment. If I had continued with her, or if I had been heartened to face the hardships ahead of me, if I had been sent to a public school more wisely chosen for a south-country child – so much time, health, young trust, young capacity for happiness need not have been wasted. I might even have become the scholar I still sometimes dream about.

Only with my mother's remarriage there began at Salterns a very different regime. Gay and lovely often, very much more *mondain*, serving many other turns. But with my father's death one thing had gone for ever – the old implicit respect for the things of the mind. My mother, very naturally for a woman of her kind and age, did not consider education necessary at all. That I should demand it was a tiresome craze I should grow out of. Once come out and dressed up, I should doubless marry someone. Meanwhile something had to be done with me. So in the end I was disposed of – in the grim Scots school, its grey barracks standing side by side with its stripped cathedral in St Andrews, on the icy coast of Fife.

I believe that I struck that great school possibly at a bad period. Certainly, given indifference at home, no worse place could have been found. It was bad luck. For at that moment, at the turn of puberty, I was in extreme need for an understanding that would ripen my own, both check and encourage it. If that had come my way –

Instead, set off three times a year on that long journey, away from Salterns, away from my brother, my aunt and from Miss Hill, parted from my father for ever, subjected, adolescent, to rigours of mind and body of which I had never dreamed – these served only to augment what was haughty and hostile, contemptuous and at the same time fearful in my character. Reserved yet crying inwardly for understanding, mistrustful yet aching for some person to trust, driven to the most ignorant forms of self-reliance by a foolish, piteous disappointment with life.

Bad nourishment for fifteen, above all bad by its disproportion. A little would have been good for me but, as it was, all the stresses were wrong, and I learned a view of the world as false as it was fearful. Forced into over self-reliance, a barrier was raised between me and my kind it was to take me many years to throw down. If I ever have. Because I was afraid of them I learned to keep people at arm's length. A fear that I longed continually to have destroyed, seizing on any gesture that looked like friendliness, making of such as I received at once too little and too much.

All the time listening to the voice of Shelley, building up another world out of abstractions, which was true, which must be true; and the crude world in which I found myself solitary only a fire-bearer's apprenticeship; and perhaps only Shelley knows how I escaped the destruction of self-pity and unteachable priggishness.

As to many generous children, it was the contradiction between the two worlds that bewildered as it hurt. Since goodness, loveliness, wisdom, adventure and high thoughts were so obviously preferable, why did people prefer ignorance, convention, commonness? All expressed in the unlovingness I felt around me on every side. Why didn't they listen to the men called philosophers who were there to show them? And to the painters and poets and great architects and men of learning? And the priests? Were they part of it or not? In theory, of course, and in history it seemed there had been lots like that. Only nearly all Roman Catholics, and Roman Catholics were wrong. And if Protestant parsons were righter than Roman Catholics – well!

Again I had had no luck. Anglo-Catholicism – I suspect my father of interest in it – had little hold in Dorset, and my faith as I was taught it had only its liturgy to attract me. Besides, Shelley had said that Christianity was wrong – though to be sure he contradicted himself in 'Hellas'. Safest to stick to God, and ask Him, because I most truly wanted to know, to show me the truth.

So it should have been easy for all – or most – men to do what Shelley wanted. Yet again I could not help noticing that they had not much wanted to in any history I had read. Any more than the girls at school, at Sandecotes or at St Andrews, any more than my stepfather with his cheerful contempt for the arts; any more than my mother with her declaration that men did not like women who 'knew things'.

If the meaning of original sin had been explained to me, if any enquiry into the nature of belief had not been counted a crime: 'you have no right to want to know about such things'. If I had not – rather later – fallen upon the *Origin of Species*, and swallowed it whole, with trimmings by Mr H. G. Wells. If indeed there had been anyone in the circle of my home of intellectual distinction and wide knowledge of the world – I should not have wasted so much of my time on my age's futile pilgrimage, on which we set out so gaily, which was to lead us through such flowery meadows and poisonous adventures into the Waste Land.

My casual dismissal up north, to one of the few schools which at that time gave a girl the same education as a boy was not without a comic touch. Some years before a distinguished soldier in India had settled near us, building himself a house for his family in the already ravaged woods between Salterns and Sandecotes. One of his elder daughters was a junior mistress there, a younger one was in the same form as I. And was everything that I was not. A girl who seemed then as good a specimen of *fabricated* genius as one has ever met – a minor example of that 'will to greatness' by which fancy, exceeding talent and amazing industry have nearly succeeded in translating Mr Aldous Huxley from one order of being into another.

A lean brown girl, she aimed at perfection, and with a quality which one saw at once was half heroic, half silly, intended to be perfect in everything. From the highest possible motives. Because it was her duty. Because her parents were so good and wise – as they were, but the remark lowered their prestige – and had made such sacrifices for her. Because also it is wrong only to do what you like, which soon translated itself into whatever you liked doing being wrong – with the sequel that for fear of doing wrong you stopped *liking* anything much.

A process of thought children used to be able to follow. (Would they now?) To which they are *not* respectful. Quite rightly. Perfection is not a proper aim at fourteen. You could see what it was doing to her very growth, drawn, intense, with lank, dark hair falling over thin shoulders and brown, pointed face. A prig so ardent she had the courage to tell us she meant to set us all an example. Set me an example. Which I thought funny and my family thought funny, and laughing over it together, forgave each other much. Once at Sandecotes Speech Day, Lady Rodney, I think, gave away the prizes, and when later on we were admiring her, Agatha, as we will call her, said: 'She has put powder on her face. I must pray for her'; and it gives the measure of her courage that it was proof against my final suggestion that she spoke as one whose face would need more powder than most: then that all women who were worth looking at powdered, who went to real parties; that my mother powdered; and would she have the cheek to pray for her?

'I must do what I think right.' I was a little sorry for her. Made uneasy also, aware that under our noses a moral monster might be fabricating itself, and that would be hard luck on her family.

Until a day came, the second lesson of the third day of the week. It was Scripture, and up to then the Form speechless by the fact that, so far, Agatha had managed to get the maximum marks, ten out of ten, for every single lesson set. Could it go on? Was it conceivable that any earthly girl would, by the end of the week, have attained one hundred per cent perfection? I with my average of fifty, leaping about like a temperature chart, with nine or ten for literature to one or two for arithmetic, was the first to tumble to what she was doing, and watch her.

As I remember, comments on a difficult passage in the Psalms fell from her lips like a budding theologian. From this rose some question on the Magnificat, which some of us so misquoted that an indignant mistress set us all to write it out instantly from memory. There was five minutes' hasty scribbling. Then she read it out and we were to correct and mark ourselves. So we did, until our attention was called off by the almost incredible fact that Agatha was in tears. At her desk, a central one in the first row, eagerly under the mistress's eye – not for her the grass-snake under the lid or the bag of sweets – she sat, her hair parted by her heaving shoulders, by sheer will-power reducing to sniffs what must have been an agony of sobs. One slip, nine out of ten – the great record broken. One slip because she knew it so well: and, as she did not fail to explain to me later, she had only put two words the wrong way round. 'And I felt I was in honour bound to count it.'

'It's a sight to see Agatha with a temptation,' said Elsie Burrows, child of a north-country farmer; who later hunted her father's pack and became a well known sportswoman in the north. Whom I have never seen since. Whom my mother did not like my knowing. To whom I owed a great inarticulate debt. For in no way articulate herself, quite without imagination, only exceeding mother-wit, her honesty and candour and good sense still make her memory dear. Had she been more articulate, had my mother encouraged our friendship, she might have broken my isolation, helped me to anchor my dreams in reality. Only a day-girl like myself, she lived during the term with two old aunts, dear old ladies, in a villa on a grim road in Upper Parkstone, where people like my mother did not call. Then one day she asked me not to be friends with her. Seriously and emotionally. Elsie was a good girl, she was sure, but she was rough (which she was) and I was quite enough of a tom boy. 'You will understand more when you are older, but these are not quite the people it is right to be seen running about with.' A point of view reasonable enough to someone who had no idea of what the girl was doing for me.

Again I did something for which I still feel shame. I ran up the garden by myself, to the black-and-white summer-house deep in the shrubbery at the top of the Lavender Walk, and the part of my mind that told me to obey my mother fought with the deeper part that told me to be loyal to my friend. For to give her up meant that I acknowledged a real wrong in her (I could always try myself not to be rough). For she was good. Rough, and hard with me, north-country hard and infinitely better than I at all outdoor things, but, as I felt deep down, she was loyal to me, loyal as she was severe to my follies. More, she even believed in me; and I was being asked, in the name of obedience, to do something that not only would injure me but that I despised.

Only to gain my mother's approval, I ran back and said I would, and she was very pleased with me, and her praise I could not bear.

Nothing very dreadful happened. I did not ask Elsie to tea for a bit. Then Mother seemed to forget about it and she came again. Only it was somehow not quite the same. And then my father died.

It was ten years later that someone sent me an account of her, of her horsemanship; and with it, cut from a local paper, a brilliant description she had written of a meet of their hounds and the run that followed it.

No such intimacy existed between Agatha and me, on whose family no ban could be laid. We were perhaps the most conspicuous little ladies of our neighbourhood, of the same age, at the same school, and as young entry our families had their eyes on us.

Incidentally, it was Agatha's irreproachable character that helped solve my mother's problem of what to do with an intelligent, idle, forward, backward, child of fifteen on the eve of her own second marriage.

For I was beginning to be superfluous and I knew it. As I learned later, the people round us knew it. The new husband, the exquisite little son, the place – these were enough. In that complex a girl ten years older than the boy, and at the least attractive stage of adolescence, had no inevitable place.

There was no unkindness about their attitude, simply blank incomprehension. Nor were these their conscious arguments. Neither my mother nor my stepfather had ever heard of education, simply did not understand what all the fuss was about. Also to her lively mind, utterly untaught, it seemed, as she explained, that any woman in her senses ought to be able to pick up enough to get along – to talk with agreeable sympathy; above all (and how wisely) to listen well.

However, a boarding-school seemed necessary, and Sandecotes would be too near; the child would expect to be allowed home for week-ends. If this school in Scotland was all Agatha's father was supposed to have said, and the girls were taught Greek and Latin like boys, and the child said that only boys learned anything, and that pious but certainly well-bred and hard-working Agatha was going there, so that the girls could travel up together – well, let her go too. And if that didn't satisfy her, it might knock some of the nonsense out of her head.

They were hardly to blame. The attention now paid, and over-paid, to the minds of children was then unheard of. Though my mother had a pretty strong notion that I was a 'difficult' case, she had simply no idea what she could or what she should do about it. Still less did she guess at the dawning horror, the rising anger and pitiless comprehension of a child working in me at her destruction of my father's books. That act was slowly becoming symbolic to me. A blood-guiltiness in terms of pure spirit. I brooded it like an Electra or a young Hamlet.

Yet a hint of my father's detachment moving in me made me see something of her point of view. I *wasn't* necessary, the new pattern at Salterns did not need me, not for my dancing its new tune. No amount of the small change of family affection could hide a matter of proportion which was nobody's fault. As well blame my father for having married again when he was too old to see his children through.

Some day, 'when I was grown-up' I should find the people who would want me, and Shelley told one this would happen: 'O Thou, who plumed with strong desire . . .'. Meanwhile at my grandmother's house there was still room for me, and wherever my aunt was; and still at home and still my most precious earthly contact, my brother had his baby need of me.

Soon he would be going to his preparatory school, and Mother had got life where she wanted it. (Or so we hoped.) Again, it was natural enough that she should want Salterns to herself. Salterns that she was busily adorning, an offering at the Beloved's feet.

No, I must go somewhere, and the alternative I had been told was some dreadful school in Paris, where I was convinced I should learn about nothing but being a young lady; alone among girls who never thought about anything but getting married, and I should never be able to be alone out of doors any more.

No, if I had to go somewhere, it might be less awful to go to Scotland. It might even be an adventure. It might be true that you were really allowed to learn things there like men learned. If I had to go away from Sandecotes – I had a vision of a place where all the mistresses were like Aunt Ada and Miss Hill, all in love with learning, all making a great adventure of it. All the girls in love with learning too, not titters and gossip, but all meaning to go on to Oxford or Cambridge and all meaning to help the world: 'Good and kind, free and sincere'. It wasn't likely to be like that, but there was a chance. Toss up, and I must put up with either side of the penny as Prometheus did.

No, Daddy was dead. Quite right, for it was time for him to do it. His books had been his funeral-pyre. Like the old heroes. It was queer. Tony had never belonged to him. Tony belonged to Mother; he belonged to me. And I must hand on to him his share in his father. The Mercy extended over young children as over statesmen, over sparrows, hid that part of our future from me.

No, I must go away and make Shelley come true my myself.

Besides, there had been a pointer for it, a 'magic'. Some terms before, Agatha's elder sister had come to Sandecotes to teach some of the younger forms. A girl, as she was then, who has since become a head mistress elsewhere, justly celebrated for her extraordinary understanding of young children. She had been very ill, and her eyes, bright with enthusiasm and suffering, touched me to some crude form of understanding; so that it did not seem fair to put her through the customary ordeal of young mistresses. And the first lesson she gave me is one I shall never forget when, after an introduction at which I began to wake up on the common forms of that metre, she read out to us the ballad of 'Sir Patrick Spens'.

It was one of the moments for which education exists, which is exactly one half of the business. One part laborious mastery, the other the moment when, in a flash of contact between teacher and taught, a new world is opened, a new power gained. 'Rapture of the intellect at the approach of the fact'; a new heaven making a new earth.

I was breathless with attention – there were more of them, were there? Lots more. It was strange that up to then I should have missed them. I think it was because, as a young child, I had been frightened by 'The Three Ravens', which, with other old songs, was in a long picture-music-book by Walter Crane, that stood on the harpsicord in the Blake room at Salterns. My mother used to sing them to me, and that one had made me most dreadfully unhappy:

> *She lifted up his bloudy head*
> *And kist his wounds that were so red.*

> *She buried him before the prime,*
> *She was dead herself ere evensong time.*

Grief and tragedy in terms exactly to a child's understanding, which was all I was then. Those cruel birds. And with the silence of childhood, I would not speak of it, but the words and their sad tune fretted me. As they fret me still.

So it may have been because of that memory that I did not go looking for those poems. Also, as I found later, the only edition at home was the Percy *Reliques*, and by that time my ear could detect and dislike the eighteenth-century modernizings of the text.

So it was that young delicate mistress I had to thank for the Ballads, for the first knowledge of that literature, perhaps the most amazing folk-literature there is; whose concentrated poignancy of statement only Homer has surpassed.

She gave us out a little threepenny edition, with 'Sir Patrick' in it and 'The Cherry-Tree Carol'; and then I remembered there was more at the end of my red Walter Scott; and later there were others:

> *Hynd Horn's bound, love, and Hynd Horn's free,*
> *With a hey lillelu and a how lo lan.*

That was like real love and true lovers, as I should find, if I had any luck, when I was grown up and went out into the world. And along with that went things like 'The Great Silkie of Sule Skerrie' that was a rather awful joke.

The point though about the 'magic' was that it was up there, near that school, that the people lived who made those poems. They didn't seem to have made any since, except Burns and the man who wrote 'Kilmeny', unless you counted Sir Walter Scott, and you were beginning not to, not for poems. Still it *was* that country. (That St Andrews was in quite another part I had only to thank my inattention to my geography lessons.) Besides, I was confused by Rossetti's ballad, 'The King's Tragedy', where a 'woman who dwelt by the Scottish sea' speaks to the King upon the Fifeshire sands. Nor had I heard the theory that when the Scots betrayed Mary Stuart and their ancient faith they sold themselves to success in this world; and that part of the price was poetry, that there should be no more 'makers' in Scotland.

So, on such casual chances was the decision taken that was to send me so far from my home; from the chalk and the turf, the greenwood and the blue, from the narrow sea which is the stream of civilization to the wind and the darkness, the icy cliffs of Fife, the 'black rock and skerry' of an alien sea.

A change which was to submit me to a process whose effect was to underline every defect in my character and, in spite of certain priceless gains, give me far less power of handling my own disposition. With one exception, for gains that were negligible in comparison with their cost.

20

In Sleep

Tony and I went out to bury a bird. A greenfinch I think, limp and still warm and pitifully soft, which had dashed itself against the glass of a window in the last night's storm. For this we had a Beasts' Burying Ground, a steep corner where the pine-woods ran nearest the house, a little below the Dutch garden. A place where the magics began, magic of that steep wood side, almost impenetrable at the top, where I believe a barrow once had been. A round bluff which, stripped of its trees, must have commanded the whole Harbour, at whose feet stood the summer-house-by-the-sea, and beyond that the flow of fields, south to the high-road and the Harbour's edge. Sheer on that side, on the other sloping more gradually, to the stables, and beyond them to the orchard and the great flower-walk, still set in a wood ring.

There beside a path, a little patch at the foot of a tree had been set apart for the burying of our pets. Since very early days, and I remember the start of it well. Years before Tony was born, when I was five or six. It was dark in the library, after tea – the old library that was then called the smoking room, my father's lair. He was reading in his chair, and logs and tobacco and fir-cones had charred together into a blue sweet-smelling fug; the white wooden shutters had been flung back and, driven in gusts from the west, the rain was trying to get in. The rain that is always trying to enter an old house, or, singing its lovely song, bubbles over in the eave-shoots, with a tune that like all the great out-of-door tunes has no beginning or end. Wind-and-leaf tune, gull-and-wave tune, bird-against-bird tune. Music men hear the end of later, when they hear Mozart.

That sort of an evening, and Mother reading aloud *The Second Jungle Book*. For the first time, and I listened trembling to the awful chase of Mowgli by the Red Dog, 'Red Dog, the Killer', across the plain to the Bee Rocks, to the river where, between cliffs of marble, cliffs blackened with honey, the Little People in their millions waited for them. Bee-roar that is the honey-taste made into sound (as I knew from our own bees). And bee-sting is a pain by itself, and I agonized at that run and that chase across the strange Indian landscape, under the Indian moon.

Till we came to the last fight, and Akela, whom I had loved and followed through so many stories (in my mind he was a wolf-Athos), was killed at last. Dead, and I wept past comforting: 'We can't do anything for him. He's dead and wolves don't go to Heaven...'

I can still see my parents' faces in the wood-smoke haze, friendly and concerned; and then my mother said – (she was awfully good at ideas, always good at them. Especially when you were little. It was not till one was growing up that the ideas didn't fit.)

'I know. We can do this –' and suggested a memorial to him in the garden. Not exactly his grave, for he wasn't there to be buried, but a memorial stone, a real one, cut by the man who made tombstones, to the great wolf.

So it was done, a stone a good foot high, with: 'To Akela, Leader of the Free People' carved on it.

This was the beginning: 'To Major, shot, Dec. 1898', 'To the Lizard and the Turtle, 1901'. Others we made ourselves with pebbles and wood and moss and inscriptions on seed-labels and flowers. Together we buried the greenfinch, my small brother and I – a burying that I felt somehow would be my last. I was going away and with that making the burying-ground over to him. As I made over the Rats' House, the room above the stables they had had plastered and painted for me, where I collected junk gloriously and called it a Museum; and all the friends of our family were very kind and gave it things. Uncle Freddy – soon to be my stepfather – and his brother had given it two real python-skins, set out at full length on baize boards. The Stump was there in all its glory on the floor; and when it rained I used to be allowed a fire, and even to stay there after it was dark. There were all my books, and sometimes Daddy would come and climb up the stone steps that led up to it out of the wood, pull my ear and make the Museum a present.

It was a good toy, the Rats' House, nourishing a child's interest in the infinite variety of objects to be found and handled and cared for; a girl-child's interest in the ordering of a house. Even the maids were sympathetic, teaching me how to clean and polish and not scamp my work. Now it was to pass to Tony, and boys are no good at house-keeping. He would fill it with a boy's business, and that was all as it should be; only another thing that had once been mine at home was now mine no longer.

I had always had a 'museum'. From the very first, in the strange, dusty, alarming, freezing or stifling loft, in the oldest part of Salterns, under the roof. There, under the skylight, among the old trunks and screens and tables and a derelict Turkish bath, between the beams that held up the roof, I had hollowed out a *cache*, and there spent many grubby infant hours, half frightened by the place, but loving it.

A very early memory, a 'magic' memory. At the same time as began that part of my life, or of any life, it is hardest to write about or bring to a coherent point. Some more tangible recollection always arises to switch it off those rails into the commoner forms of memory. I mean the extreme part that awareness of the supernatural played, from the beginning, in my life.

It was different from my belief in God, my belief in Apollo or Artemis. Not less real, but different; and the link between both experiences was my belief in the Guardian Angel I had so often to evoke. Then, between the long spells of oblivion in a healthy child, would come spells of 'awareness', breath-catching delight out in the woods or appalling 'night-terrors', so strong that even today I dislike to remember them; that only a mixture of health and faith kept from marking my life disastrously.

Faith, I believe, even more than health. God was there, and in a different way from Apollo or Artemis, though they were real too. More real to me than Our Lord or the Saints. And since He had made everything, everywhere, why bother about Church? And indeed, one reason why it satisfied to evoke the ancient gods was the satisfaction they gave to the sense of loveliness the Church as one knew it starved.

Beauty and Liberty – if they had not been so often denied in the name of the Christian faith, should one be trying Science as a substitute quite so much?

For in the same way that I was told that desire for learning in women was against the will of God, so were many innocent freedoms, innocent delights, denied in the same Name. (And there my home was reasonable; it was what I very soon noticed in the world without.)

It is an old story and will repeat itself, so long as men reverse that profound clause in the Athanasian Creed, which tells them not to try and convert the Godhead into flesh, but to take the manhood into God. Quite enough has been written about this misrepresentation, justly and unjustly, by all of us who have been wounded by it, actually or by excuse. For it has nothing whatever to do with the truth or falsehood of the Christian Faith.

Yet, this much is true – if we had not all suffered by it in our most delicate years, few of us would have 'theorized ourselves silly', so as to stand now, paralysed and hypnotized, in the name of Science, into incapacity for any objective search for truth.

It has taken me as long to get over it as anyone, and it has been a most difficult recovery. Indeed, if you consider our present disbeliefs a plague, a Black Death of the spirit sweeping over Europe, real recoveries are rare. Rare, but carry this blessing, that, once recovered, you cannot take that infection again.

So from the very first there rose consciousness of the Deity, and of bright ministers of His, better than any saint (of which in a Protestant household there was little said) who, under the holy and glorious names of the ancient gods, you could turn to with joy. Never shall I regret it. Then, rather later, I was to discover Dionysos, and with him a whole new range of experience; and how he was adored at Delphi and buried there, and the road that Apollo takes yearly to the Back of the North Wind. The eternal conflict, right down to the roots of Yggdrasil, between him and the Far-Darter, the Muses' Leader. And the World-Ash came into it all right – being another bit of how men had seen the way God made the world.

Obscene or cruel myths are kindly kept from children; and if they come across them, they do not notice them, and a little good-will works wonders. Actually, by myself, by the time I grew up, I had worked out a sketch for myself, with modern trimmings, of the same religion as Plutarch. As Glover says: 'Radiant with amiability – and everything a symbol of everything else, and all is beautiful and holy.'

Until the war.

Yet, no less than the men of Plutarch's age, I was often and intermittently aware of a much smaller, nearer, form of supernatural life, an immediate earthly 'unearthly'. Ever since I can remember, and from this came the night-terrors, as well as the delicate thrilling awareness out in the woods.

Of every sort of kind and quality, in and out of doors; in patches, and often, as in the case of the great pine-tree, especially attached to things. God and your Angel took care of you through it – the Angel who was later to stand beside you, as his daimon by Socrates.

'It' was infinitely less than God. The thought of God could send 'it' scattering in an instant – if you remembered in time. Only there were bits of it, come upon suddenly round corners, so terrifying that they caught you before you could remember Him. It was awfully interesting too. Things to explore when you were grown-up. And some of the gods were even 'like' it – Hecate, of course, and Loki; and because of 'it', in another, grander way, people died when they saw Pan.

All this I found out for myself, in the ancient garden at Salterns and in the woods, in the salt-marshes and by the sea. Very much as primitive man did. At the same time I knew nothing of the long course of antisepsis, delivering man from this awareness as from an unprofitable obsession. Exceedingly necessary, yet condemning it throughout, first forbidding it because it was true; then, as in our own day, because it is false. Until we have lately reached a point which denies the whole existence of spiritual reality; and, when that proves too difficult, a more recent school will have it subjective at all costs. The next step, if people would see it, may open the way for man to start again (if that was the way he started) on his spiritual pilgrimage. Letting in again primitive animism with all its bogys into a world that has denied God.

Fairy-books had nothing to do with this. Fairy-books I understood from the first to be art, not life. And, often with some contempt, judged them as such.

This with occasional exceptions, as when, occasionally, some primitive content, some genuine 'bogle-work', got through the clear-cut prose of Mr Andrew Lang. There was a horror, called The Red Etin of Ireland, who had a song about eating people, that woke you up at night. There was a Russian story of a man without a heart, whom I was afraid I should meet and afterwards I did. Above all, there was the castle that the woman sought so wearily, carrying her baby up great mountain sides; Soria Moria Castle, that lies east of the sun, west of the moon. These, and the Blue Bird Prince. And in these last three, the thing that moved me was in some way the sense of truth. Prophecies they were or images of what my own future would be.

Then later there was to be all Rider Haggard, my distant cousin; and later still the Dark Tower, which is the beginning of the knowledge of the Waste Land. Which is the approach to the Grail.

These came later. The elements I knew from the start, without books. In a sense, my growth was and has been a mastery of it, a learning, a familiarizing, accepting and rejecting, a charting of that unknown. With the help of heaven, from traditions of experience handed down, and from my own experience. Early terror and tip-toe curiosity, matured to wonder. Wonder and the use of reason upon unknown and subtle material, a hierarchy in the making.

> *There is Cabestan's heart in a dish –*
> *No other food shall count but this.*

Learning to walk warily among the endless illusions and pitfalls of that country, Kilmeny's daughter, returning often from places she could not describe; one foot on our earth, the other in that other, the world in which Coleridge and Thomas the Rhymer were free. Thomas, who, little as I knew about him, was one of my first loves. 'Thomas the Rhymer' I used to whisper, and 'Thomas of Ercildoune'.

'True Thomas lay on Huntlie Bank' – it was not till long later that I read the ballad, and was frightened by the familiarity of it. I knew it all before, and what it was like when there was neither sun nor moon, but 'they heard the roaring of the sea'.

'Kilmeny' – a poem that is two kinds of a poem, a lovely, truthful, mystical narrative, on a theme worked out later by Poe and 'changé diablement en route'; but more by the now-forgotten George MacDonald, who wrote *The Princess and Curdie* and *At the Back of the North Wind*. A poem it might be too fantastic to suppose descended from the Scots Chaucerians, down the romantic stair.

A poem that has just one verse, a stanza that had nothing to do with the rest or with the high tradition of European 'making'. Five lines that have their source in archaic experience and terror, quintessence of ballad, quintessense of Hogg when he had forgotten his culture, the Hogg who in 'Queen Hynde' jumbled with my own knowledge. Hogg, for an instant, become a 'maker' again.

It is not Hogg speaking, not the half-equipped man of letters, not the ruined drover. But the shepherd of Huntlie Bank. The poet whose lyre had only one string. Or else it is Huntlie Bank speaking, articulate with the ghost of its earlier shepherd:

> *In yon greenwood there is a waik,*
> *And in that waik there is a wene,*
> *And in that wene there is a maike,*
> *That hath neither flesh, blood, nor bane;*
> *And down in yon greenwood he walks his lane.*

Kilmeny's daughter – but the pure child can meet the greenwood lover and take no more, and more, than any kiss.

Kiss or token – and be delivered from all lovers. Be even a little careless about lovers. Except the lover who is the token of the greenwood love.

Kilmeny's daughter – these things, wherever you go, you do not leave behind; cities cannot touch them nor men's disputes. Learning can be their adornment – with their knowledge, *The Golden Bough* would not have been gathered off the withered tree.

One way to it was from the deck of the *Vanity*, staring towards the land. Portland and the Chesil and St Aldhem's Head, and behind their grey walls and towers a high country of dim green. With the hissing sea, the yacht rose and swung. On a thing which, unless he were very careful, would kill man. Very young I understood the difference – man had not been given sea in the way he had been given the land. It was a long game of skill and caution and danger, catch-as-catch-can, that he played with the sea. A game that, very often, the sea won. What a business it was with the tides – how they must be waited on and waited for, who would never wait. And no one but Our Lord had ever stepped out on to the green and blue backs as if they were ground. A thing it would be fun to do.

Sitting on the hatch I stared at the shore, and at the downs rising in the summer haze. The land seen eternally from Salterns, across the Harbour to the Purbeck Hills. A land it became my profoundest desire to know. A desire that was later, in part at least, to be satisfied.

But first I learned it from the sea, learning it as far as Cornwall and the mouth of the Dart. Summer by summer, fine or wet, all the years until my father grew too old to hold the helm.

Until out of the watching a perception arose which I tried to tell – to make clear – to myself by saying that this coast I knew so well, bay by bay, cape by cape, could be seen double. That there were two versions of it. Or that it had an existence in two worlds at once. (A double aspect of a place that has been described once in a story by Mr Metcalfe called 'The Bad Lands'.)

There ran the coast, and that was what you saw on a map; what you landed on, quay or shingle. Places at the same time, from sea or on shore, with another aspect and identity.

In 'another world'? What world? In one sense the rest of my life was to be a search for the answer to that.

For the same knowledge was always turning up – in books that were 'great' books, and books that were not great at all, only with some turn of that knowledge. Books, like Rider Haggard's, which only that knowledge made great.

Hardly ever in people. Perhaps people would come. One of the rules was that you must not seek. Or ask. When, at the best, the best you could say – or write – was no more than an indirection.

It was at that time I began to have the dreams.

There have never been more, at most, than a score of those dreams; when on each waking one has felt that some gain, some positive knowledge has been added to one. Knowledge of what? Of *studia perennia;* of a chart – a map to show what those places 'really' were?

The first one was of the well. It was when I was a baby; and there were corals and pearls and a tower of pure, dark water. On its floor you went into a room beyond which was light; and there were two women in it with low voices, looking. Many years later, a young student reading at the British Museum, I found the Orphic Tablet, and the first dream leapt back to my mind and I knew it for the same place. Different trimmings, out of 'Arethusa' or even *Alice in Wonderland*. Only it was the same, the conviction having with it a particular lucidity, an identity of atmosphere, a factual quality of which not even the rising tide of fashionable psychology could dissuade me.

That was the first. The next, first of a series which has continued at long intervals throughout my life. Of a poignancy, a nearness to that which I most desired which makes their memory ineffaceable.

What one would like to stress, at this time, when our dreams are all subject to examination under one single and none too flattering set of formulae, is the extreme difference of their *quality* from the ordinary dream state; their factual nature, as of imparted knowledge. Or, more nearly, of a state of living attained.

For one thing, they are unforgettable, as easy to retain in essentials as the ordinary dream-stuff melts away. This, when their content is not of any experience ever undergone by man. Nor can they be induced, I have tried that, by any drug, stimulant, suggestion or desire. They may be rarely preceded; once or twice I have known them fade away, into ordinary dream-stuff; but between the two dream states there is an instant of change, as of a barrier passed, as between two levels of consciousness. Once, at least, in its relation to the future, came up to more than Mr Dunne's quality.

Lately they have become very rare. Possibly because the conscious mind, recording and analysing, may have established a check.

They have 'something to do' – that is, sometimes, they are not wholly, I think, unrelated to one's state of perception when moved by art or by natural beauty. Or again with the state in which one works easily and well.

Just as they have nothing whatever to do with one's devotional life, or with any of the states of prayer. Mr Huxley can say what he likes. They don't match. Again akin and perhaps most akin to the 'magic' knowledge that came to one as a child; but not to the enlightenment that comes from prayer. Variations on two distinct orders of experience; and that last to be confused with no lesser experience (as one used to think) however poignant, however significant for life.

Part of one's excuse for writing this is the confusion that exists to-day between levels of spiritual experience. Now that it has gone out of fashion to deny their existence (which was never very easy to do) they must, it is felt, be somehow disinfected. That is, at all costs, kept subjective, lest they provide the discredited supernatural, let alone theism, with a new leg to stand on. (A leg that might be compared with Fenrir's chain which, though forged of cats' footfalls, stones' roots and women's beards, yet bound the Earth-Wolf when Thor's cable broke at a snap.) At least that is what its opponents might think, when Mr Julian Huxley is at such pains to assure us that, in essence, St Thomas Aquinas in meditation, or any of us at a concert, or even taking a ticket for lovely Lucerne, are in an identical state of subliminal uprush, of essentially the same order and directed to the same end.

It was a good thing he did. For one thing it raised the issue. As it needed to be raised. Most of us had more or less slipped into the notion that a sunset was an equivalent for a formal act of prayer. 'One instinct from the vernal wood', and all that. That what was good enough for Wordsworth was good enough for us. More than justified again when it provoked Father Knox to his exquisite analysis of Mr Huxley's unrevealed religion.

For which, in gratitude and humility this note is added, in contrition for past follies. For I, who had less excuse not to know better, was taken in by the same claptrap for many more years than I care to think.

Not quite dishonestly. It is particularly hard at this time for the unscientific not to be paralysed by science. (The science they get, popularized with a seasoning of scholarship, and thoughtful sixpenny reviews.) We were on our honour to use our minds, and Mr Lunn's Hegira from Stagira knew very well how to disguise it. Science also, not usually written by scientists, but by men making use of science to draw their own conclusions and boil their own eggs. And eggs these days are eaten very hard-boiled indeed.

It was William James who noticed a curious, pathetic yet unattractive, form of asceticism, common in his day, and still, I think, implicit – a fear of believing the best. As a New Englander he rather admired it; yet even he felt forced to point out that his countrymen need not feel that it was cheating, even in eternity, to suppose anything but the worst.

To make it an act of cowardice to believe in the Providence of God – could puritanism go further? And this, unconsciously, has persisted; not nobly as in James or among the learned and wise of Boston, Massachussets, but stupidly, with a kind of cynicism, a kind of brutishness; descending, as now all such things descend, to the people by way of the press.

> *Scio, Domine, et vere scio, quae non sum digna accedere ad tantum mysterium propter nimia peccata mea et infinitas negligentias meas. Sed scio quod Tu potes me facere digna.*

The first Latin prayer that I learned. A prayer which might have served all through. Which, in a way, *has* served. But to turn again for a moment to the future – if I had not been sent on that journey to the north, there to learn too young the meaning of isolation and endurance beyond my years; to a school at that time, for all its impeccable piety, so arid of devotion as to separate utterly the idea of life from the idea of God – if this had not happened, I should not have begun to wonder so early what the Stoics were about, alternate states of perception and faith with one cold little sentence found in Aurelius: 'If there be a God, all is well. If chance rules, be not thou ruled by it.'

The reading may be corrupt, and how angry my mother was when I asked her, in all innocence, what she thought of it! It seemed then that I *could* not learn that grown up people did not like those questions; that they were not interested; had never heard of being interested; thought it wrong to be interested.

And when I reached St Andrews I found there were even fewer available people interested than there were at home.

With one exception – the lessons for two years I was to have with one mistress, in literature and scripture, four hours and their preparation which often had to make up for all the other desolate hours of the week. For these no follower of the arts, no musician waiting for the singer's first notes, the conductor's baton-tap, the great dancer's first steps; no young citizen, crushed in the crowd, waiting for the statesman to speak, waited more hungrily than I. For the scurrying entrance of the little dark woman, sallow, with burning eyes, and ivory fangs of stuck-out teeth. The pace of those lessons, their urgency, their invective, the searching questions shot out; the sudden silence of her contempt, the rare golden silence of her praise. Her scorn for our ignorance and folly, her lightning acknowledgement of our understanding. At the time it seemed to me impossible that there could be any of us to whom such lessons did not mean rebirth.

21

Two Drawing-Rooms

IT was proper before my mother's marriage there should be a great re-decorating of the House. One age was over. Victoria gave place to Edward, and my mother's last Spring. It needed doing; it would be fun to do. One Salterns vanished and another appeared – far lovelier, and I had my share in it. In those last holidays we worked together, my mother and I.

It was I who suggested that the old vestibule that led into the hall should be knocked out, right and left, enclosing on one hand what had been the storeroom in its flagged, airy, shadowy space. Restoring it on the other side to the original shape of the House, by knocking out a thin wall and leaving only a single square shaft to support the head of the stairs.

This led to the question of the two drawing-rooms which filled the whole west end, the Little Drawing-room looking out on to the drive, the Big Drawing-room down the lawn to the sea. Rooms, built on sometime in the eighteenth century, which rose, with elaborate cornices, right up the roof, with only the lofts above them. That most mysterious of the whole range of lofts, the only part of the House I was afraid of. Where I was not encouraged to explore. To this day I do not know why, nor why I feared it; only my imagination said it had a white spot about it. A 'patch', when you saw it in your mind, that was not pure white, that glowed like a not-quite-clean mist.

There was no image, let alone any story about it. I never got further than the little mist. It had a door, at the very top of the front-stairs, where their delicate line came to an end in a little straight run of gallery; and, looking down from it on to the great black lantern in the well of the hall, I hated that door.

A door I felt, and felt more certain as I grew older, that *was* the door on to a mystery. A house-mystery, and some way to a Butts secret. Only to something that was bad for us. It was hardly ever opened, and when I was little I did not like to think what would come out of it. Until

I realized that nothing ever would. Would stay within where it was, distilling. An essence? Something like that, only in stillness of stillness, the stillness of the still. Salterns was full of stillness, coloured quiet, colours that moved, but oh, so quietly. Colours and shadow and coloured shadows, but always colour. What was in the loft had no colour, and its quiet was not the house-quiet. Quiet that always moved; this did not move at all and, although infinitely remote, was in some way hostile to it.

These qualities – these essences attach themselves to old houses. More especially and naturally to great houses. At Crichel there is a ring of gold laughter that breaks as you enter; and at Knole, if you listen, you can hear the house-pulse beat.

Later my mother did a strange thing to that door. Someone had painted her portrait, a portrait she and her family combined not to like. So she had a frame made, glazed with a lead-latticed window to open and shut, complete with catch; and this she called 'The Face at the Window' and hung it there, disposing of a bad picture most charmingly.

The Big Drawing-room was separated from the other by a huge curtain, of some kind of gilt wool, nobly draped, from a sketch, I was told, made for my father by Dante Gabriel Rossetti. The fireplace mounted to the ceiling, tiers of black oak, divided by pillars, each panel representing a scene from some legend. Wood from a church, patched with tolerable copies, the whole thing a Victorian-Gothic-Pre-Raphaelite fabrication, but effective enough; the effect, as with so much else at Salterns, of the influence of Rossetti on my father's taste.

Yet something in his taste and character, at once indolent and sure, forbade him to make his house into the usual Pre-Raphaelite monument. For one thing, William Morris, apart from his printing of the Kelmscott books – whose Chaucer we had – hardly interested him. It was Rossetti's love of the pure medieval, the actual antique – even perhaps a memory of the 'Gothic' romances of his boyhood – that had formed his taste. Also he had inherited many things which were anything but Gothic and some of them were very lovely. Those, with the Blakes, had all to be found room. Above all, my mother as well as he knew how to make the most of what we had – and more perhaps than all the House itself knew.

So huge oak cabinets stood in the shadows, and high gold chestnut bureaux, bright with brass; delicious eighteenth-century rosewood chairs, whose seats she added to the world's fine stitching when she embroidered them. Straight-backed chairs of Dutch marquetry, yellow and gold and green; and in the dining-room, there was a final 'Gothic' piece it took two men to lift, 'the Bishop's chair', another pastiche of black oak, with two whole lions for its arms.

In the Library there was comfort – with which the rest of the House had singularly little to do, and our servants' rooms were a disgrace. As, apart from one or two fine pieces in my parents' bedrooms, our own today would be considered ugly and comfortless; and the bathroom put in for the first time was one of the changes to do my stepfather honour.

Heaven knows that restoration was needed, and it was gracefully and skilfully done. A green and white Salterns came out of it, white walls and plain green carpets, and ancient lumber and indifferent pictures cleared away, and all our finest things displayed in clear space; brilliant brass and silver, and a blaze of flowers in tubs and boxes and jars.

Flowers in brass tubs, growing – I remember campanulas, very tall, that the bees used to follow, so that all summer the hall murmured with them. The wall whose far end, next to the Blake Room, in the new part of the House, my mother had filled in with a mirror sheet, running up from floor to ceiling, giving a lovely transparency and a sense of something limitless to the long irregular shaft that was the spine of the House.

When everything else had been decided, with a touch of genius, she unhooked the hall's huge lantern to replace it by a delicate brass candelabrum to carry light like stars. (Not real candles. Electric light in a countryside without natural power was still unknown, but there was that strange system known in those days as 'chauffeur's despair'. Lighting by carbide, mixed in a garden shed, mixed with a strange stink; and laid on much as gas is laid on, but by no means so certainly. Whose sole advantage was the delicate light it gave.)

With this went the opening out of the hall, its white ceiling spaced with lozenges, a coat of arms in each. Then the destruction of the conservatory and the 'lifting' of the entire House, on the lawns and sea-ward side, on to a terrace of Purbeck stone. A terrace spaced with rough jars of local pottery, from which again flowers streamed.

To do this, quite rightly but a secret sorrow to me, another tree was sacrificed. Not the obvious sacrifice of thinning out, which left the great ones intact. Which needed doing, as my father left to himself would not have touched a twig. Yet he and I had had a special love for the one that grew at the very top of the lawn to the left of the dining-room window.

If the eighteenth-century idea of 'conceits' ran to follies – and there were many in Dorset – Bond's Folly, Bankes' Folly – the nineteenth-century took it in trees. Hence the monkey-puzzle and the yucca, and all sorts of strange and usually hideous conifers. With these went the palm, wherever it could be persuaded to grow, carpet-bedding and paths paved with coloured pebbles – for which in Dorset the Chesil Beach was surely reponsible.

Of all these Salterns had its share. What must have been a cargo off the Chesil at one time ornamented the paths. This when I was a baby, and somehow they disappeared. To be replaced (early again) by horrid cinder scrunchiness. Then by gravel; and then, very firmly, by my mother, with turf. Like the archaeology of buttons where, as Professor Glover says, some happy man's life-work is awaiting him, the epochs of the English garden seem never yet to have been gathered into one satisfactory book. By my time carpet-bedding had gone out, but I remember one old gardener, before the days of our famous Jack Norman who came as a village lad and rose to run the place, serving my mother with intelligent and faithful enthusiasm. (A red-haired, sweet-tempered Irishman, of real natural gifts, and to my mother a species of John Brown.)

But the old gardener I remember grumbling to Nurse because my mother would not let him compete with Mrs Dawson-Damer's gardener and grow a royal crown and cypher out of some species of miniature plants.

In secret I too admired old Mrs Damer's bed. It was like a lovely game to make things grow like that. Only, by that time, the ideas of Miss Jekyll had come in to set the taste of all England, and as much nature as possible allowed in our gardens again.

A most vital and necessary change but, like even the best changes, it brought a tiny and not quite necessary loss. They were really very charming, those small jewelled beds, and in any complete garden there should be room for a floral embroidery of its mistress's name.

Yuccas though we had in plenty, their horny trunks sprung up eight feet high, topped with a whorl of savage spikes, a ruff of green daggers, sharp as swords. Monstrous things they seemed, alien with a flower-history behind them that was not the history of our flowers.

Until one year, out of the centre of the ruff, one of them sent up a spike, rosy and tender, like flesh. It curved a little, and after a time there burst from it a shallow arc of white bells. Bells of white wax, bee-stormed and insect-crept, that crowned for weeks the wrinkled grey trunk and, as I remember, rotted off it slowly, as flesh rots away. A lovely dreadful thing. And it would not happen again, so I was told, for another twenty-five years.

A quarter of a century. So it should have happened again, some time ago. Only there is no Salterns now. Long ago the yuccas were hacked up, with their daggers and their secrets, burned or rotted in an alien land.

There remained the 'ornamental pines' and of them again we had our full share. Even a monkey-puzzle. I was told that my father sacrificed it for me – for him it *was* sacrifice – 'because the child might hurt herself against it when she starts to run about.'

Of these the chief was the great macrocarpa, standing at the foot of the lawn, on the bank above the fields. Not the tamed, domestic, stand-the-climate, windbreak advertised today, but a real macrocarpa, high and hideous, standing indecently by itself, flanked by the green beeches and beside a cherry-tree. A huge cherry-tree, not much good for cherries, but a snowstorm in spring.

That went, and rightly. Though, with my father's tree-love, I saw the necessity, knew more than anyone else about its common and uninteresting, its dryadless soul, I was sorry for it. It was, I knew, a vulgar tree: the others would not speak to it: it had shot up like one of those fair-giants, who, in consequence, are weak in the head. Its virtue was its cones, like little bags of purple leather, suddenly shrunk into puckers, a kind of tree-tortoiseshell. One of those trees that do not belong; that grow too fast and have no proper root: that think they can show off by their fast growing, when the slower the better was the rule since trees began. Though perhaps the yews overdid it, refusing in less than fifty years to become a tree at all.

Though that was worth it in the end, when you thought of the longbows. Or, many years later, the yew I was to see in the old Romney churchyard. Six hundred years old, and still widening in power and strength. One with the Church, before which it stood with its arms out. They had cut their bows from it for Agincourt. Then, long years after, such bows as Latimer learned to draw. Drew with the weight of his body, beginning with a little bow for a little boy. The English longbow, whose use no man can learn unless he and his bow grow together.

The other tree, the tree outside the dining-room window, the tree I really minded about, was round. Not like a macrocarpa, a mop or stick or one of the maids' feather brooms, but more the shape of a pawn, round at the bottom and diminishing round to the top. Goodness knows what it was, but it grew, bulging out, right down to the ground, its foliage like feathers of green leather, aromatic and very acrid to bite. The white fantails that cooed and strutted along the roofs and around the house – an overtone with the bees – used, for some reasons of their own, to get inside it. So did I, or raced round its fat sides with Daddy after me; and he is inextricably mingled with the memory and the being of that tree.

It went. Inevitably, and properly. And with it something that I felt united him to Salterns. Or, as a spiritualist would say, had he wished to haunt us, he would have found it harder without that tree.

To return – as this book seems to write itself, winding in and out, like the streams of Poole Harbour scouring their passages through the mud out to sea – to the drawing-rooms, and the hands that time laid on them.

They must until then have been a perfect 'period-piece'. Miniature of that matchless description Mr Benson in *As We Were* gives of a whole historic house. Very high, dark, gleaming and crammed with furniture. Their walls covered with a Morris paper, dull pomegranates and squares, I think, of turquoise and bright gold. Of such quality as to weather into a dim richness, with the carpet's deep blue and yellow and red.

In my earliest day the furniture was a suite of yellow brocade and ruby velvet, many pieces of it, including a mysterious seat, three seats, more or less back to back, set into a pillar of shining mahogany; and many cushions, some heavenly soft, some comfortless; and in summer a dark floral chintz, which, indestructable, was re-dyed for the restoration a uniform clear deep green. All of that imperishable quality when degraded taste was still executed by the standards which had once made the English school of cabinet-making one of the delights of civilized man.

This with its oak chimney-piece, a black seventeenth-century cabinet the size of a house; and in the Little Drawing-room, above the fireplace the painted rumble of an old coach. A huge mirror, gilt-framed, opposite the great fireplace filled one recessed wall, an equally vast sofa below; and as I have said before the curtain draped across the arch between the rooms, heavy as the drop-scene of a theatre.

The windows were our sorrow. The rest of the House had kept its early glazing from before the days of plate glass – small oblong panes, divided by strips of turned wood. But in the drawing-rooms my father's first wife, 'the late Mrs Butts', whose taste for hand-(and home-) painted china, chimney-piece fans and a particularly scratchy kind of brocade cushion with tassels, still lay heavy on the House – had insisted on their removal. So that nothing but the most expensive sheets of glass – and in her day windows were not opened – should impede the view to the sea.

(If, as we said with scorn, that *was* her reason, and not an early-Victorian contempt for old-fashioned things.)

There they were and they were wrong and we had to put up with them. For the rest, shadowy like all the House, and to a child enormous, the rooms were crowded with the same dim richness of things. Pictures all over the walls, that clacked when the wind blew through. Early nineteenth-century pictures, water-colours, all in narrow gold frames on wide gold mounts; small strips of pale colour they seemed, laid on gold. There were also the earlier ones that I so greatly loved, eighteenth-century work, pictures of Italy, of mysterious mountains and woods. Painted in infinite detail, thickly with Chinese white, giving them a mysterious bloom – the blues and greens of jade and malachite and lapis; of forests I knew to be pictures of both mortal and immortal woods.

Woods – this I knew from our own and from the New Forest – were not like that. Perhaps it was because they were Italian woods. But I did not think so, not altogether. Only that the men who painted them were inside the meaning of woods.

Until I made a discovery. What they must have seen. What had happened when you saw woods, any woods, like that.

These were in their antique frames of gilt, carved and pierced. And there were others, even earlier, on copper. Little scenes of battles, many figures, very distinct, running about; and strange towns and strange houses; and one had a fire, painted very red and yellow, on snow.

These paved the walls like gold panels; on the floor you fell over things as you ran. (Until you learned that it was wrong and clumsy to do that.) Into a gate-legged table, of oak like black glass, with silver odds and ends shining all over it. Once when I was very little I saw my mother fill two silver vases on it with rosy flowers and their leaves and, with a young child's stimulus to pure colour, thought that silver and pink and green were so delicious I wanted to eat them. Like an ice in stripes, or that lovely paste of almonds that pretended to be fruit and one was not allowed. Then, that this pleasure was in a way better than eating, for you *always* wanted it. Things to eat, however good, made you stop; but every time you even thought of this you got the same lovely feeling like a taste, and it never made you sick.

All the silver things were interesting things, all sorts of boxes and candlesticks with snuffers, and animals made out of it and toys. In fact, the 'silver-table' of the period. Then there was another table, whose top was a glass box on legs, that had even better things in it.

Laid on dull green velvet, boxes of gold and ivory and tortoiseshell and shagreen, and that work in enamel laid over shell now no longer made and called, I think, piqué work. Seals of cornelian and beryl and amethyst and, best of all, ebony boxes, their lids set, under glass, with birds. Unknown coloured birds, made most exquisitely out of feathers, that I was told – how rightly I do not know – were made in South America by the Indians the cruel Spaniards killed. Which could not be made now, were a 'lost art', like the sword-hilt and guard, of steel embossed on gold, brilliant steel (until they let it rust) in scenes of pastoral, which it was said that Louis XV had once given to a prince. There was a lump of amber with flies in it from the Baltic. There were watches and miniatures and patch-boxes and jewelled pins. Junk, but some of it very good, and fine training for the eye and the taste of a child.

If you ran to the great mirror you saw the room repeated. Stood underneath thinking about *Alice Through the Looking-Glass*, and like Alice; and when you ran into the mirror and out round the corner of the lawn in it, where would you be? Rubbing your nose into the glass, you could see a little further and a little further, and it was directly when you stopped seeing in the glass that the fun began. There was the beech-tree and the pond beside it and the queer dark fir behind that. Then, when you stopped seeing, the looking-glass world began. Only not the same one. There would be another set of magics. Always you were deliciously on the edge of knowing those magics, but never quite. It might have to wait until you were dead.

Then, as you ran away, you fell over the chest with the pagoda tree. Old polished wood, carved and painted and gilded. Called a dower-chest, and it came from Italy, and when you were going to be married there it held your linen and your silks. The pagoda-tree had jangled down and spilt everywhere, gold off its gilt branches, seals and rings and earrings and étuis, rolled away under the brass tub full of ferns. Or right across the room to the fire where the lazy-tongs hung, the steel pincers on a three-foot spring because the late Mrs Butts in her crinoline had been so fat; but no good really to pick up the little hard things you'd knocked down. Best to go down on the floor and make a good job of it. The floor from which you could see the fire picking out bits all over the room, dark wood and pale brass and gilt, gold and silver, porcelain and glass and the great mirror itself; and the mirror said it the other way round all over again, each fire-note, but fading off round its borders into deeper shadows than the deepening shadows of the room.

Only it was never possible to curl down over that fire. With the family contempt for comfort, the two chairs that stood before it came from India, of dark teak, carved in an open-work of foliage and fruit and birds. Eastern work, made by men who did not sit on chairs, and cushionless, more dreadful for the human frame than it is possible to conceive, their springless brocade seats less easy than many stones.

(Later, gilded, they became part of another chapter in our lives; but plain or gilt, I always disliked them. Unfriendly exotics, that were not true exotics, being made to be sent away to the West.)

Chairs, so the family legend went, a ship's captain had brought from Bombay, sometime in the seventies. Dumped them on Poole Quay, and Lord Wimborne, two Lord Wimbornes back, had offered him twenty-five pounds for them. This he was hesitating to give, when my father, riding over from Salterns, saw them out in the rain, gave the man the money and brought them home.

The room was as full of things as the peacock's tail, in a gilt peacock that stood before the fire when it was out, was full of eyes. Not many photographs – that had long 'gone out', but albums, thick books of brown and gilt leather with clasps, and thick cardboard pages also gilt at the edges and grim ancient photographs, men with hair growing in strange parts of their faces and women with hair in nets. And one whole mysterious set that must have been in a church, of a procession with choir-boys, and the photograph had taken their cassocks scarlet, and it was about something Aunt Ada knew and liked, and Mother didn't and said it was 'extravagant'; and Daddy didn't explain.

These were on a table – a table I loved; a round table on a gilt leg, from Italy, and its top all made of marble, coloured bits of marble made in a pattern. Gone temporarily out of fashion, we were fools to dispose of it, as I remember we did, to an astute dealer for a song. But it was exactly against the period taste. Taste I learned as canonical, almost taking it for granted that, except for Dante Gabriel Rossetti, the art of making beautiful things had perished off the earth just about one hundred years ago.

Then there was the great cupboard, right away beside the curtain, along the dividing wall. A seventeenth-century cupboard of black oak, which was alive. More alive than any *big* thing in those rooms, and at one time I thought it had a thing that lived in it. Not a bad thing, a kind of lob-lie-by-the-fire, who did nothing in particular for the maids, only came out by nights and danced the House.

These things and so many more I have forgotton. The 'Sunday toy', a little figure of Humpty-Dumpty, beautifully made, with face and hands of painted kid and a body of rose silk. A hollow body, but for a single glass marble; I was *never* allowed to unsew him and take it out. And 'the marble in his bags', as Daddy said, made him fall about, but whichever way he fell, even a header off the highest chair, always made him land upright.

Then there was the velvet bag with the gold cords, that *always* hung on the glass bell-handle beside the fire, and had a piece of embroidery in it that was never finished. And the little oak footstool which was all one was allowed to sit on when visitors were there. And on the top of the great cupboard were the three jars, the biggest jars I believed there were in the world. A vast round one with a lid, and two with open mouths and a thick lattice of china up their throats. Late Ming, red and blue and burnished gold on a skim-milk ground. Earlier they would have been superb; even today they have a certain magnificence; and as a child I admired them as a child admires all things very much larger or very much smaller than, as they say here in the West, 'they belong to be'.

The rooms were lit, very delicately by a few candles and the deep-set fire, and very dimly from the high white ceiling by the second lantern. Twin to the one that lit the hall, again of wrought iron with bottle-glass panels leaded together, and in the centre of each panel the same coloured eye. Only this time all dim, sickly yellows and greens and a thin wine red; and the illumination as it turned slowly on the endless points of reflection the ghostliest I have ever seen. Pure Gothic as the nineteenth-century Romantics conceived it.

How I wished we had a ghost at Salterns – not the tree and wind and leaf and garden potencies I knew, but a Real Ghost. A Grey Man or a White Lady, with a proper story, who put in regular appearances. So that one could say to 'the other girls': 'If you will come to tea and stay till after dark, you'll see our ghost.' No, we hadn't. Father and Mother, though regretful, were perfectly firm about it. And about the 'other things' you couldn't tell them. No child can. Its instincts of self-preservation, even with the best parents, far too sure.

Though, as Mother agreed, there ought to be one, and as for about the garden she loved and served so well 'nothing would surprise me less'. And once, when I was about sixteen, I think I may have seen one.

It was by Bryant's Wood, the very steep wood at the back of the House, where on one side our property came to an end. A steep black pine hill, and at its top a much-loved common, leading down to Sandy Lane, and then more woods, the short way to Sandecotes. A high bank with a gate in it, and on one side a thick shrubbery, marked our boundary. From the gate into this ran a path, dividing almost at once into two ways, both leading on to the drive, one towards the stables, one towards the House. Across this path, close to the gate in the bank and before the divide, ran another. A very long path, running all the way up through trees and rhododendrons and laurels from the Old Lodge to the very top of the orchard and the croquet lawn. Ending at the black-and-white summer-house in the woods. From the lodge to the gate, known as the Back Path, it was this upper half of green under-tree tunnel that was known mysteriously as the Lavender Walk.

Except where, for a few yards, it opened up above the terrace opposite the front door, as dark a path as I have ever seen. A sandy tunnel, grown across with savage roots, polished to ivory by the feet of years. A path that no one used except the coachman on his way up from the lodge, and I, running wild; and on Sundays and Saints' days by neighbours who attended the Chapel on the heath, and who used it as a short cut.

In particular, Mr Browne, Mrs Browne and the Misses Browne; and more than once, after Mrs Browne had said she had sprained her ankle but had visibly blacked her eye, they protested about those roots. A protest that, I remember, we turned down with scorn. Was it not enough that they had the use of the path, without grumbling about Our Pet Death-Trap, as I called it, unreproved? To my father it was obvious that the lightest hand laid on one of those gnarled monsters might injure a tree.

I do not remember how it was settled, but the Brownes continued to use the path. The Brownes and the Pontifex family. All most respected, early inhabitants of Parkstone, before that happened to Parkstone which was to happen to Salterns, and the quiet gentry who had made their homes there.

Evelyn Pontifex was at school with me. Dorothy Browne, though also of the same age, was not. (A very lovely child, she grew up and went off on her own adventures as I was preparing to do. Evelyn Pontifex did not.)

Their feet, on high days and holy days, were the only ones that trod that path. Then I, one evening with the light striking level through the trees, came down Bryant's Hill and entered our grounds by the gate. (On whose high bank there grew the most wonderful clump of club-moss I have ever seen. Out of a rotted tree-stump, an emerald mound, a wonder.)

At that instant, in the long sunlight, there ran in front of me across the main path, a woman dressed in black. Coming up the Back Path, she seemed to flit across, under the arch of laurel, to the slight turn where it became the Lavender Walk. Very lightly she went, without a sound, and swiftly over some of the worst of the roots.

I followed, but in the Lavender Walk there was no sign of her. She had not turned back or she would have passed me. There remained only the divided path on to the drive, a matter of a few feet.

She was not on the drive. I ran up as far as the stables, and there was the coachman, washing the carriage. Then down to the back door, and there the maids were, sitting with their sewing, beside the bay tree. No one had seen her. Nor could she have hidden herself, on the wide drive or the close shrubbery paths. Why should she have hidden at all?

Left with the memory of the sudden transit of a swift, soundless figure, a small woman in a dark mantle. In the scattered gold of sunset, in a wood, a figure that crossed my path for a second and was gone.

22
Death-Duties

'*Now* what on earth are we to do with them?' my mother said, and together we went into their dimness, into the gildings and reflections and shadows, prepared to strip them in imagination.

She had on a period hat, perched high and built up at the back and sides with close bunches of curls. (Curls made of her own hair, of course, but part of the hat rather than her head. And in her happy manner she would unpin it and cast it from her, curls and all.)

'The matter is – you can't paper a room this height, and the patterns they've sent down I wouldn't be seen dead in a ditch with –'

'Or Uncle Freddy's "back of a cat-fight in hell",' I said happily, for I loved this.

'Hush,' said my mother and giggled. She was very much in love.

It was then I had my inspiration:

'Whitewash it then,' I said, 'and turn out everything but the best things we've got.'

This was what was done. I don't know if my mother had thought of it herself or not, but she accepted it. Paint to be exact, the stark white just broken; and after it the walls soared, pure and bare; and the shadows fled away and the noblest of our furniture stood out, the small pictures vanishing with the trifles and the gilt. On the walls hung a few family portraits; for brightness there were flowers *en masse*. For further brightness – and this was very happy – in every division of the chimney-piece stood a jar of our best china. Good early Ming, chiefly rose and white, part of the collection of a Robert Butts, who had been Bishop of Ely in the eighteenth century.

All the trifles vanished, and the rooms took on a stateliness, a simplicity that in small country houses of the period was then quite unknown. A shock that went round the neighbourhood, and food for days of gossip at the whitewashed drawing-room of Mrs Butts.

There remained though, hanging on the inside of the arch between the two rooms, what I used to think of as the Family's Eyes. They had

153

always been somewhere in the room, and in our family for a very long time. Two pairs of mirrors, round mirrors in round ebony frames, and inset in the glass of each were eight diminishing mirrors, sixteen times repeating all that passed. Repeated with exquisite fidelity. One of the pair had painted within its ring of eyes a bunch of flowers. Rare these and not made now, and one of my first introductions to the secrets of the mirror-world. Mirrors, as Lord Peter Wimsey says, that with cats and bells don't bear too much thinking about. Believing them in some way bound up with us. Butts-eyes.

The death-duties on the estate were heavy, and my mother was left to deal with them, wholly ignorant of business, not well advised and in love. Reasonably enough, something had to be sold – leaving aside the prudent but hard and self-denying method of raising them by a mortgage on the House and land, and then by rigid economy, paying it off. No such scheme was, I believe, even suggested, and the money had to be found.

So she decided on the sale of the Blakes to wipe out the death-duties, leaving a balance sufficient at least to raise a memorial to my father in the Chapel. Since there has since been some controversy about this, I would like to put it on record here that, to a woman in her position, the solution was an obvious one. Except that, in execution, it was carried out without due thought – and indeed sufficient knowledge would have been hard for her to obtain. But a sale made without due thought for the future, the future she was parting with, the future that was sacrificed to the present.

For at that time, only a few years after the publication of Ellis and Yeats's work on the Prophetic Books, the interest in Blake was at its beginning. His work was beginning to be known. All my life I can remember people calling at Salterns with introductions and asking to be allowed to see them. So they represented a security that should have been held on to at all costs, a maturing investment. This my mother did not understand, nor anything of the intrigues and intricacies of the picture-dealing world. It was a lesson she was never to learn.

Actually helpless in their hands, she tried to stick out. Twelve thousand pounds she got, for a collection which W. B. Yeats told me ten years later would then have fetched fifty.

Everything was sold. Not only his chief works, the great paintings in tempera and water-colour, which again, ten years later, filled a room in the Tate, exactly as they had left our walls. There were sold also portfolios of sketches and engravings, the superb copy of Young's *Night Thoughts*, Blair's *Grave* and many others. Even his engraving cabinet which Brother Aubrey had taken for his own; I remember in the centre of its door he had added our crest in brass.

The miniatures only were kept, now in my brother's possession. The only three Blake ever painted; my great-grandfather, Tom Butts, his friend who was at the War Office and an early Swedenborgian; and apart from the Blakes added many beautiful things to our house. Things in the main we no longer possess. He and his wife Elizabeth and their son, my grandfather. Very fine miniatures, sensitive and transparent in tone and, for all their formality, with something of Blake in the line and the modelling of the bones.

The rest went. My brother was a baby. I too young not to accept the necessity as absolute. (If only my mother had not been so indignant at the small fortune left to me. Indeed it seemed to make her very angry – I even heard her speak of 'driving a coach and horses through your father's will.')

I remember too the night before the men came to pack them, going down to the Blake Room after dark, and playing on the harpsichord a tiny Beethoven suite for which I had a passion. Called after desire and pain and delight, it must have tinkled out sweetly from the instrument it was composed for. I had no intention of playing a dirge – only – I hardly know – to express an apprehension I could not clearly formulate, first intimation of an enormous and fatal loss.

When I went upstairs to say good-night to my mother, she was crying. Not angry with me, but as if she were a little afraid.

A piece of quick luck followed for the empty room. A short time before his death my father had bought a new portfolio, reproductions of the Gainsborough and Romney portraits of the Althorp Spencers. By a new colour-process – I have never seen lovelier – and there were very few of them made.

As my mother said, in a room that was pure Jane Austen, they went 'better than any Blakes'.

So that room, now renamed the Picture Room, lost that which made it unique, as our family its unique possession. Yet perhaps not its loveliness. For now from its green walls, above its cabinets and between its delicate sconces, for *Nebuchadnezzar* and *Sir Isaac Newton* and *The Lazar-House of Death* there smiled down the 'portraits of a serene aristocracy' in place of the mind of Blake.

Incidentally, the room began to be lived in.

For its eight rosewood chairs my mother had embroidered seats, in pale silks, urns and formal foliage; to the House a lovely gift. Covered with green silk against profane use, those covers were more and more pulled off, and the chairs drawn up round as lovely a fireside as I remember. White wood to the ceiling, and the panel above the mantel inset with four eighteenth-century paintings of satyrs and nymphs. The hearth was lined with peach-red tiles, the fire of wood and fir-cones in a classical copper basket. In one corner stood a great unstrung gilt harp.

(The harp my mother practised so as to please my father; and it was one of the stories she told against herself, how she heard him coming and began to play to surprise him, and how he came into the room and said: 'Mary, would you mind doing that when I'm out of the house', and the relief it was that she would never have to practise that harp again.)

There were the card-tables folded back in their demi-lunes against the wall. There were china cabinets of the same rosewood, full of Sèvres and Dresden and Bristol, figures as 'fresh as youth, as rare as love'. I did not love them as I loved the things out of the East.

Better than the one in the drawing-room, the curio-table by the windows had in it an even better collection of toys. Not so mixed or mysterious, but 'a box of delights'. More or less in period with the room – there was my great-grandmother's toothpick box, a finger of ivory, her cypher in gold under a crystal, the tiny box carpentered with minute copper nails. Green velvet inside, faded and silver, a mirror in the lid for her patches, the pick a twist of gold. There was her Dresden scent-bottle in its case; and watches and snuff-boxes and patch-boxes and more miniatures; and a box of transparent agate, filled with coloured wafers expressive of all the refinements of eighteenth-century sentiment.

Underneath it stood a box I loved, of brilliant marquetry with a lock of pearl. A War-Office despatch-box belonging to my great-grandfather, I was told, but it does not seem likely. Now and then, when I had been very good, I was allowed to help take out the things from the curio table, and polish them with chamois leather and silk and help my mother to rearrange them. For which I am very grateful, training as it did my touch in handling rare and delicate things. A joy of the senses, so much that they again became live things, their life communicating itself as Chaucer says, 'accordynge to its kynde'.

One thing in particular, an amethyst. One long crystal, cut I think in an octahedron. Cut for a seal, with a belt of fine gold below the head. Only the face was empty, uncut, a transparency waiting for its device; and I hoped some day it would be mine, and I would cut my own upon it.

From a shallow bow-window, the Picture Room was flooded with light; on pale green and white and delicate woods the light fell. The delicate quiet broken only by the beat and the chiming of another of my father's grandfather clocks.

A clock to go with the room, of marquetry, with an enamel disk on its face which told the age of the moon. A pair to the one as you entered the House, tuned to a second with the rest, calling the hours with music, in time with many a whirr and grunt and rustic tick. Brass faces, steel faces, enamelled white faces painted with haymakers and flowers.

Company in the House. Its voice, until, after his death, they ran down, and very few were ever wound again. My mother tried to at first, but she had none of his precision. It was no longer a rite, and my stepfather, I suspect, disliked them. At least, when he came, he did not take them over; as I hoped he would, inarticulately regretting them. Another thing had gone which held my father's memory, attached to the place the memory of him. He of course had something better to do now than hang about Salterns – only – it was a question to do with *pietas*, a piety no longer in practice; and particularly important with rhythmic striking things like clocks. Whose business is with repetition and with time. Which speak. Whose stopping weakens *mana*.

Whose silence implied that life at Salterns would now go to another beat, the entry of a different order of time.

With the hall opened out, the morning-room flung into the old library, and the disposal, this time at Sotheby's, of many more of my father's books, there remained only one room quite untouched. His best work, the dining-room, another tall room, panelled, floor and ceiling, with plain panels of very fine dark oak.

It was a most beautiful room. A few family portraits. A high plain stone chimney-piece, raised to a central block that held his cypher, and on it another clock. A seventeenth-century clock of gilt brass, made for some Butts, domed and pillared like one of Wren's churches, the engraved steel face between delicate pillars of burnished steel. A lovely thing, and its winding twice a week another ritual, its striking pure silver; and it opened at the back with bright exciting doors, which had architectural scenes engraved on them. About fifteen inches high, under a glass shade made long before the domed horrors of Victorian days, of thick bright glass, bright like crystal, with a cut block above through which the sun divided into colours. It stood between two bronzes, Hermes and Artemis on horseback. Late Renaissance, good but not very good, and a great puzzle to me, who had learned not to call them Mercury and Diana, and liked my gods like the ones on vases, plain, and did not understand flying draperies and expressive gestures and technique.

The dining-room had three doors, of the same panelling, very silent, very heavy. One a real door, the other two for deep cupboards; and above each a coat of arms, our own, and my mother's and that of my father's first wife.

The furniture was proper with the rest, black oak, bright with silver; a huge cabinet for china, recessed back above into three small cupboards, their keyholes hidden by the wood sliding back like a bolt. All carved, lions and masks and foliage and fruit, all bright with centuries of polish, and one tall one beside the chimney-piece, without silver, but with the Bishop's legacy of blue and white china from the East. The Whistler touch.

The oval table was lit by four candles in silver sticks, the only light when we dined alone; and the cloth hung down in folds, the beautiful stiff damask of those days; and underneath it, never seen, was a piece of blue and silver brocade. Last remnant of a pair of curtains my grand-father had brought at the Longwood sale, in memory of Napoleon.

Another pair of whose curtains used to hang in the drawing-room, whose crimson and yellow may have accounted for the upholstery of the suite. Faded but self-supporting silk, banished with the restoration to make blotters and cushions; and I too young to feel the tragedy of the hands that must have parted them, staring out across the empty sea.

The dining-room curtains themselves were very different – an instance of my father's taste and flair for finding the right thing. Often copied today in cheap fabrics, but then rare and superb. Of the heaviest unbleached linen, printed with Jacobean birds. Blue and green and orange, pheasant and peacock with sweeping tails. Hung beside windows, unlike those of the drawing-rooms, which had kept their original country panels of wood-framed glass. And above them and on each side of them, separated from the actual windows by a heavier moulding, in each division a coat of arms. My father's own work, and so an amateur's, and they had even run a little; but the hard heraldic colours had weathered most beautifully, as if into a tiny restatement of the 'palette' of Salterns, the whole range of colours dominant there.

On top, in greater elaboration, the full escutcheon; and set beside it, for a 'canting' device, a great gold bee. Down each side the arms of our kin, Bacon and Drury, Graham and Aubrey and Fitzhugh – the sun struck through them, and made pools of colour on the polished boards; but at night, when the white outside shutters had thundered together on their oiled runners, their colours, no longer pieced by light, stared down on us like masks.

It was a very beautiful room, beautiful in conception and in execution; which I know gained us the admiration of the people who understood such things.

In which, I believe, stripped, the boarding-house breakfast is now going on.

The one room in which no change took place. The one room at any time one might meet one's father's ghost.

23
Tiger-Tiger

RESTORED and cool, its shadows lifted, the House awaited my stepfather. This also is the place to describe him, whose coming cut more than one of our lives in two. Whose coming, as I faintly apprehended, brought something fatal with it, and I of necessity was not yet acquainted with fate.

His arrival was really a return. For months the conventions of widowhood sent him away from Salterns, where until my father's death he had been our most constant guest. 'Uncle Freddy', not yet called 'Tiger-Tiger', with his brother Bertie, the two men constantly at the House, walking over to it from their mother's house in Branksome Park. Some four or five miles away from us, through woods. Woods that ended on top of a range of low hills; then down their sides and across a shallow valley on the landward side of Salterns, continuation of our heathland, where the waterworks stood. A gaunt brick building with a single tall chimney, pointing like a finger at the sky; and beside it, banked up by the heather, a series of fascinating reservoirs, the water a different colour in each. One gushed into the other, a crystal bar like a tiny fall or a giant tap. Past these they would walk, along a heath-path to a bank that marked our furthest boundary, not half a mile from the House, but a curious desolate place, heather and swamp and white grass, where all my childhood, seeded from the dark wood belt that divided the moor from the garden, a young wood was springing up. Young firs, shapely as Christmas trees.

To a place where our land rose again, fifty yards from our boundary to the summer-house-on-the-hill.

The path would lead them to it, the silver track of pure sand; and it was at the summer-house, now re-christened 'the Butts' Arms', that my mother and I would go to meet them. Built, as I have said, for Brother Aubrey, where, it was said, even Daddy could not hear him practise his violin; it was all one complete room. With a trellised porch knotted with ivy, dwarfed and moulded by the wind. And inside it had furniture and a real fireplace. And over the fireplace a steel engraving of *The Prisoner of Chillon* very much resenting his dungeon.

We used to leave the key outside under a square of cut turf, and inside there was whisky and soda to refresh the men after their walk. But just below, beside a rhododendron thicket, there was a marsh-pool, called the Smugglers' Pond. Whether they ever used it or not I do not know but all that part of England lay in the heart of the 'free-trade' country, barred with sunk roads in every direction up from the sea. And on the crest of the sand-hills, above the pit between Salterns and Lilliput, a ghost was said to walk. Ghost of a girl, whose lover shot a preventive man, and she had seen him hung at Poole and walked back in silence and flung herself over there.

So Nurse said. Certainly some of the Salterns wells were hollowed out for cargo; even in Daddy's day, before I was born, my Cousin Graham had caught our skipper, Musselwhite, hauling up brandy out of the star-reflecting water. And gone shares for his silence. And it was Musselwhite who did not believe in my father's new telescope, not even when he told him he had seen him on the yacht's deck scratching his left whiskers at midnight, by the light of the moon.

Always there was something strange about that air-dancing hill, thigh deep in marsh and heather, and the little round house on top. A place that made you glad that when you were alone there the Chapel bell reached it, that its one note rang across the moor, as if it were breaking in on the air that blew about up there.

A most solitary place and a look-out. From it you could see across the Harbour to the hills and, on your left, the open sea. Between lay marshes, marshes and the curved Harbour road; and on the rising land to the right, the slum-village of Lilliput; and beyond them the expensive new houses of the gentry, built along that road, commanding the sand-and-heather Harbour cliffs.

An airy brilliance, but I did not like that hill. Always, on the stillest day, little winds fretted about it. Peevish airs, with a whimper in them, as though some miserable old unhappiness, ineffective and spiteful, fluttered there. A sea-and-land mark commanding the whole countryside which I did not quite recognize again until some months ago I went, in Wiltshire, to the spur on the downs on which the last gallows in England stands. A place that carried me back again, half-way, to the time when I first read Dr James's 'View from a Hill'. One real and one imagined place, both exactly the same place as the steep white pebbled path run round a single room, the place where we used to meet my stepfather and his brother, and called 'the summer-house-on-the-hill'.

There were four of them, only surviving sons of 'old Mr Hyde' of Sindal, in Kent, whom I have never seen. Out of sixteen children, the only surviving boys. Eight remaining in all, four boys and four girls. Four of them living with their mother, long a widow, in a large red Victorian house in Branksome Park. Whose door as you crossed it, let you back into finished Victorianism at, I believe, its deadliest; untouched by art, almost impervious to spirit, incomparably less alive than my grandmother's house; where, like an old queen bee, in her eightieth year, the mother of so many children reigned in what was left of her hive.

Hive from which no strong swarms had stormed out to replenish the garden of England where they were bred.

Four brothers, descended from the elder branch of the Clarendon Hydes, still wealthy and until lately exceedingly rich. A family doom was hunting them down – in restrospect it was as though one could hear it snuffing at their heels.

The eldest, John Hyde, lived apart in the New Forest, unmarried, with a life-long friend. Arthur Hyde, the youngest and a soldier, had married out of his world, and lived in the north, in disgrace. Freddy the second eldest and Bertie the second youngest lived with their mother, and with two unmarried and one widowed sister.

Into Johnnie, a hunting man and a great whip, all the vitality of a dying stock had been poured. True *viveur* of the nineties, he made you think of the Regency – a member of the Jockey, a founder of the Pelican Club. No beauty like the others, but with the perfect distinction proper to a man of his kind, and with it an extraordinary tang of life. I adored him, for the few times we met were one of those revelations of life that force on growth in a child. Too rarely we saw him at Salterns; he did not like my mother, and in some subtle way his presence made her conscious of her virtue; but, if ever one lights candles for the dead, one does not forget one to Johnnie Hyde. He could sing too, rousing later my youthful spirits to the highest pitch of enthusiasm by declaring that the only woman he had ever wanted to marry was Vesta Tilley. I heard him sing comic songs, not like an amateur; and once, as it should be sung, 'Drink to me only with thine eyes'.

The other two brothers were, or had been, outrageously good-looking. My stepfather was simply the most beautiful man I have ever seen. Many a young beauty of our age I have known since, now when young men take care of their looks with a kind of sub-Rennaissance pride. But few to compare, none to surpass that tall, slender, dark elegance that first caught my developing eye for such things.

Beauty and stupidity to match? No – a lively – not intelligence, but sensibility, starved. For what food I do not exactly know. An unstable inheritance, bad training, delicacy of stamina; a flair for life, a weakness when confronted with it. Too fine for common convention, not strong enough to break it with impunity, he had run through many phases of the not-quite-satisfactory younger son. His soldiering he had never taken seriously; his diminished income was a mere bewilderment to him. Women at his appearance became usually irresponsible – while he remained indifferent. Not like his brother Arthur, a flirt. A man I am pretty well sure capable – and perhaps only capable – of one profound all-enclosing love. Capable of it, and incapable of finding it, seizing it, holding it, sacrificing not only to it, but for it.

Unless indeed he had already done so – and lost.

Manners so incomparable as to ravish whoever he might meet. Yet, though they came from the most cheerful heart, were no more than the outworks of an entirely perfected reserve. In him ran nothing but the most ancient blood in England, a thing he never thought about – he very rarely thought about anything – but on knowledge of that, as it used to be understood, was the measure of his attitude to the world. Reserve unconscious from its very depth, a flawless barrier, not only between him and men, but between him and life. More nearly, as my mother once said, in restrospect, laughing: 'There were just three families in Dorset your stepfather felt he could *naturally* know'. To which one added to oneself: 'If it were not for her, ours would not have been one of them.'

Yet all this is crude, and not very like the truth. It will have been told quite wrongly if the reader's comment is 'Snob'. There was not a grain of snobbery in him. Rather – and this is more like it – he breathed naturally a different air. Perhaps – almost certainly – among us he never found a climate that suited him, fish out of some crystal stream whose reaches he never mounted, for whom the right leap had never been blown out of the intractable rock of human affairs. He might not have been happy at Versailles, but perhaps at the Court of St Louis, where the knights wore fair clothes 'that their ladies may love them more' and praised God in one. Perhaps in waters we see running only in the imagination, that the arts have abstracted for us, and the romance of history, out of the dusty actualities of men. A world that smiles down on us from Gainsborough's canvases. But I put him earlier. With him went 'the gold and the silver, the vair and the grey'. Not the world of the provincial nineties for a not at all successful younger son.

Imagination would have saved him – had he been trained in the use of such imagination as he had. Imagination based on reality and nourished by it, and from a spring on to its shoulders a man may catch a glance of a wider reality, the health of a serener air. For in him there *was* latent a quality which made him a perfection fallen among imperfections, and wholly, and this was his ruin, unable to adjust himself to them. Creature of a far wider world than any *nichée de gentilshommes* clustered on the north side of Poole Harbour. A work of that *rare* loveliness thrown up by each generation, which in my own the war did all but wipe out. Or left inferior specimens – of the men who are the brightest feather in nature's cap.

> *Jeune homme sans mélancolie,*
> *Blond comme un soleil d'Italie,*
> *Garde bien ta belle folie.*

Yet it was the *belle folie* that betrayed him, not of necessity but, as we used to think, 'of the silly way he was brought up'. A delicate boy, not sent to Eton with Johnnie, but brought up largely abroad by tutors, with whom he travelled about, petted now and then at little German Courts. Crammed for the playboy and nothing else. Then an army-tutor of doubtful character. Then India, polo, high-play – though India made a shikari of him; and his story I loved best was how he went up the hills after snow-leopards, and rough turquoises for the woman he loved, determined to get across the frontier in those forbidden days into Thibet. He did not get into Thibet, but he got the turquoises and the leopard; and he had seen and never forgotten the Himalayas from the snows, under the night moon.

Only, as you could tell from his stories, his experiences brought him so far and no further. There were things he could not co-ordinate. A source of bitter nostalgia for the days before he knew what care was; when his beauty and his riding and his kindness seemed all that life asked, and women and men loved him and the rest could take care of itself. Which it did not. He could not even fully express that past. Only his soft brilliant eyes would turn to stare smouldering at the fire. Half-burned out stars, stars whose central fires were waning. Waning, or not properly blown upon? Who could tell? His health was going, and at forty-eight, where was he? Making a marriage at which people, for various reasons, would shrug their shoulders.

Fine memories though they were – of Ireland and the Empress Elizabeth hunting with Bay Middleton, of London in the eighties at its most brilliant; and after Kipling and Surtees his favourite books were *Experiences of an Irish R.M.*

Books, little fool that I was! I was too proud to read, who now know their quality as much as he did. Who probably never thought of that aspect; only that in them was as good a life as in all his travels he had discovered; and I can never read the story of that run, where Sally Knox and her cousin come racing together at their banks, without remembering my stepfather. For, from the time he was stationed at the Curragh, he had fallen in love with Ireland, like many Englishmen of his kind. Better for him perhaps if he could have returned there, worn out his life fast in the sports he loved, not foundered at a Dorsetshire bank, unhorsed in a world he did not know, was incapable of knowing.

If he had wanted to help in the upbringing of me and Tony, if he had taken our affairs in hand or taught my mother to understand them (but there, only too soon, instinct suggested to her the principle of divide and rule). If he had made friends with me as I grew. If, finally, for us all, he had not met and trusted one man. Trusted him or allowed my mother to trust.

Instead, it was that the ruin brought on our family, out of all the members of our household, came through one who was the gentlest of us, and in some ways the best.

The tide of which I have so often spoken rising in our land, tide of planless, suburban, mediocre change, was of all things the most detestable to him. The most incomprehensible, the most utterly to be ignored. (Remember also that in the place he had no traditional roots.) Already in doubtful health – I will mention here, as it is known, that at times he drank too much, and be done with it. A man easily affected by it, whose constitution, especially after a bad hunting accident, no longer left him tolerant of much alcohol. So were his brothers, Arthur and Bertie. A curse of congenital desire for it supposed to have come into the family with the Musgraves, two or three generations back. A habit that shortened all their lives, and the same thing was said of Johnnie, the eldest. But Johnnie died at a fair age, almost in the saddle. A very different proposition of a man.

Johnnie Hyde in his house in the New Forest had regained for himself something in that world which is 'forever England'; bursting through conventions like a tiger through a paper hoop, through the horror of his own sisters and of virtuous matrons who hastened to attach to him that curious word of the last generation, which carried such a variety of implications, the monosyllable 'fast'. Head of the family, he had money enough to keep himself amused, amusements which became legendary. The brother I saw least of – who was the one I most desired to see. (If only mother, so I thought as a child, would marry him – only then, what would become of Mr Percy Moore?) And he, for some reason or another, did not like my mother. Thought her, I believe, prudish yet too strong-minded, and in some way a danger to his brother.

So that his story, apart from our rare meetings and the superb impression he made, for me is full of gaps. And the only person who I am sure knows it, who lived near him at the time, near him and his friend Gerald Lascelles, the Chief Verdurer of the New Forest, was his cousin, Horace Annesley Vachell; and how I wish he would tell us that story before it is too late.

Though he had done well as a soldier, Arthur Hyde, by reason of his marriage, saw little of his family. So, there were Freddy and Bertie, more or less stranded at their mother's house – even as a child I could see that something had gone wrong.

It was Uncle Bertie who provided the more or less finished picture – sketch of the Awful Warning we should have heeded, more fully worked-up. Exceedingly tall, slightly lame from an accident, a leg broken in Australia and badly set; and want of exercise increasing his weight he looked like a caricature of his brother's beauty, gone loose and gone fat and gone soft. Completely amiable, with a taste for music, amiable and irritable, that combination only spoiled men know how to achieve. I do not know though how he managed to be spoiled, for his sisters were a grim commentary on the whole business. Only the extreme deference which in those days, in a family of distinction, was shown to the boys could have explained their acquiescence, their subservience to two such failures about their house. My stepfather it is easier to understand. His beauty – there is no other word for it – and in those days his brilliant high spirits masked so much. Masked what Bertie Hyde unmasked, the failure, the almost extinction of a family which, a generation before, counted itself among the proudest commoners in England. Women from whom a lively child shrinks, lenders of many badly written and improving books. *'Little Henry and his*

Boozy Bearer' as Uncle Freddy used to say. And though their one sister-in-law was in herself an admirable woman, and one who had produced a son, we never saw her at Wilderton.

So all that complex of affairs, dull to a child, and then somehow painful, I never learned in its details for somehow they made you feel sorry for them, and that again did not seem quite fair.

Only that when I grew up, whatever happened to me, I was not going to be like them, or look like them or lead the sort of lives they led. Aunts I had to call them, who would run off home to my own dear aunts with almost passionate relief.

Aunt Isabel, Aunt Evelyn and Aunt Dorothy. (What a superior set our own were!) Aunt Isabel, of almost dreadful austerity, tall, composed, always in black, dull black that fitted like the dress of a woman out of a Noah's Ark. As at an earlier period the clothes of all dignified women seemed to have fitted, but not at the turn of the nineteen hundreds, not the soft and gracious or provoking lines of my mother's dress. A plain gold cross hung round her neck – another relic.

Aunt Dorothy in replica of her, but with what a difference. Aunt Dorothy, youngest of the sixteen – their mother had borne Johnnie at seventeen, before she had been presented, before she had been at her first ball. And, as sometimes happens in such families, Aunt Dorothy was a little 'wanting'. A tiny doll of a woman, her hair not in a netted bun but in the once fashionable fringe, cut out of a top-knot of loose curls. Actually the 'mongol' type to perfection, her little bright teeth glittered, her little voice chirupped like a bird.

Both were slowly dying in that decorous, super-comfortable red house, as hideous as I have ever seen, but where monstrosities jostled splendours and treasures out of the past.

Yet, in spite of angular skirts and high starched collars, waists bound with a petersham ribbon, crosses, lockets or pince-nez hung on flat breasts ('It beats me,' my mother used to say, 'how they manage to *get* their clothes thirty years behind the times.') both had, as photographs showed when they were young, something of their brothers' beauty.

Both waited on their mother, as the workers in the hive wait upon the queen, distilling the royal jelly; only in their case out of something like their own life's blood.

All three, including one of the married sisters, were antithetic in their charmlessness to their brothers' outrageous charm. All three were intensely dislikeable to a small child. Not one of them had any use for children; still less, one suspects, for the ready-made family of their favourite brother's wife.

So there was only one game to play when you were taken to call on 'old Mrs Hyde'. Or, strictly speaking, two. The old one, out of the strata'd possessions at Wilderton to pick out the original 'Hyde things'. The other – a secret game – what was old Mrs Hyde thinking about?

Mysteriously old she sat in her widow's weeds; far, far older she seemed than my own real grandmother, the 'prettiest' old lady I have ever seen, still light-footed, tiny and active about her house. Wearing her weeds for 'old Mr Hyde' whom I had never seen, who had married her when she was sixteen, Sir Ralph Darling's daughter, and there was – I think on her side – Napier blood in her, blood of Napier of Magdala, whose soldiers said had been a cruel man. A wax, translucent face, yellow inside its snow-pure crêpe, and very silent. What was she thinking about all the time? What *did* old Mrs Hyde think about?

Of having sixteen children and losing eight; of having started too soon and would she have married old Mr Hyde if she'd been to a ball first? Of why they were not so rich now; or why her beautiful children hadn't married other beautiful children and hadn't had more, so that she could sit in the middle of them like a real queen bee, like the photographs of Queen Victoria? Of how awful it was to live at Wilderton after Sindal or why old Mr Hyde had liked sal volatile instead of whisky and soda to drink? Or where her knitting had gone or her spectacles, or of the person who had given her an elephant's foot for a workbox? An elephant's foot with a grey leather top sewn with grey buttons. Set in silver and the elephant's toe-nails polished till they shone like his tusks. Or why her sons weren't out in the world doing great and important things or what time was the carriage ordered or what would there be for lunch? Or after the awful job of having them all, was she too tired to care what became of them?

There must be something that old Mrs Hyde thought about.

It must be easier now ordering lunch, now that old Mr Hyde was dead of sal volatile – Heaven forgive me if he wasn't, but that was the idea I got into my head as a child. They had always far more to eat at Wilderton than we had at Salterns – my mother brought her nursery up frugally and sensibly – but meals at Wilderton remind me of Lucine and Louisa in *Mr Knox's Country* and how their cousin Flurry said that 'it wasn't cracking blind nuts made them the size they were'. Only the Hydes stayed thin. But old Mr Hyde was a gourmet and one that could not trust his temper; so that at the end of each meal the butler used to hand him a notebook with a gold pencil, a book with 'Lunch' or 'Dinner' printed inside; and if the fish was wrong he would write beside it: 'Fish – flabby', 'Sweet – sickly', 'Pie – pig-food', to be sent out to the cook.

I used to wish I had been there then. It would have been interesting to notice. For there was something that made it deadening to go there, and at first I could not see what.

It was not the garden, though after Salterns that was dreadful – acres of shrubbery, and round the house a few dull formal beds; it was not the best behaviour and the best clothes. It was not even that they did not like you or in the very least want you there.

It was – one day I got it – it was that you never heard the very least interesting thing said.

It was not that they talked about dull things or difficult things or things that you did not understand. Then you could have listened. It was that they never talked about anything that mattered at all. Not even when they were by themselves or in the secret place of their hearts. Like being a houseful of people who got no fun out of being grown-up.

Oh how different from Salterns and from Milnthorpe, where, in their different ways, something interesting was always going on! All this when I was a child, and I did wonder if my stepfather when he came to live with us would bring that sort of vocal silence with him.

He did not, and in a way he did. And no doubt I have exaggerated in my account of that house. My mother was probably far nearer the mark when she said: 'My dear, the Miss Hydes are *dull*. They can't help it and don't mind it. So we must make the best of it.' Adding: 'Still, it is a mystery how they came to have brothers like that.'

As for the treasures there, I do not remember much, for I was never allowed to run freely and make out what I could for myself in that house. Only one thing I remember clearly, one thing over which my mother and I used to weep. Called the Anson Trophy, which the Admiral, their ancestor, had brought back from China. We have lately seen that sort of work imitated in pearl-shells and wire; but this was the real thing – an under-sea forest of jade and coral, crystal and pearl. Arethusa risen out of the sea-depths, from 'the bowers of the ocean powers' but brutally hurt. Given to the children to play with, and broken and badly mended; until finally it stood neglected in the

Wilderton drawing-room, under a square glass case, in a condition it tore the heart to see.

The house's chief possession was its silver, a collection going back to the time when Charles II had given all the Hydes gifts. Silver, as my mother said, 'that will go to Johnnie when his mother dies, and since he leaves no children, then to Freddy for his life.'

But it did not happen like that. Not at all like that.

There were two other sisters who had married – 'and who,' said my mother, in a moment of rare candour, 'wouldn't marry to get out of that house?' Not a remark she chose to apply further. Or perhaps had need to. One of them had inherited a touch of the brothers' spirit and more than something of their looks, had married a country parson, due for preferment, and raised up a band of girls. Girls now women. Hyde in type, with something added to them no Hyde ever had. Something equally given, equally taken away. That strange charm replaced by vitality of quite a different kind; strength for good works, lives wholly absorbed in administration and in the Church. All girls, and children of a girl. As though indeed that name was to be written in water at last.

As for their mother, she dressed the Hyde beauty in the same clothes as her sisters – with mutton-leg sleeves in the years of grace 1900 on. Yet it was strange to see how even such clothes young maternity could soften to grace.

The last sister, Aunt Evelyn, now dead at a great age, was one of those women about whom it seems impossible not to apply all the cruel jokes about a certain type of woman that were ever made. As her brother said cheerfully: 'Evelyn married a blind man, and six months later he was dead.' It was the kind of comment she asked for, for from that day to her death she wore full widow's weeds, down to her handkerchiefs bordered an inch deep in black. On she lived and on, all by herself; and more and more legacies came to her, money and precious things, as she lay bedridden in another replica of her mother's house. Shrunk to the size of a little child, she lay in her bed, her invalid's ears wide open, ruling her household like another queen-bee, only this time in an empty hive.

Every year her family expected her death, and they thought it had come at last when her butler committed suicide. Instead, it did her good; she is believed to have put on weight – the death-bustle, the stir of scandal and affairs putting new life into her.

Until, not long ago, she died, having outlived them all, the company of those beautiful dark rose children born nearly a century ago.

Dark red rose children, 'the fairest and the freshest flower'. A set of delicious pastels showed them, bare-shouldered babies, like the children in Winterhalter's painting of Queen Victoria and her family. Even the boys wore love-locks – it was the fashion then and their mother could not bear to sacrifice their long flowing curls. 'And when you think what they must have looked like, you can forgive her,' my mother said.

To bear and rear so many. To lose so many. (Another son, Vincent Hyde, grew to manhood, was in the Navy and died young.) To see none but one boy and one girl fulfill in any way their promise. Again, out of sixteen, two only married; out of sixteen, one son born.

Arthur Hyde was something of a figure in his day. He distinguished himself in South Africa and, stationed for long periods in Ireland, broke hearts there. Like all of them a finished athlete; like all of them with entrancing manners, entrancing looks, and a delightful habit with it of missing trains. To say that he was coming to stay meant with Arthur that he was thinking about you, the telegram announcing his arrival that he hoped to see you in due course; so waxing and waning, fading in and out of his friends' lives like the Cheshire Cat.

Then he, who had left so many women of his own kind in states varying from unhappy bewilderment to amused surprise, appeared one day with a very different sort of wife. A country girl from the north became Mrs Arthur Hyde. Their issue one son and a posthumous child, again a girl, but in that dwindling race, the only one struck with the pure Hyde stamp. When the last comes to the last, in the woman is the race.

171

24
Départ Pour Cythère

WHEN my mother's engagement was announced the neighbourhood sat back and said: 'We thought as much'. Adding (if only it had not been such obvious sour grapes), 'All those Hyde men are *fast*.' This descending to a mutter about 'coming down to live with their mother when they'd made a mess of their lives'. Implying that the best-looking of them was making off with the richest widow in the neighbourhood and no good could be expected of it. Then – and this reached my ears also – 'what will happen to those chidren?'

Here I think the men of the place checked their women. For all the brothers were men's men, and the Bournemouth Club rallied to my stepfather, especially the old soldiers. Men who had been my father's friends, who knew how welcome during his life my stepfather had been at Salterns: that no one more than my father had realized what was likely happen on his own death. Which, of course, was true. I knew that. Could remember my father treating 'Uncle Freddy' – who called him 'Sir' – very much as a son. From Daddy who knew how to give good presents, this to my mother was his last gift.

At very least it pleases one to suppose this. My father was no fool. Also, a just man, knowing that in his desire for an heir, though he had given her everything, he had taken in exchange my mother's youth.

Now she was all sails set – *'départ pour Cythère'*, and Redfern making her wedding-gown of cream lace and sables and Parma violets.

(Only not the lingerie to go with it. It is curious – I know no one thing that did more to separate me from my mother, a distress my brother most fully shared, than her inability to realize that what is worn beneath must duplicate in its fashion to the last stitch what is worn above; that the shabby corset, the coarse shift are all false doctrine, heresy and schism of the toilette. Let alone that men are sensitive about things like that. Especially men of my father and my stepfather's experience.)

It was no use. Over that part of her trousseau she could be

172

persuaded to take neither interest nor care. Nor – and this was beginning to be bitter – would she allow me any but the dullest and plainest and often the scantiest quality of underthings. There was undoubtedly some touch of pathology here, the question somehow confused in her mind with genuine modesty. Due, perhaps, but I do not think wholly, to her Victorian training, her wrong initiation; which had led in her case to a decidedly corrupt horror of the accompaniments as well as the processes of sex.

Off to Cythera – forgetting that she was a bad sailor.

Again, forgetting not to remember that there had been for many years another woman in my stepfather's life. A married woman of family, separated from and I believe ill-treated by her husband, whom he had most profoundly loved. A woman of his own kind, who knew her world, who went like a bird, in days before divorce was conceivable. Their love was his romance. It was for her sake, I think, that he left the Army. (Just after his majority, so soon that he would never be called 'Captain' Hyde.) They had even travelled together, in Ireland and in the South of France; and, long before they were known, in the Islands of Hyères. For that reason he would always talk of them, Hyères and Porquerolles and their nightingales – always in relation to sport and to the friends he had in France – with a lightness that I felt hid longing still. Somehow my mother had it at the back of her mind what she would not admit – that he was giving her his second-best.

He may have been. With the judgement of fifteen I could not make out. It would be so hard on Mother if it were true. What I could see was how the romance of it all had bitten her. Nothing had ever happened to her before like that. A moral romance, a strictly virtuous adventure, and one of the best-looking men alive redeemed by her from a siren. Tannhäuser up-to-date.

I noticed also that she hated the memory of that woman. Hated while she feared it: envied while she feared.

Long ago they had quarrelled, my stepfather and his Artemis. When his engagement appeared in *The Times*, she lowered her stock in my eyes by writing to him a letter, as quoted by my mother, of malicious enquiry: '. . . a widow, my dear Freddy, with a ready-made family?' A letter he showed my mother and she told me. Partly I think in fear, turning to her for protection from the passion that still gnawed him. For I knew that after their parting his health had broken down utterly and that for years he did not sleep. Had gone away as far as Australia and joined his brother Bertie, who at that time was managing their Queensland estates. And it was in the isolation of the bush, under the alien stars, each alone with his memories, hard riding all day and, the day's work done, only their family memories behind them, that both men had begun to drink.

If he turned to my mother to exorcize a ghost, he came to the wrong woman. I think I know what he thought she was, that he saw her as the Absolutely Virtuous Woman of Charm. He was wrong. She was far more complicated, had far more character than that; needing above all, now that her romance, her first independent adventure had come, a man of stronger intelligence, stronger character, greater knowledge than her own to direct and make fruitful her immense potentialities. And have no nonsense about it. Some of which my father had done – especially the no nonsense. But he was too old. She needed a lover and a master. He a mistress and a mother. Neither of them had the least idea of the rational examination of themselves, their desires, the potentialities of their situation.

I had an idea the future would be a chancy thing, but pride was what I was clear about. Pride that my mother had carried off this man so many lovely and passionate and famous women had wanted. It was my mother now who wore him in her cap. For keeps? Of course, only what sort of keeps? A woman in love – for her part she felt about him very much what the young Queen must have felt about the Prince Consort. Though she was heiress of England, it was *his* sacrifice. Maybe it was, but hardly as she meant it. To impartial eyes my stepfather was doing pretty well for himself. Certain sentimental old gentlemen, notably Colonel Everett, were anxious. Came and tried to persuade her of something I do not know but which made her very angry. The women's jealousy came out more obliquely. Chiefly, so I gathered, in approaches to my mother's elder sister and suggestions for her to transmit that my stepfather was not all that he might be. Equally spiteful, equally the one way to make absolutely certain that the marriage would take place.

Only, as I did wonder, was Colonel Everett in love with Mother and thus jealous? Or was it that he had truly cared for us all?

Darker hints were not wanting, even to the insolence of suggested doubts as to my brother's paternity. Suggestions to which nature gave the lie, whose pure rose and white and moon-washed cap of hair signed him more than his father's son. Son of every Butts ever conceived, his little ways, his wiles, his dawning tastes – our family in miniature.

That talk died quickly. A far nearer version was given in the

Bournemouth Theatre, where a touring company arrived with *Peter's Mother*, a recent London success. A play taken from a novel in which a young wife, married to an old man, sends her lover away for the sake of her little son. In the last act, some years later, the husband dies. 'Peter' is growing up. There are complications, and the final happy reunion.

At least this is all I remember about it; but my mother and my stepfather, engaged, were sitting in the stalls among an audience who knew them: and it may have been sheer self-consciousness but, in her account, all eyes were turned on them. Anyhow, in delicious confusion, they left the theatre together.

Manners change. How naïve and provincial this sounds today. I remember it vexed me at the time – it was a stupid thing to have done, not what one expected of Mother. Certainly our robuster temperaments would not underline such a situation by running away.

Then married they were, during, I think, the first term that I found myself alone in Scotland.

Three things my stepfather – not called Tiger-Tiger until years later when I was grown-up – brought with him for a dower. Three things of great importance to our collectors' eyes. Not the Anson Trophy, as we had hoped, who would have given it a proper home, saving it from the further mishandlings of time. It belonged, I think, actually to Johnnie Hyde, who for reasons of his own seemed to take little pleasure in his brother's marriage.

Instead, he brought with him a clock, early eighteenth-century work, by a famous French clock-maker. A most lovely thing, about two feet high, in a rather simple case, carved scroll work in green and white and gold. A perfect time-keeper, I used to think it spoke French; neither its tick nor its chime were in English. Like the best French rhetoric, vibrant, musical, hard. It never cleared its throat or stammered, nor did it burst out into deep song like the now silent Salterns clocks. It stood in the hall; you saw it as you came in through the front door, always correct, replacing my father's chorus. As if it were pleased with itself, saying: 'What do you want with those barbarian giants now that I am here to inform you of the exact hour of night or day?'

The second was a cabinet of Chinese lacquer, ivory and shell figures on black and sprays of almond and peach, brass-hinged with dragons. Inside were many drawers of the colour of polished blood, and it stood on very indifferent gilt console legs. A fairly good piece, in excellent state, but rather late, and most unsatisfactorily raised. For half the point of those cabinets is their support, their lifting on to what is actually a table with elaborate, typically European legs, whose curves and flutings should be those of a counter-elaboration, one style answering another and completing it.

It also stood in the hall, its drawers filled with an exciting collection of shells. On its top, well set-off in the cool light, against the bare white walls, a very large jar of *famille verte*, wild horsemen careering on pink El Greco horses. A very fine piece if it had not been badly injured on one side, to which a dreadful nursery tale was attached.

In the old days it had stood on the top of a dining-room cabinet, always high up, so as to be out of harm's way. One day, many years before, there had been a spring-cleaning, and my father, who at such times used to prowl the House like a tiger barred from its lair, had been temporarily got out of the way. His orders had been that the jar was never to be moved, but while he was away the cook, heaven knows why, unless it was with the idea of washing it in a bath, carried it off up the back stairs. (Stairs that were a little dark precipice, at whose foot was the cellar door and the gents; later, in those hardy days, the telephone, and the door to the kitchen and the servants' hall.)

Meanwhile my father, unable to bear it any longer, had returned, gone up by the front stairs, and with the tiger's instinct came round to the top of the back.

To see, rising slowly to the level of his feet, the cook's head, with the great jar clasped to her in her arms .

Then it is said that he spoke only word: 'Woman!' At which she fell, instantly, backwards on to the stones below, her stout body breaking the jar's fall.

'And what I shall never forget to my dying day was the Captain's face as he spoke that word.'

The third part of my stepfather's dower was something that must be almost unique. Two boxes that had belonged to his great grandfather, the Colonel Wildman to whom Byron sold Newstead Abbey before he left for his Greek war. Boxes made to fit into his travelling carriage, which were with him at Waterloo.

Of dark red mahogany bound in brass, each one fitted inside with the full Corinthian's *batterie de toilette*. On a lining of dark blue velvet, cut-glass boxes and bottles of all shapes and sizes, their lids in silver-gilt repoussé, complete even to a tiny funnel for perfume – that in itself a toy worthy of a goldsmith of the ancient world. The whole the very finest work of the period, a perfection of the cabinet-maker and the silversmith. A lovely thing to possess, and my stepfather's dressing-table also very creditable with its tortoishell fittings. I wished my mother's looked like that. But hers was strictly utilitarian, the workshop from which an elegant woman emerged. Nor could either daughter or, later, son get her to see that Venus' tools, to do their work right, must be worthy of the goddess.

These things he brought with him. Beautiful things. Beauties on his own standard of beauty – if you except the legs of the cabinet – the very best.

They stood together on the terrace, in the sun. My mother's fairness shadowed by a lace parasol, by the hat tilted down, built-up with curled feathers at the back of her gold head. My stepfather in his grey Hampshire hat, an inch of scarlet from his mother's parrot or the blue of a jay's wing, shot in the woods, nicked with a tiny colour bar.

His darkness, her fairness; her golden womanhood, his extreme grace. Strength touched with fragility, and the most finished bearing of a man that I have ever seen.

Beauty that, as he aged, wore to a shell, a transparency; his olive skin sallowed to wax, his cheeks fallen in, his smooth black hair whitened to a beaten silver cap. A dried shell, for the swift grace of my childhood, stiffly but still beautifully erect. His temples concave discs, his temper grown unsteady by suffering, half-persuading me as a young woman that all that delight had been only skin-deep after all. But only half. In my heart I remained profoundly attached to him. Because beauty is its own witness. If my mother had been content to build from that.

I know now that he cared for me. Would have shown it always had be been allowed. (Evidence that came, years later, by strange ways. As truth does. And peace.) But long before the end I was grown-up, the war had closed down, my own life was beginning to open and he had made himself no place in it. At Salterns far too many things had happened – things I had no share in, things I was not asked to share.

Things I hated or feared, despised or laughed at or did not understand. Things I longed for. Things at which I despaired.

If I had known then what I know now – it is the old cry of infinite regret. Only at that age ignorance is one of the terms of existence, of being alive at all. Life which can never be learned at second-hand.

Only, had I ever had it presented to me what was happening at Salterns, I suspect even then I should have left it to its own devices.

My world by then was beginning to flare ahead with the tumult of the post-war world. All standards seemed gone, all values discredited, or at least stood on their heads. Anything was possible, but safer to bank on the worst coming to the worst. Yet I managed to snatch motherhood out of it and love. Found the Prince in the Tower, travelled with him and without him the country East of the Sun, West of the Moon. Passports run out there, in that country; not to be renewed this side eternity. For the rest, with the rest of my generation, went off to find ourselves thigh-deep in the mud of the Waste Land. Joined the number of those who did not stay in it, who were due to travel another road. Across the Waste Land to the Dark Tower, past the horse who 'must be wicked to deserve such pain'.

'Quaere reliqua hujus materiae inter secretiora'. But not with Count Magnus on the Black Pilgrimage.

All of which lay years ahead of the day when, for the first time, at King's Cross I joined the school train for St Andrews in Fife.

25
Regiment of Women

It is a belief of mine that much of the pagan reaction today could be traced back by subtle ways to infant distaste of the hymn 'Gentle Jesus, meek and mild'. The last two adjectives the very last in the dictionary to recommend the faith of its fathers to the natural child. Especially when they used to hear them applied to the last-arrived curate, with scorn.

Unless corrected quickly by others, that hymn in the past sowed seeds of rebellion in many children's hearts. Knowing little beasts, not anxious to be pitied for their simplicity. Anxious to be rid of that simplicity and touchy when reminded of it. 'Jesus, Rex et Sacerdos' a likelier master for a strong child, to whom meekness and mildness as it understands them is the usual weapon of an inferior. Recognizing, when as an adolescent it first opens Nietzsche, only a further development of the same precepts.

Not that my home insisted much on that hymn. It was Nurse who taught it to me, my fantastic touchiness about language causing me to detest it, its sense apart.

I left a home heathily and moderately devout, where a little ritual was allowed to train the senses and draw the heart, to go to a place where the beauty of holiness was not merely forgotten but long assumed to be integral with some form of carnal sin.

Nor is what follows in any way written to the essential discredit of a great school. That has been too often done, usually by young men for whom their school was far too good. Besides, for a few years after the war, when all our institutions were under review by a generation very properly disenchanted, it was a way of staunching one hurt by another, like applying a counter-irritant to a continual pain. Also a quick cut to royalties and a little publicity. And, in certain cases and to some degree, justified.

So now one finds it difficult to judge how much to say. Which again becomes a matter of indifference when one remembers that so

179

great an institution has a back broad enough to bear any criticism one unsatisfactory scholar can make.

Nor have our great girls' schools come much under review, so priceless a part of our inheritance as to be considered above criticism.

For heaven's sake let us be grateful to them. Their foundation was a mark of one of the few sure goods of our age, the lifting of the taboo laid on women against the free use of their faculties. That most mysterious of all taboos, running as it does through primitive society, having its origin perhaps in a 'magic' fear of her; which in modern society decreed that she should be reared in ignorance and irresponsibility, her sexual functions, at one and the same time, too disgraceful to be mentioned yet the be-all and end-all of her existence. A process brought into intolerable relief by the added leisure of the nineteenth century which did so much to take from her the wholesome and delightful work on which depended the well-being of her household.

All this has been said, was said in my youth, *ad nauseam*. Worth repetition because we have begun to forget what the state of affairs was like. Or how easily, as in Nazi Germany, the liberties we now take for granted may be lost. For in my own childhood, outside questions of strict morality, I was taught, when my mother got down to brass tacks, that the final reason why such and such a thing must not be said or done or learned or thought was in ratio to its sexual attractiveness. That was not what it was called, but men were supposed not to like this or that, 'have no use for such women', did not marry such women and, most dreadful and shameful of all, 'said things' about such women. Matters that had no conceivable relation with sex, yet sex was dragged in, mysterious, all-pervasive, unexplained and somehow shameful; and every sane instinct protesting, one winced away, shying like a colt as at some blood that should be coursing through a body but spilt and fly-sought in the dust.

Most women of my age and my kind will remember something of this. (Nor was any woman more afraid of the rising tide of feminism than the average matron, happily married or not. For their shrewdness showed them its fallacies, its liability to extravagance, its tendency to side-step off on to an essentially false basis and preach sex-war.)

From the beginning, to be given a real education was the one desire of which I was sure. Like a little animal running in search of the herb it needs, without which it cannot thrive; without which I knew I could not come to my proper good, but just as surely to my proper harm, a nuisance to myself and to those about me. And at that moment in all the world there was only my blessed aunt to back me up.

It was for the salvation of intelligent girls that those schools were founded. Public Schools on the boys' model, there are many now; but first of all St Andrews and then its great sister-schools, Wycombe Abbey and Roedean. Founded, with Cheltenham, about the same time as Girton, to go one step back and fit girls for the universities. More than that – change the whole concept of their training whether they went on to the universities or not.

Not since the Middle Ages, when the great abbeys took girls and instructed them in all courtly and gentle knowledge, had such an effort been made. In effect to hand on, exactly as to their brothers, the whole traditional culture of Christendom. To fit them further for an active attack on life, as mothers or scholars or professional women, accustom them from the beginning to activity and responsibility.

Superb women in our grandmothers' time, Scottish gentlewomen in particular, in a land where education is a passion, where for generations it has been to some degree shared, found their fitting site in St Andrews. Seat of our first university, where already in my day the women worked with the men. Nor was the money lacking to give their ideas dignity in the eyes of the world.

Dignity, yet, with all that nature had done on that wild coast, an almost complete ugliness. Again, in a land become afraid of the *making* of beauty, its creation by the work of men's hands; 'beauty-shy' as though, as some believe, under an ancient curse.

Another task too they had before them in those days, as, I do not doubt, they have today. One that does not go into prospectuses – to civilize the parents. Especially the mothers, in those days robbed of their dear girls; sent away from them to learn things they had never learned, to be dressed with iron severity and hardened out like young Spartans in icy barracks and playing fields swept by the Lapland wind. *'Vent de Russie'* as the old Mademoiselle used to say, blowing in hail like grey crystals on the coast of Fife.

'Black rock and skerry' – the School stood in St Andrews Bay, back of the tiny port with its 'wynds' and its fisher-folk, where for fear of infection we were never allowed to go. In the nook of the headland on which stands St Rule's Tower, but for its tall battlements more like a primeval monolith than any work of man's hands. Beneath the tower, the churchyard about it, like the anatomy of some huge beast, what is left of the choir and the nave of St Andrews Cathedral. More than what

181

is usually left of the cathedrals and the great abbey foundations of Scotland; where, I believe, only three of the ancient parish churches are still in use.

The boundaries of the School and its playing-fields are the Abbey walls. Still thirty feet high, set with towers and, above the sea, in the farthest corner of all, in a wilderness of dandelions and rank grass, beside the squat red drum of the School's gas supply, a tower that had been the pigeon-cote, pierced with countless stone niches for the monks' birds.

There was another tower, much higher up, beside the tennis-courts and the nets and the gardeners' sheds, which one could climb and sit on its parapet on holidays or on playground leave and, rarest of all blessings there in my time, think.

Inside the walls there were acres of wide playing-fields and courts, grass and gravel, for all games, hockey and lacrosse, cricket and tennis and fives. From north to south, along the western wall, nearest the tower, ran the Houses; in my day Miss Sandys', Miss Sanders', one I forget, then Miss Abernethy's, two huge stone barracks between four. Then a partition wall; then, in a garden, in the angle of the south wall and the west, our own House, the Stewarts. A house divided in two, half for us, the other half the Head Mistress's House.

The only old house. (The Shermansons and the Pearsons stood away in a wood outside the walls; the Day Girls had no house.) A long, low, antique Scottish house, stone-flagged; and our half had a graceful stair mounting its white wall that glittered by night. Stony-white by day, but with something that was gracious about it, something that wasn't school, that had once been trodden by different feet.

Our front door did not lead into the playground, but on to an outer court; and rising opposite, joined by a passage with cloakrooms and lavatories for the other Houses, stood the School House. A high, huge, grim, efficient building, with a tower and a clock, a clock whose voice rang out high and far over the bare Fifeshire fields.

'And the Klangê of cranes that fly across the sunrise' – I used to watch the wild geese passing in the East – 'bringing to the dwarf-people battle and death'. Think that the geese were the cranes, until the voice in the clock-tower told me it was time to go out or come in – at any rate stop what I was doing at the moment under this new life's iron rule. After the gentle work at Sandecotes, the freedom at Salterns, the discipline seemed unintelligible.

A *rappel à l'ordre* I needed badly, the punctuality and exactness I learned – at home it was chiefly meals and not to keep the carriage waiting – have been the greatest use to me ever since. But at first it seemed like a great machine – pitiless, not always *sensible*; not explained and so made logical. It frightened me, making me sulky and rebellious; and since that was no good, acquiescent but unwilling and sulky. I can still hear that tower-bell in my sleep.

All said and done, in those years the great School had not fully ended its experimental stage. And it is only experience that gives suppleness, the grace of perfect adjustment. Girls there were to be turned out into something more than young ladies, citizens and scholars; above all, mothers who would not fail their children by prejudice and ignorance. Or their men by – this *was* somehow implicit though never a word was said about it – by not being gentlemen. Utterly right, all this had yet to be carried out. It was carried out, yet it still seems to me at that time with unnecessary harshness and lack of sympathy, a rule of thumb – and a Scot's thumb at that.

Again, as young ladyhood should not be the first consideration – our homes should see to that – it was liable very considerably to be overlooked. For by rule of thumb, if we were to be taught like boys, boys we remained once our lessons were over. Boys, not only in the classrooms, but on the playing-fields; boys in such little leisure as we were allowed; boys again in the authority of the house-prefects over the younger girls.

With the result that what *is* desirable in the state of young ladyhood was considerably forgotten. In those days certainly a vicious tradition of false refinement clung to it, yet the result was one on which the authorities had not reckoned, one of the little games Fate plays with the finest intentions of men.

The ideas of the School were becoming popular, but not among the intelligent gentry of England and Scotland alone. In a way it had succeeded too well. It was a rather expensive school, and (again in my time) had begun to appeal to the parents of manufacturing families in the industrial north, potters and cotton-spinners and people from Bradford. Men who would all vote Liberal and believe in progress and free-trade; rich bourgeois families, recently enriched, in which the Victorian tradition was still going strong. Large families whose sons were busy getting into public schools and rather amused in the holidays to find their sisters' games up to standard, being put through the same grind.

Only homes without the remotest notions of our culture, the long tradition of 'gentle' things. Often newly-rich parents, gentility their idea of gentlehood and the School's fees no object.

To take such raw girls and knock the gentility out of them was the first task of any decent authority. Snobbery, purse-pride, false sensibility, with all that goes to make up 'schoolgirlishness' had to be done for, and done good and hard.

It was. Girls of sturdy stock became visibly hardier, less silly, less pretentious, more able to play for their side. Yet – again I am speaking of more than twenty years ago – I do not think it crossed the mind of Authority the effect such girls, in the upper forms, would have on children from gentler homes. Little ladies of whose breeding there could be no doubt, from homes which in those days would not have thought those north-country 'industrials' proper to know, were thrown together with them unchecked, often again under their thumbs. Naturally ambitious girls, who *had* to get on in the world, invariably became prefects and games captains, and the contacts were often painful and bewildering. And, to some extent, in the Stewarts at least, a certain amount of bullying went on.

This should not read like pure snobbishness. In spite of iron rules, those girls had more money than anyone else. And money and the ceaseless striving for personal advantage they brought with them as their concept of life. In my House it altered 'tone'. It was not that the rest of us cared tuppence who had money or who had not – the fine Scots equality in such things was in the bones of the place – but many of those girls were not Scots.

That small minority was aware of money, money and getting on in the world, and of nothing else. They would get on in the School while they were about it, instinctive practice for what they would afterwards do in the world. Not in learning, that was not 'done' as it never is, but in games and by a prefect's authority. They would lead and the rest could toe the line. An amusing study in retrospect.

The School, using the most effective instrument of group pressure among the young, did its best for them. In their homes ladies still cherished ill-health and a set of taboos reminding one of the intolerable vulgarities of the female world in the time of Charles Dickens. All this had to be knocked out of them. And it was. A high standard of hardihood, courage and endurance was set. Lessons the others needed less.

Yet it seemed that to attain this so much else was sacrificed. The public-school standard rigidly applied without, almost as a point of pride, the least enquiry into individuality. (How later I envied my brother at Eton, with its sensible liberty, its blessed privacy, its chance 'm'tutor' gave a boy of finding out what was going on in his own mind. If only we had been given even a share in such things.)

Instead – yet over and over again it must be remembered that schools cannot, and in general should not, be run for the exceptional child. Only I was not really exceptional. Oddly mixed in development, very childish and very old for my age. Thoroughly spoiled, they thought. Yet I was all good-will, anxious in all humility to learn, not uppish or priggish in the ordinary sense. Only of rather solitary upbringing, passionately aware (and at home encouraged in this) of what I called Interesting Things; as unprepared as Shelley for the run of youth's barbarities.

If a mistress had ever said a word of counsel, wise criticism or encouragement; if they had ever allowed me to explain my difficulties. If I could have told my people about it when I got home; if I could have had the friends I wanted. Instead, one or two of the prefects helped make it unfashionable for the friends I might have had to become the friends they might have been to me. My father's daughter knew how to answer injustice with contempt. Not wisely, not at all intelligently even. My books should comfort me. Very soon, my books rather than my work.

I was not really lazy, only utterly bewildered as to what they wanted. And for another thing, my body was at its most critical stage; after the gentle south the iron cold of Fife was an exceedingly great strain on it.

It was an awful cold. To this day my body shrivels at the finger of the east wind. Not the gentle sou'wester of my own land that could never blow too hard.

> *Western wind, when wilt thou blow,*
> *The small rain down can rain?*

whose prayer I was too young to finish yet.

There was also a pettish matron who for a time allowed the rough Scots maids to fill up our hot water bottles at bedtime from the kithen; who then forbade it, saying that it must be done only from the bathroom tap. Taps which never ran hot at that hour, and what was more you sensed the ill-will that lay at the back of it; that she did not want us to be warm.

A regime that nearly killed more than one delicate child. I

remember two little maids, beauties, motherless children of a colonel with his regiment in India, sent to us rather late straight from their ayahs and, even to the eyes of barbarians in their middle teens, we could see that their lives were being made at least as hard as they could bear.

When I left I did all I could to fling away the memory of those years. Years, so it seemed then, that I had wasted – that had been wasted for me. Now I see that both were true. Now, today, the part of the system which seems least wise was the absolute separation between the girls and the mistresses. A custom which, with the idiotic mimicry of children, we adopted for ourselves and made sacrosanct; calling it 'sucking-up' for a girl to be seen exchanging a single word with any person in authority, about any concern but her work.

A little encouragement goes a long way. What would I not have given to have asked one question of the great teacher I have spoken of about those amazing lessons, whole phrases of which I can still hear as they left her lips.

Yet only once, for one moment in all those years, did I ever speak to her out of school, outside the stark classrooms of the Fifths or the Lower VI.

Stark they were, their walls bare except for an occasional map. With one exception. Heaven knows how it got there but, by its mercy, in the Lower VI form room (I think) there hung, on a roller, unframed, a very fine reproduction of the Hermes of Praxiteles. There, of all places. By what divine accident? To be stared at in the long hours of the winter evenings' prep, when the gas whistled and the pens scratched and the chill air hung like a gauze, air except in summer nearly always diaphanous with moisture. Blown off the sea, sap of the hilly, stream-fed land and the dew off old stones.

Hermes 'smiling in divine kindness at the child outstretched on his arm' – in that grim land, reminder of another world. Where there was laughter and immortal loveliness and gold weather, an infinite number of memory-miles away. No. Not far off at all. It was inside you, and just – just as one was becoming so miserable as almost to forget – the Gods had remembered. Remembered you and hung him there – who did not, I was pretty sure and on the whole grateful, think enough of me to let me die young.

Sent instead a theophany, a shining-out of a God.

186

I thanked God for it, adoring His son, Hermes, the Caduceus-Bearer, the Leader of Souls. (By then I was older and knew all these names.) He with his brother, the Far-Darter, he of Pytho. Phoebus Apollo with his sister, Protectress of Maids, of me – 'even the Twins whom Fair-haired Leto bare'.

In this we were very fortunate that, two of us together, we were allowed out for walks, and once in the Sixth Form even by ourselves. So that the whole of St Andrews, all of the town within bounds and the countryside round it, trudged by innumerable walks, became as it were 'made over', a piece of the earth possessed. Which is the only way it is possible truly to know any place.

It is to the Scots character that St Andrews must owe its foundation. On so indented a coast, weaker races would surely have avoided the place. A short headland on one side of a great shallow bay and notoriously one of the coldest spots in a cold land. Where there can never be anything but a poor harbour, and that made in the teeth of nature's most serious opposition.

Teeth is correct – for on the eastern shore of St Andrews Bay the earth runs under sea in a series of reefs as dreadful as the mind can conceive, searching for dreadful places over the coast of the earth. Knife laid alongside knife, under-sea teeth, razor-backed skerries parting the heavy waters of the North Sea as butter divides on a hot knife. South-east the cliffs ran for many miles, beautiful cliffs, not very high, grassy and flowery and tinkling with burns. Miles along their tiny coves stood rocks with names – the Buddha, I remember, was one of them. Rocks it was an endurance to reach, an exploit to climb. Our House Mistress, Miss Stewart, a notable athlete in her day, had climbed them all; and to do the same was the ambition of each of her House Captains.

It was on the East Cliffs – out alone by myself in the last days of my last term, that I had an adventure. Adventure that was to be the first of a series of adventures, but I did not know that.

It was a brilliant, icy June morning – 'The Spring comes slowly up this way.' I was going to leave. Soon I would wear shady hats that I looked different and, I was beginning to see, more pleasant in. Take off the hard round white straw with its pale blue house-ribbon. Never wear that sort of hat again. I had failed in my examination for Cambridge. The School was annoyed and ashamed of me, but my people didn't take it seriously enough to care. I was not proud of myself – indeed I was ashamed too; only I knew it wasn't altogether making excuses to know that if they hadn't over-worked and under-encouraged me, allowed me to *explain* what I didn't understand, I should have got through, maths or no maths.

Actually, so I afterwards learned, the mistress who coached me in mathematics left the School soon after I did, and, not long after that, rather mysteriously died. A woman who hated teaching, who hated girls and especially this girl, often careless and inattentive, too nervous to explain her fundamental difficulties in logic which at times made the whole business incomprehensible. Quick enough also to sense that her teacher was a neurotic and to shrink from her.

By that time I was in a bad nervous state. Three years of repression and criticism and loneliness had worn the nerves of adolescence to a state of alternate numbness and over-sensibility. And I had no one to take my troubles to, my home becoming more and more a place where I had no place. Where the only place offered would be a prison. Nor had I, except in point of growth, got any older – bruised back on to myself so as to be in some ways less developed than the eager child of three years back.

It is all rather pitiful to remember. 'The Regiment of Women' can, I imagine, be more particular than men's in its severity. Women, architects of a great experiment, now splendidly under way. Content with their work, and particularly without pity for one whom the experiment did not seem to suit. A want of sympathy that can break out into active dislike – all the sharper for being half-conscious and in need of false props. There were one or two mistresses, I feel even surer now, who, when they thought of me at all, hated me. And with the awful candour of youth, I looked at that fact and at them. Not with resentment, but first with pitiable bewilderment, followed by a kind of detached ironic scrutiny. So that was another bit about grown-ups. I have forgotten the details, but one of them managed to involved me in some scrape with another girl, magnified it and so arranged it that I was left as the person nominally responsible. The same mathematical mistress, I think. I was about three quarters innocent, and quite unaware of the storm raised behind my back. Until it broke, and I found that I could not explain. I bore myself innocently until it was shown me that I looked guilty and was sent for by Miss Stewart.

Then the affair suddenly blew over. But in the opinion of the House, unpopular as I was, it had not been fair. Yet I fretted myself because of it, which was very bad for my examinations. What was worse, learned no worldly wisdom from it, only a poisoning touch of cynicism; getting it more and more into my ideal-fed young mind that grown-up people on the conventional side were, *ipso facto*, not to be trusted.

By this time I was leading a life entirely in two worlds – the school-world with its deadly pressure, and a world within, where every song that Shelley ever wrote sang in a kind of super-chorus together:

> *Oh Thou, who plumed with strong desire*
> *Would float above the earth, beware!*
> *A Shadow tracks thy flight of fire –*
> *Night is coming!*

In a deep window-seat, in a corridor of the old Stewart House, at winter dusk. The sun setting behind the School House, ice-blue sky and torn rags of gold cloud flying in the roaring east wind. The wind from Russia. The whole night hurrying up fast and a single star out – I have never seen the host of Heaven glitter more diamond-hard than they did on St Andrews nights. After play, after tea, in the blessed quiet of a half-holiday evening when there was no preparation; and the meaning of 'The Two Spirits', the poem in which is all Shelley, suddenly made itself known to me.

Nothing is more mysterious than the 'seizure' of a personality by a work of art. A work of any of the arts, which may have been familiar for years, suddenly, like an act of focusing, falls into place. Becoming lucent, intelligible – extra-dimensional? Whatever phrase you like, but the person to whom it happens is in a state of enlarged being; at the top of their powers, but in tranquillity. An experience not of strangeness but of intimacy. 'At that instant her mind was ennobled in Islam' as it was said of the woman in the *Arabian Nights*.

It is always happening. Nothing is known about it – nothing worth knowing. Except that so long as it goes on happening no spirit is ever quite lost. Just then it was often happening to me. Nor has it ceased to happen.

I was saying the lines over to myself when a girl passed. A brilliant creature, daughter of rich stockbrokers, I think, with a house in Surrey, and she very proud of how worldly her home was. Sent to us, I think, least she should become too precocious. Which she had.

It was one of the glories of the School that sex-nastiness was considered such bad form as to be practically unknown. Girls who felt like that about it at least kept it to themselves. She was in some sort an exception – I remember how absurd she used to look in our austere short skirts and belts and tunics of blue serge. She got singularly little encouragement, though to our mixed horror and joy she kept a pot of rouge among her handkerchiefs and put it on. Largely, to do her justice, to see if a mistress would spot it.

At the same time, she was intelligent and, though she despised me beyond measure, there was some sort of recognition between us, based on the easier, in some ways wider and worldlier, life of the south.

In all, she was not shocked and I was not shocked, but what I took for granted, she was curious about. Despising me, it irritated her that she could not quite despise. Both of us were sorry for the other, and equally irritated by the other's incomprehension.

A very pretty woman in the making, she stopped beside me in a bad mood. Said almost every nasty thing one young animal can say to another young animal about tastes it does not share. And I, hurled back from my cloud-ride, and falling with a crash at the feet of the School House, folded myself inside my resistance, inside which I had lived so long that it seemed like the child in *L'Homme Qui Rit* who was being made into a dwarf. About which too I used to have a waking dream, an image, a terror that they had cut off my breasts.

'You don't know what it's about – leave me alone.' Knowing she wouldn't. Knowing, as I thought, more and more for certain that there was no bridge between the lives these people lived and the lives Shelley told us to lead. In the faint light her little, clean-cut, scornful, sensual face looked rather like a devil's. A sentence about 'the World, the Flesh and the Devil' passed in my mind. For a moment I hated her and was afraid of her. Knowing, this time correctly, that she summed something up. Something which had its attractive side. That I should want to play with and would not be allowed to play with. Because – I did recognize that – I had been given Shelley for playfellow.

Suddenly she spoke almost kindly – and kindness was so rare in those days that it made me at once want to cry:

'Come down to the schoolroom and join the merry throng. Our schoolmates, our playfellows, our *virgins*.'

I thought: 'You won't be one long.' Whatever that meant. I wasn't very sure. Perfectly indifferent, only she made you think of things in a queer way. We went down together. It was the January term and she began to tell how, on her way back from an almost grown-up dance, she had been snowed up, and how exciting it would have been to have passed the night with the boys who were with them in the car, under rugs.

Would it have been? I hadn't thought of that. Only she seemed, with her rouge-pot and her boys and her talk of getting married and what you did when you were married, to be like an enormous bit of the world. That was what 'knowing' meant to her. To her, and to very few other girls in the House, but again I knew enough to feel that there was something special and pretty good about that. Getting to know things about being married before you ought to know – that was her knowing; and she was brilliant and did what she liked with rest of the House and I envied her. Was that knowing? Not the knowing 'the Ionians sought as the bride of their devotions'. The phrase had not been written then, but that was what I had come so far north to find. Knowing that it might be found at Cambridge, if I could ever get there. But knowing, if you were to believe Mother, men did not want women to have. Did not like women who had. Did not marry women who had. (Did they like any better women who wanted to find out things they were not supposed to know? No, they didn't – if that was what Mother meant when she talked about 'having a pure mind'. Only she used it to say that you shouldn't want to read great books because they were 'coarse', and there you found that the only thing to do was to take no notice.) Besides, I had never thought of marrying anyone. And I was so plain that it wasn't likely anyone would want to marry me. Perhaps not quite so plain as all that, if that mysterious thing Mother spoke of as 'fining-down' ever did happen to me.

One memory chases another, and this story has run away from the adventure that morning on the Fifeshire sands. It was the last week of term. The last week I should be at the School. I walked fast along the cliffs. It was delicious to be alone. Alone, in the middle of the morning, not in School; although I hadn't passed and the mistresses looked at me with annoyance. Justifiable annoyance. I had wasted their time. Worst of all, I had let the School down. There would never be a whole holiday because of me, because I had got a double-first. Soon I should never have to go to school again. I had got very little further in thinking about life than that. Except that there would be Tony to play with – Tony with whom it was already possible to share Interesting Things. Interesting things and beautiful things. Otherwise I had no plans. Only I was so tired already inside.

I walked fast – impossible on that coast to dawdle in the June wind. One tiny bay succeeded another. Out of the wind the stones were warm. I scrambled over another headland, hilt of another jagged knife-blade that the sea never ran up as it did in Dorset on Dancing Ledge.

Half-way across the next cove I was stopped short. The sun blazed palely above, but on the dry sand I had walked into a pool. An air-pool, it was grey and whirling, and as if full of specks; yet, under the unclouded sun, it was as if out of it. In dead, spinning cold I turned, not faint, but blind. With an immense effort, *wrenched* myself out of it. Tore on and sank on to a rock on the further side. What had I struck? It looked all right – or perhaps (I know more about it now) as if a patch of air in the mid-beach had gone dead.

I went on but, returning, it was a great effort to face that little bay. I crossed it higher up by a cliff-path instead of by the sand.

Returning, I had no one to tell. One or two enquiries produced no story about that beach, no evil meeting that took place and left its mark there. I have never found out. Any more than I can ever forget the instant sense of terror, of something inimical and deadly, of having stepped into a *focus*, a column of energy, cold and vile and hateful, spinning there.

Nothing like *that* had happened to me before, as strange as it was unexpected. I had walked into something, but what it was, and what it was doing on a Fifeshire beach, to this day I have never found out. And when, many years later and in a very different place, the same thing happened, the fear and the evil were left out and only the spinning strangeness remained.

26
Cheiron's Pupil

ON the further side of St Andrews runs an utterly different coast, a sample of nature so opposed it is hard to believe that they can lie down side by side. Inland from its beaches lie the great Links, the greatest links in the world, the mother of all golf-links. For ten men who know St Andrews for its University, the one man who knows it for its School, a thousand know it for that triumph of endurance over climate that sends men there to play the gentlest game. Golf, for whose play sweet weather is implicit.

From the Royal and Ancient Club House they sweep away, parallel with the sea; the three courses following the shore-line, from the city to where the Eden river ends them and bisects the bay. Half-way to where the smoke of Dundee rises under hills.

The Links were once dunes, that no man's land between the foreshore and the real earth. Mimicked mountain ranges blown up off the wide beach, wind-moulded and then grass-starved. Captured and knit into shape by the kind of grass that will not grow anywhere else. Bound and trussed and laced by it to form a land of its own. A grass-world, a bird-and-rabbit world, a barren kingdom but a kingdom to itself.

All over the earth you find such places, wherever the sand and the wind have free play together. In a kinder land, there was Sandbanks and High Horse Manger; and another across the Harbour mouth toward the Studland beaches. There the heather came down, close behind, and there was a lake behind it – there often is a lake. A piece dropped out of a spring sky, a transparent turquoise, enamelled in reeds and wild duck, fringed in osmunda and bog-myrtle – a piece for a Chinaman to paint – the crystal water of Littlesea.

There was no lake behind the St Andrews Links – no Scot would allow that – only the railway line for boundary. Patched with the greens' unflawed emerald stuck with scarlet flags; the rest in the rough, a bank of loose sand, the shape of a wave *reversed*, with blown grass for

193

crest, dividing them from the beach.

Such a beach! At low tide, half a mile of hard sand to where the Eden sped in its shallows, until one came, wading, to its midcurrent, swift and spiked with tiny grey waves, like the stream in the story that parted lovers forever.

Half a mile out of dove-pale sand, hard for riding, only I was not allowed to ride there. Half a mile to a line of breakers. Always breakers, grey, thunderous, a huge roll of them as far as eye could reach; and between you and them at certain tides a starring of myriads of empty sea-urchins. Few shells, coarse weed, little else but those sea-urchins, empty, clean, dry and spiked. Rather dreadfully alike when you came to think about it. What was it like, sea-urchin land, at the bottom of the North Sea?

There we would often walk, two and two alone, ant-size, on the vastness of that beach. Beach as wide as the beach at Hendaye, nearest of all in the western world to the 'long and wonderful beaches' where the Pyrenees join the Basque country and Roncesvalles is not far off. But at Hendaye the sea comes like a lover to the earth his mistress. Not like the Scottish sea.

'The woman ye met by the Scottish Sea . . .' Oh, the land was full enough of poetry. Only not the poetry you thought it would be. Not like the ballads, or only a whisper here and there. More like the sagas, and the goddess of that sea was Ran. Aphrodite had never set foot on it, but Ran with her net full of drowned men, her net set with teeth. 'The Laughter-Loving, the Golden' – what would those stark men with the cold sea in their eyes make of Her if she came up the beaches? Send for Auchterlonie, the professional, to drive her back or the caddies to throw sea-urchins at her? Or send for some old professor to bid her be gone in her own tongue or throw his old plaid over her? At very best, dress her in one of their scarlet gowns with its facings of chocolate velvet, lead her inland to a hall and give a grand discourse about the sinful, naked thing that had come out of the sea? That I said to myself would be the sort of thing to happen if the Foam-Born blessed St Andrews with her feet.

> Car tu es la très-belle, la très amoureuse,
> Car tu es la Mère de toutes choses.

I knew nothing about that yet, for the first time in my life in a world where physical beauty counted for nothing. Or rather, where its presence made men uneasy, as at a forbidden thing. Forbidden or only allowed under the utmost safeguards, as when nature had put it there past any avoiding, or some man like Wordsworth put it into philosophy; or let in sideways by a man like Carlyle, in a torrent of words whose subject should disinfect it, being about something safe like the sinfulness of sin.

Only their cakes were all right, and beautiful was the only word for the way they baked bread.

Also we had in the School, walking among us, her voice full of humour and kindness and 'the grave music of good Scots', teaching us every day, one woman most beautiful to look at.

Almost the Melos Aphrodite, come to school, come to Scotland, turned Scots gentlewoman, turned schoolmistress, turned athlete, but with us all the same – a junior games and mathematical mistress, Miss Lindsay, known in my day as 'Slup'.

In a school where 'crushes' on mistresses were as nearly and effectively taboo as possible, she was deeply beloved. A girl there herself in its earlier days, she had gone to Cambridge; as I was told, scraped through her degree but was one of the first women to make her name as an athlete.

'The great grey-eyed Athene stares thereon'. I think she did. And with her kindness, a kind of golden good humour poured from her, something that made you think of a great and splendid boy. How such a woman remained unmarried is a question to which no simple answer presents itself. Except perhaps the simplest – that in her youth, she married herself to the School.

Yet, young as I was, sometimes I longed to dress her – for intelligent women 'the plain Jane and no nonsense' epoch was in full swing. Curl the corn-gold hair she wore twisted in a knot, simple as the Goddess's, display those superb shoulders; with the right make-up accentuate that pure, sweet mouth. The iron tradition held, and I never spoke two words to her; yet, to the stupidest, the least satisfactory pupil she ever had, she was more than patient, more than kind. Once or twice we caught each other's eye.

In some of the lessons I have already spoken of, given by the mistress, whose name she has asked that I shall not give, she spoke on the Prophet Isaiah and his phrase 'the Lord's remembrancers'. Words it never occurred to me to apply to any creature, dead or alive, at St Leonards, St Andrews, Fife. Until later I remembered Miss Lindsay, walking, her head bare, in the playground on a grey day; understanding that was exactly what she had been to us, had we known it, even then – a 'remembrancer' of the blessed Gods.

Oh, there was poetry about all right. Only never before had I thought of a world where poetry was only highly respected once it was inside a book. The longer time printed the better – it was farther and farther away from the man who wrote it, the things that happened to him and made him write poetry at all. Again I was puzzled. Of course it was rather like that in other places, but not with Aunt Ada or Miss Hill. Any more than with Mother with the things she really liked.

The only poems, so I gathered, either about this time or perhaps a little later, that were respectable outside books were poems like Wordsworth's. They were like an extra, rather superior if you could do it, kind of going to Church. That and Burns and Scott, but they because they were Scots; and the less you asked about what Burns was like as a person the better. I remembered too my mother, when I was very little and had said to her that Dante Gabriel Rossetti was a much greater man even than Daddy because he could make great poems and pictures and Daddy could not, and she had assented in a worried kind of way. Making it quite clear that the man was one thing and his poems another. In which I felt again that she was at once entirely right and entirely wrong. (For up to this time, the only ideas I had for myself about life was to be a poet and nothing else.

Before I went north I had begun to try; it was my great secret, my great delight. Perhaps it gives a measure of the change effected, that while I was there and not until more than a year after I had left did the capacity to compose a line return to me.)

Then, a little later, I was to read in Plato about the poet and the bees: λεπτον γαρ ὁ ποιητης και πτηνον και ἱερον; and accepted this: which is after all the last intelligible word on the subject that man has said.

Poetry didn't matter at School; poetry didn't matter in St Andrews; poetry didn't matter in Scotland; poetry didn't matter anywhere really in the world. (It must matter somewhere or all the poets would have died of broken hearts, for want of some one to listen to them while they were at it. I wasn't a poet yet, but I sometimes thought for want of someone to understand that I should die too.) Yet, in the same place, in a world of such frigid and timid indifference, we were taught more about poetry than anywhere else in the world.

Unique schooling – in the following years I was to learn much, from famous masters of their subjects, but none that so kindled the mind as those swift hours with that mistress in the gaunt classrooms in the Upper School of the Fifth Form and the Sixth.

I cannot find the words to thank her, let alone to praise her as I should. Only it seems to me that some record should be left of those lessons, teaching that went to the heart of the matter, like no other I have ever heard. So that there are in the world today several thousand young women who, in their girlhood, willingly or unwillingly – it is strange how unwilling some of them could be – were enlightened, instructed, frightened, abased, set on fire, reduced to tears, much as, a very long time ago, certain Athenian youths were instructed. Beside a spring – the spring outside the city walls from which so much of the mind of Europe had its beginning.

It was a quiet autumn morning of my first term when I first saw her hurl herself into the classsroom of the Fifth and glare round at us. Children from Lower V, picked children, promoted at the beginning of the school year, a handful of new girls and I among them. I had been warned: '. . . the most awful lessons, and goodness help you if she doesn't like you. She hates all new girls, anyhow.'

She took our names, then informed us that this year, little as we deserved it, we were to have the inconceivable honour of studying with her some of the works of Edmund Spenser. Our green Globe edition, our little annotated textbooks, lay before us on our desks.

'Today we will begin with the outline of his life. Names, places, dates, I shall expect you to remember. If you remember nothing more, it is not only I who will have no further use for you.'

She began. I had never listened to anything so fascinating in my life; and it was then that I began my school career only too well. For our preparation was an essay on his life; and when, three days later, she stalked into the classroom with our books, it was mine she snatched from the pile and read aloud to us.

An exploit the whole form, among whom were several in my House, were perfectly determined should not make me conceited. It didn't. I was quite bad enough at other things to keep me in order. It was not conceit. It was happiness. Here was the wonderful thing I had come so far to find, the difficult, easy thing. Nor had I the wit to hide that I found it delightful. Not because in one way it was easier, whose preparation took the last ounce out of me. But when everyone else was at least half afraid – and to girls who could not keep up her lessons were a source of genuine terror – I can see now how the very sight of me, radiant, at my ease and a new girl – must have irritated: of worldly wisdom I had none yet.

Why should they be jealous when they were so much better than I at nearly everything else? Once I heard them discussing it: 'I tell you, it's not all swank. She likes it – poetry and all that – she knows what it's about.' I broke in and teased them, and could not fathom the real hostility that went with it. No one at home or at Sandecotes, because you liked poetry, called you a freak.

But a freak was what they called you here, in a process of long-continued jeering whose result was to set me into almost a life-enduring mould of mixed timidity and contempt. Over-sensibility and not always secret insolence, one of whose further results was a dislike and distrust of my own sex, and an inability to debate easily and unresentfully it has taken me years to overcome. If I ever have.

A hardening process, in part most necessary, whose natural bent was towards an almost idiotic candour and trust. Only, like so many things at that time in that great School, it was overdone. Nor by that time did my home provide explanation and antidote. My mother was busy with other things than the complicated reactions of one unattractive girl to her fellow men. Nor a woman capable of taking education seriously; of backing up a mistress or a discipline, or of explaining or defending her child. Nor, as I have said, out of school was there the remotest contact between scholars and their teachers. Explanation on a point in class might not be asked outside. It was not *done*, at least in my House; and I certainly never had the courage to think of it.

So that the sight later at Eton of my brother's opportunities seemed to me glimpses into a paradise it was now too late for me ever to enter.

I see now that the authorities were waiting for me to fall into line. Take the stamp of the School and the stamp of my House – a thing I had to learn to do. While by a particular harshness ensuring that I should do it as awkwardly and as reluctantly as possible. They – I quickly tumbled to this – wanted me to adore the place, uncritically, did they? Well, after a term or so, I decided I wouldn't. It is the old tale. What they could have had instantly by reason and love – for there was surely enough to admire – they demanded as a right. And they weren't fair when you had tried your best, blamed you for not understanding when they wouldn't let you ask. Shelley said you had to keep an eye on people like that. They could want. To be more accurate – I see now that this was what lay, very timidly expressed, implicit, at the back of my mind.

The usual deadlock ensued, a real state of strain, as I went up the School, never doing them justice or myself justice, capable of submission to anything but what I felt to be *au fond* unfair. It was fair for them to be angry when I slacked; not fair when they gave me no encouragement to do anything else. In my last year they even stopped my literature lessons because I gave too much time to their preparation – lessons which alone by that time gave my days there any point at all. Examinations were their excuse, but I suspected by that time that they took pleasure in it. Justly, as I still believe; and idiotic as psychology. For half an hour's friendly talk with my House Mistress would have won me over. Won me to enthusiastic submission, for I was still the gentlest, most trusting, most persuadable child.

Only with a child's savage sense of justice as yet undaunted by the world. It hadn't been fair. However hard you tried you couldn't please them. Until it become not worth trying any more. Till it became too awful to try.

Until in that place where people were apt to laugh at the English there stirred in my Saxon sturdiness of blood, the little song of Kipling's I had lately read to Tony, in the nursery, on holiday evenings over the fire:

> . . . *with his sullen set eyes on your own,*
> *And grumbles, 'This isn't fair dealing,' my son, leave*
> *the Saxon alone.*

> *You can horsewhip your Gascony archers, or torture*
> *your Picardy spears;*
> *But don't try that game on the Saxon; you'll have the*
> *whole brood round your ears.*

Only you couldn't finish it. What brood had I to come bee-stinging round the heads of those uncaring women, those unjust girls? My brood didn't care. There was precious little of it to care anyway.

All this, of course, is vastly over-articulate. The sum of what I felt, its essence, who had my own growing to do; and knew by those who should have seen to it that I was being hindered, not helped.

Hindering myself too – as a child does when, for right and wrong reasons, it feels all its world against it. And, lest I seem both to excuse myself and to condemn too much, let me say again that no school ever designed by man can be run for the exceptional child. For one thing – it would be that child's ruin, who needs above all others a dose of this world as he will find it and the common run of men. And favouritism is to be shunned at all costs, or anything that fosters in the brat a sense of superiority.

How to remember this and do the child full justice? Our recent experiments seem hardly a solution.

Or rather the solution lies to hand, in the most ancient simplicity familiar to us all. The antique balance of deep love with sound discipline, cheerful sense with understanding, imagination with hardihood; the child left alone, equally taught to play for its side. A training dependent on systems only in the second place, the first dependent on a group of persons come together by vocation to hand on the whole of a civilization, on a common measure, yet according to the needs of each child. A tradition and an adventure, a treasure-hunt with a grind. A tradition whose image is the wise Cheiron, the bringer-up of heroes, or the goddess, Pallas Athene herself. Κουροτροφοι.

A thing that cannot be had to order, for which there is no fool-proof receipt. Yet it gets done. Undoubtedly St Andrews supplied the cadre for it. Only, when the day's hunting was over on Mount Pelion, the war-games and the exercise of arms, the dancing and the playing of the lyre, surely Cheiron laid his horse's length down by the fire and talked to the young heroes about their ancestors and their family scandals and what he had seen galloping about the earth, and what they would have to expect of Gods and men. If only our Cheiron had been allowed to ask us to tea.

27
Atthis

'GIRLS! You will turn to Isaiah, the First Isaiah and the Second Isaiah, and read what was in the mind of those masters in Israel about the future coming of Our Lord.'

Mysterious lessons: 'Behold, a virgin shall conceive, and bear a son . . . and the weaned child shall put his hand on the cockatrice' den.'

'. . . the calf and the young lion and the fatling together; and a little child shall lead them.'

'But he was wounded for our transgressions, he was bruised for our iniquities: the chastisement of our peace was upon him . . .'

'Instead of the thorn shall come up the fir tree, and instead of the brier shall come up the myrtle tree . . .'

The fierce black eyes stared out at us, like an eagle. It said, '. . . there is no beauty that we should desire him'; and who cared that this woman had nothing that makes a woman beautiful? How common she made all our looks, the classroom 'à l'ombre des jeunes filles en fleurs'. Bright curled hair and delicate skins and clear eyes and bodies like Spartan maids. Yet we were no more than puppets, dolls she was trying to make come alive.

Here were no sour grapes – the sour grapes the young are always on the look-out for. All this was true, for the loveliest girl as for the ugliest. Free for all who could bite on it, bread of life for foul or fair – 'Ho, every one that thirsteth, come ye to the waters . . .' It was something in us she cared for that the world would not care about; that the world would try and kill, or that the world would buy.

'In the year that king Uzziah died I saw also the Lord sitting upon a throne, high and lifted up . . . Above it stood the seraphims . . .' Like Blake. He knew and Isaiah knew, and Ezekiel – 'by the waters of Babylon'. And she knew also. She was a Welsh woman, from one of the countries of the Sanc-Grail. I sat over my Bible with bowed head.

Head that lifted, to follow her, breathless, again: 'I spake to the people in the morning and at evening my wife died.' The man who went

201

into the valley of dried bones and a voice said: 'Son of man, can these bones live?' And he answered: 'O Lord God, thou knowest.' That was the Waste Land again. For a second I shut my eyes.

For all our sober dark blue clothes, we were bones covered with sweet flesh, primrose-cool and sweet. And we were no more than those dried bones if we did not learn what these things meant.

'. . . with twain he covered his face, and with twain he covered his feet, and with twain he did fly.' No wonder Cowper, who *was* a poet, wrote a hymn and said God moved mysteriously. There were Thrones, Dominions, Virtues, Principalities, Powers, Seraphim, Cherubim, Archangels, Angels. They were the same number as Dionysos' Nine. Then came man.

Isaiah said to God: 'Here am I; send me.' 'Will you,' she asked us, 'remember Jeremiah's answer?' (Here for a second her eyes, which except to put one of her terrible questions never glanced at us, turned, so I thought, towards me.)

'"Ah, Lord God! behold, I cannot speak: for I am a child."' She tapped her Bible and emphasized: '– but both went. That is the double answer of the living soul when it is first spoken to by God: "Here am I; send me." and "Ah, Lord God, I am a child".'

'Good morning, girls' and she would spring down from her desk and be gone. Her tiny form shooting down the bare corridor – to what must be her holy and mysterious life alone. Alone in a stone house near the School – I used to look up at its windows with longing – where she lived, so I remember, with a young French-mistress.

In those days it was still more than possible to teach French without an idea what it sounded like; and our teacher was usually known as 'pauvre veuve', from a perfectly dreadful book by Erckmann-Chartrian about an intolerable young woman 'uplifter' of the Revolution, who at every possible or impossible moment 'fondait en larmes'. A book with its rhetoric, its empty moralities and emotions, we took for a roaring joke. Until even the authorities saw the point and replaced it by Daudet; and the next summer holidays sent our teacher off to France to hear what the language was like when it was spoken.

That first year's work on Spenser and the Prophets – four hungry hours out of each week, hours one was famished for, hours that went by so terribly fast; hours, I am now ashamed to say, prepared for, reckless of consequences, with time stolen from other work.

Hours alone that restored confidence, a desolate isolating confidence, but still confidence. Self-respect, and what had become a grim joy that I was hated for my ease at the thing the others feared.

I was not hated in the least. It might be a good thing to teach the naturally solitary child a little group psychology; or that a shade of protective colouring is good wear. What I had done was make them all uncomfortable. There *might* be something in it. Of course there was something in it: only it wasn't a thing to revel in – you might at least pretend to be scared stiff with the rest.

For in reality the School was exceedingly proud of that teacher.

Our House Mistress, Miss Stewart, was a remarkable woman. One of the first distinguished woman athletes, a classic and a great lady; who in middle life had something of the man about her, a boy, even, mixed with an *élégante*. Her House was equally distinguished, for games and sound learning; and there was a touch too of the world about her not all the House Mistresses shared. To girls of her own kind, girls of breeding and fair wits (she was no intellectual) and an infinite capacity for playing games, she was a loyal and intelligent friend. She simply did not know what to say or what to do with any other kind of girl. It had been her life's work to give to the right kind all that was soundest in the training of a boy. To make forever impossible the old false values of female education, female accomplishments, female enthusiasms – the old formulae that once proved so nearly fatal to a girl as naturally shrewd and sensible as the old Queen. (How she would have profitted by St Andrews! As Dr Randall Davidson once said, regretting the limitations imposed on that great character; 'Remember, she never had anyone to play about with and knock the nonsense out of her.')

To more than one generation Josephine Stewart gave simply this best, fought for it in an age when people still shuddered at it. Because of her many women of my day and after *have* had the nonsense knocked out of them and, running in harsh weather like young deer, learned to play for their House or their side, take the rough with the smooth, learned a loyalty and hardihood and truthfulness they would never forget.

'All those Stewarts wash behind the ears,' I heard on Speech Day one father say to another at the Sports, still hardly crediting that girls could run and jump, bat and bowl, field and throw as they had seen them do. It was about this time the first School Team played the Scottish Internationals at hockey, and only lost by two goals. Three, I think, of our House were in the team, among them Phyllis Guillemard, our captain, a beauty and perhaps the finest all-round athlete the School had so far turned out. A good intelligence – we went up the School together – a gardener with a green finger, a generous heart to go with it; she was equally admired and loved. Nursing in the war, she died of malignant influenza and was buried as a soldier is buried, as much a loss to England as any man who fell. For in losing her the world knew it had lost a creature of the rarest quality, the equally-proportioned young person.

She played in that match, left outer, I think, passing to the centre forward with the most exquisite precision, shooting her goals like young thunderbolts; and the whole two hundred and fifty of us roared and rocked and yelled together; and Miss Stewart, who had played in her day for Scotland, umpired, striding up and down the boundary line in her white swagger coat, her silver whistle at her lips.

We all yelled together, one united yell, for once one voice, all unkindness forgot. As we did later when the House, under Phyllis Guillemard's captaincy, won the School silver shield, and Miss Stewart was proud of us, smiled at us all, even at the worst of us; stood us a huge cake and a special kind of half-holiday. And when not the faintest touch of vanity or of self-consciousness could be seen in the heroine of it all, only double practice, help at coaching the backward; when even in school her work did not suffer nor her garden go unweeded, then our House Mistress must have been that her work was good.

We began with *The Shepherd's Calendar*, cunningly, as I saw later, to lead us to the Pastoral; to Arnold and, best of all, to Theocritus. Lessons on the text, with little miniatures inset, bearing on the ages, their ways and personalities and beliefs. But, above all, to tune in our ears to the subtleties of the English poetic speech, unutterable, like the laughter of the sea.

> *Ye dayntye Nymphs, that in this blessed brooke*
> *Doe bathe your brest,*
> *Forsake your watry bowres, and hether looke,*
> *At my request:*
> *And eke you Virgins, that on Parnasse dwell,*
> *Whence floweth Helicon, the learned well . . .*

This was how running water was written. I used to compare it, at a place a mile from the School, where a burn flowed down a little valley called the Laid Braes. A Scots stream running deliberately between smooth brown rocks, roaring in spate, clotted with yellow foam; in summer singing on a single note.

The Shepherd's Calendar is a good text also for the mealy-mouthed, not only the exquisite 'April Eclogue', but many a couplet full of ancient sap and that tang of living earth which, as she taught us, is one of the particular glories of our letters, one which Spenser had learned direct from his master, Dan Chaucer.

Again, it was at the 'April Eclogue' with its flower piece that she paused, staring out at us again: telling us to mark it, for there was more to come.

Some wonder I guessed 'embodied in the mystery of words'. 'You'll know about it all next year,' a prefect said – 'Milton.'

Yet perhaps the most memorable of all these was the hours spent thrusting on our blunt ears the significance of the 'November Eclogue'. That exquisite trial-piece, so little known in comparison with the 'Prothalamion' and its pair; its linked music so sweet the senses faint though never cloyed by it.

> *Up, then, Melpomene! the mournefulst Muse of nyne . . .*
> *Dido, my deare, alas! is dead,*
> *Dead, and lyeth wrapt in lead.*

> *All musick sleepes, where death doth leade the daunce,*
> *And shepherds wonted solace is extinct.*
> *The blew in black, the greene in gray is tinct . . .*

> *The knotted rush-ringes, and gilte Rosemaree . . .*
> *Ah! they bene all yclad in clay;*
> *One bitter blast blewe all away.*
> *O heavie herse!*
> *Thereof nought remaynes but the memoree;*
> *O carefull verse!*

Here was all sweet sorrow. Very different was Edmund Spenser's complaint that nobody wanted his poetry but himself:

> *Cuddie, the prayse is better then the price,*
> *The glory eke much greater then the gayne:*

Why was she so anxious to impress *that* on us? And what an awfully bad time poets had to look out for. (I was going to be a poet – was this what

Nurse used to call a Warning?) Before I got here I'd begun to be a poet,
only, when I showed a bit of it to Mother, she said she didn't think I'd
ever be really good. I knew she was mistaken, and the only thing was
not to show her again for fear she made me afraid to go on. (Youthful
defence against over-suggestibility.)

Yet it seemed that people were beastly to poets even at the court of
Queen Elizabeth, when people called England a nest of singing birds.

> *And if that any buddes of Poesie,*
> *Yet of the old stocke, gan to shoote agayne,*
> *Or it mens follies mote be forst to fayne,*
> *And rolle with rest in rymes of rybaudrye;*
> *Or, as it sprong, it wither must agayne:*
> *Tom Piper makes us better melodie.*

That sounded like us, with Music Halls and things, and the kind of
thing Uncle Freddy liked in the theatre. But oh the words! the words!
the lovely archaisms and alliterations, sturdy food for the child I was to
bite on and digest. With extraordinary tact, matter and manner were
expounded to us, their alliance and interdependence, combining in the
justest proportion pure aesthetics with devotion of spirit.

> *O Pierlesse Poesye! where is then thy place?*
> *If nor in Princes pallace thou doe sitt,*
> *(And yet is Princes pallace the most fitt,) . . .*

The English court didn't seem quite the right place now. Unless you
counted Rossetti's drawing of Tennyson reading *Maud* to the Queen.
Did King Edward really *care*? Also it seemed very important to be in
love, and I'd never been that. Except that there was one girl in the
House I wanted very badly for a friend. Had for a friend for a bit. Until
another girl had come and taken her away, and I hadn't the least idea
how to put up a fight. Too stupid and too proud. Also learning, as the
lover has so often to learn, that the very intensity of need makes him
strengthless towards the beloved.

Now that I look back on it, it was a queer business. A rehearsal,
had I known it, for much that I was to endure later. I can still see her,
her head like a Holbein drawing from that great portfolio now in the
possession of the King. A man's bones, in type not unlike Henry
himself, square and blond, with witty, ash-grey eyes and a delicately
freckled skin. Male bones and male energy, no beauty but immense
compensating character and a thin cynical mouth. My nature-made

protector, who in the right way would have knocked the nonsense out of me. One on whom her own irony preyed, her own variety of mistrust. A nature demanding the satisfactions irony keeps sweet, and so far starved, with only her own temperament to feed on.

One – as I guessed then and know now, for later I found her counterpart and our friendship has never been broken – who would have use for all of me, on whom no part of my nature would be wasted. The friend for whom it is worth becoming all that one has it in one to be. A cotton-spinner's daughter from a suburb of Liverpool, where all those families seemed to live. Not, so I gathered, one of the successful ones, where was wealth pouring in they had not yet learned to spend. Rather on the outside of that prosperity, possibly even a sinking ship. A large family with several brothers, with the tang of male life about it; and she would grow into a woman that men like. There were bits of home in her. Also, in one way, we were both rational creatures, critical of orders whose purpose we could not see, of the pettiness of school taboos. Delicious flashes of understanding – we swanked together rather secretly in the playground. Reading *Barrack-Room Ballads*, adoring the irony and the bad language, extremely pleased that we went home to a house full of real men. Swanked in our long blue cloaks, their hoods lined with the paler silk of our House. Hoods thrown back, whatever the weather – a point again of etiquette – from my red curls, from her sheaf of corn-brown hair.

Yet, as I soon and rather sadly discovered, her cynicism made her in reality more afraid of public opinion than I. In her protest against the innumerable petty tyrannies that undoubtedly, at that time, had the run of the Stewarts, there was something timid, something essentially negative. A negation I knew that I could fill.

It was my first great attempt at friendship, touched with the sexless passion of my sex as well as my age. Who would not have understood explanations out of Plato or of Lesbos. Knowing only that here was the friend I wanted, to whom I could give, from whom I could learn. And with it went sweetness which, as I knew from the poets, must be love itself.

Then to make a mistake I was to make again, which it took me a long time not to make, thinking that, because we shared the same tastes, she had the same assumptions as I.

For she had promised me that we were to finish our time at school together. To be the important school friend, who went over to class with you, ran with you before breakfast, shared 'silence', shared

Sunday and Saturday long walks and all the ritual of school life.

In my second year she was to be confirmed. I, some time before, at home. And that Saturday afternoon, the evening before her First Communion, we had walked the playing fields together until dark. Under blue and gold cloud-rags, in the Russian wind. Talked of celestial things. (I may say that preparation for Confirmation, given by a clergyman visiting the School, at that time was a compound of bewilderment and boredom calculated to suggest to any intelligent child that the business was a dreary farce, imposed by custom, in which even the authorities had hardly the least belief. I am sorry, but it was so. I remember what we said, and what certain lectures on religious matters given by the same man, once a week, were like. Lectures, to the Upper School only, given to tired girls, in the evening, entailing extra or scamped preparation, difficult even to criticize, whose effect was a boredom so awful as to be the only quality that remains.)

Lectures of which Doria had had a double dose; as preparation for a sacrament a means for insuring that such a nature would receive it with a mixture of indifference, dislike and a hardly amiable contempt.

Crossed with a certain uneasiness – was there really nothing in it after all? Questions that kindled me to a sudden steady flame. I knew those lectures – she was to forget them. Their substance even was not to the point. She was only to think of the infinite ways there were of knowing God.

'If I could believe it was true – out here with you it looks as if it was.' Then she grinned: 'Keep me to it. I'll need it. You don't know what a difference you've made.'

The difference she had made. Did she know that – my life was suddenly filled and brimming over? It was all all right. How simple it was. I'd come up north simply to be able to do this. Hand on a little of the lovely things I had learned to someone else who needed them. It was as simple as that.

'Keep me to it' – I did not know that to nine people out of ten it would not be a sacred word. Or rather that they go back on it because it is a sacred word. Or that a girl of Doria's character would be guided by the reaction next day, the feeling that those hours out in the playing-fields had at best been too good to be true.

It happened so easily. For a day or so I left her alone, fearing to underline what had passed between us. Meanwhile, another girl in the House, a chic, pretty girl, essentially second-rate, but on school standards equally at the top of the second rate; a thruster in a sweet pert way, with, I remember, legs like bedposts that didn't match the rest of her – got Doria as easily out of my hands as one took a pencil out of another's pencil-box. A thing one could forgive.

But not the insolence of triumph – a wounding, an underscoring of the solitude and the loss. Solitude, because it had been broken, now unbearable; a quasi-serious, spiteful little flaunting. Child of a father in some regiment not long back from India, she may even have impressed Doria from Liverpool. Whom I, family-tutored, saw as the perfection in embryo of the garrison-hack.

It lasted a year and a half, and settled it whether I should make a success of life at St Andrews or not. A time of desolation and abandonment I can never quite forget. Any more than the girl forgot her victory. Nor was it difficult to see that Doria deteriorated with her – from one point of view at least. Fell into line, knew her second-quality oats, cut out her sarcasm and quick judgement, her vivid curiosity. Learned to take seriously a whole number of stupid pretences which were doing their best to make us a less living, less intelligent community than we might have been. For in my time there was wonderful stuff in the Stewarts alone, ground out and ignored, mocked at and under-fed.

This I saw, watched Doria being blunted, acquiescing, going up in form and team. Who at one moment had the makings in her of as keen and as antiseptic an intelligence, a wit and insolence towards life as I have ever known.

In a very private notebook, lost later in a rather cruel way, I wrote down about it the desolate truth. Except for my work I had given up trying to make writings of my own. Except for that one red notebook for putting down, very occasionally, things it would hurt if you did not try to give them a shape. It was only one sentence but, when I read it through, I saw it was the right sentence; and tried, because it had made the right sentence, to be glad even of the hurt. Because that was how writing was done.

Only it was the last sentence in the book. Not for several years did I try to write again, years after I had left St Andrews for ever.

Once it nearly came right. We both had measles, we two and a fortuitous batch from other Houses. I was very ill; then recovering deliciously, the poison gone out of my blood, and convalescent, found myself almost alone with her, in the great echoing stone 'San', with its blunt Scots nurses and its blessed idleness.

On a spring evening I sat by a window, looking out over the

playing-fields and combing my hair. Noticing that it was growing in again fast, all little tight curls and tendrils. I was seventeen; there was a gentle langour in my blood and a dim sense that some day this would all be over, as a little tune came into my head:

O mon amant,
O mon désir,
Sachons cueillir
L'heure charmante.

Singing it, I saw Doria standing by a further window, a strange smile on her lips. We began to talk awkwardly. A few minutes later, a faint halloaing drifted across, across the young grass and the gravel path which divided the hospital from the playing-fields. Some of the Houses, on their way back from play, giving their daily hail to cheer up the invalids. As we waved I could see among them Doria's friend, doing all she could to attract her attention, a whole discreet scene mimed of fidelity and devotion and 'look-out'. And Doria, moving to a further window, signalled reassurance.

Then I understood whence came all those constant notes and gifts. She was alarmed. But it was too late now. All this was coming to an end, whether I got to Girton or not. It was coming to an end. I should be grown-up and be done with it.

Purified from sickness and by it I returned to the life of the School. (Too far away to go home, it did not occur to my mother to send me anywhere in Scotland to convalesce.) Sent back too soon; other girls were sent away to recoup, so for a few days they let me go more easily.

We had given a term to the first book of *The Faerie Queene*. That she had said, smiling grimly, had been his notion of Despair. A cave all hung about with skulls and the romantic properties of woe, but the meaning of it all not Despair but Delight, the rapture of the blessed on the far side of the grave. Despair's meaning to tempt a man to seek it before his time. (A point most exquisitively brought out by Charles Williams in his great book on the English Poetic Mind, showing Spenser's Despair to be no other than Hope with a different set of properties. And the wrong sort of Hope at that.)

'Death is the end of woes: die soone, O faeries sonne!' – the delicious words swam in my mind with all adolescence's luxury in grief.

Sleepe after toyle, port after stormie seas,

Ease after warre, death after life, does greatly please.

But for a certain hardihood of race, bringing me, then and later, as near to the thought, even of voluntary death, as any young desolate of the eighteen-fifties.

Then came 'Lycidas'.

A whole term given to Milton. On whose 'Allegro' – at that time I was all for 'Il Penseroso' – I sent in a cocky essay and was snubbed for it. Which was very good for me.

Then, in the last weeks of the last term we should work with her, came what, as I had dimly guessed, she had kept up her sleeve for us. It was the toughest thing we'd done, I realized that. Nor did she ask for our comments on it, insisting only on a rigid 'getting-up' of both notes and text. Then she began to tell us what 'Lycidas' was not. It was not, like *In Memoriam*, a personal lament. Milton cared little enough for Edward King. Not was its world the world of Theocritus; its flower-piece would never bloom at once, like Spenser's, not like Shakespeare's. Yet, as she said, curiously anticipating the judgement of Aldous Huxley, it remains the most stupendous production of the English poetic mind. Perhaps of any mind, at any time in poetry. The reason being what one had to find out.

Considering all things, 'had' was good. Much the class cared about the English poetic mind. Only there was something that crushed us into silence, and that not the elaborate notation or the 'stiffness' of it, but the charged line.

To this day I cannot see how she did it – unless Milton did it for her – but word by word, line by line, verse paragraph by verse paragraph she built up in our minds a sense, a conviction, not of music or sweetness or loveliness or any box of delights, but of one overwhelming beauty and overwhelming power. Beauty and truth in absolute fusion, in absolute balance, knit together and rooted and grown and crowned and winged by power. Power like Nature's self, whose supreme attributes are loveliness and power. She brought us to it, as to the foot of Olympus, where 'the seat of the Blessed Gods stands fast for ever'. Leaving us there. With other poems she had made us strive like a lover; here, before each hammered word, she left us to adore. As well wrestle with a mountain. 'Jacob was sent an angel,' she said grimly. 'Lycidas is too great an angel for any present here.'

It was the end of the Summer Term, almost our last lesson. 'Next year you will be in the Sixth and will see no more of me. If these lessons have meant *anything* to you, you will perhaps take this hint. In our Scripture studies you have heard of the patriarch, who fought with an angel for his blessing. So much for him. There are blessings that are fought for – and others that cannot be earned or snatched, which are given only "without money and without price". I have brought you up to a certain place; remember that what you make of it is for your lives to show.'

The swift charged silence followed. Outside, below the high windows, a cry from the High Street, 'Caller herrin'; bare-foot lassies passing with creels of fish on their backs. The wind fretting. A gull. The eternal accompaniment, some way off, of the sea. Then it seemed that all round us, round us and in us, above, below, in our bodies, in our blood running and our hair growing – something vibrated. A soundless sound that was the base of sound. That must be going on the whole time if you could hear it, like the pulse of everything you had to be very quiet to hear.

Only now it was growing into more than a pulse, more like voices far off, into a chorale, a Gloria. The Music of the Spheres? I knew I should hear it only for an instant – if this was an instant. 'Translate! Translate!' my mortal being cried. Meaning that this hearing would vanish, and I must have a mortal word to call it by, an image to recall it.

Like an organ when a stop is pulled out, the sense of it increased. Another part of me noted that she was still at her desk, reading out the last paragraphs of 'Lycidas' and that the hearing was released by those words. Released the throbbing that was in everything, the pulse that had turned into singing. And the words and the pulse were two different ways to what the naked mind cannot conceive, much less hold, for itself.

In solemn troops, and sweet Societies
That sing, and singing in their glory, move, . . .

The words had swelled out and become – like the blood running in our bodies and the light out of everywhere. 'It is like what is meant by the Logos in St John', my mind said; and for a little I was not conscious any more.

No one noticed. My narrow desk held me up, and the sweet air blowing in across the courtyard blew me back again into ordinary perception. When I could hear and see again, she was answering, brusquely, questions about a forthcoming exam. A little later, I watched her rush away, along the passage to the head of the stairs.

212

28
Night and Day

A GREAT many things had happened in my last year, the year that Miss Bentinck-Smith arrived to take over the School. A well-known Anglo-Saxon scholar, a woman of the plain-Jane-and-no-nonsense epoch; an extreme change, so we all felt, from our old Head, Miss Grant. Julia Grant, who had taken over the School from the almost mythical days when Miss Dove, its first Head Mistress, had left it to found Wycombe Abbey. To do for England what had been done for Scotland, and to make its mothers sit up. Which by all accounts she had. Only leaving behind her a woman as delightful as any I can remember. Type of the Scots gentlewoman who is also a scholar; a scholar, lovely to look at, and, I have heard, a brilliant hostess. A slight, gracious woman, her signature the most beautiful I have ever seen; when she left us, there were storms. Miss Dove had formed the School when the present Heads of Houses had been all junior mistresses. Now, for a generation, under Miss Grant, they had played together, like an old team, one into the other's hands. And Miss Grant, as she aged, felt she could leave the School to them in peace.

Miss Bentinck-Smith, by all accounts, did not. I rather think she found herself in the position that so pleased Dean Inge when he was sent to St Paul's – only in her case she was anything but content to be a cypher in the hands of what was, in effect, her Chapter. Felt herself wasted as a new broom, determined to put down her Council of Eight and run the School herself. So that there were wars and rumours of wars – of the weekly Mistresses' meeting breaking up in tumult – of the mysterious House Mistresses' meeting, held, if I remember, once a month, breaking up in something as near a fight as is possible for nine middle-aged ladies of high academic distinction and full habit of body.

Of all this I learned no more than was perceptible to a girl in the middle school, and can answer for very few of the actual changes she instituted. Two only were immediately perceptible – when more than one elderly mistress left, to be replaced, such we understood was the decree, only by young women (supposed again to be her protégées) who had recently taken a First, and by that species of infatuation which overcomes the scholar's mind, irrespective of whether they had the remotest idea how to impart what they had learned. I remember one amiable young thing with the highest Oxford honours, whose notions of teaching history I can honestly say gave me a distaste for the subject that lasted nearly twenty years. A subject for which I had left Sandecotes with a passion. There were even rumours that she asked no better than to get rid of the degreeless mistress of whom I have said so much – to find her, *Laus Deo*, too strongly entrenched in the very fabric of the School's love as well as life.

Nor was our new Head, in my day at least, ever popular. Partly for her austere manner, at once, so we felt, school-marmish and rough. Partly because for a time she took School prayers, not in a frock, not in her Doctor's gown, but in a sort of robe, like an embroidered dressing-gown, a source of great glee to the older girls. 'A maternity-gown,' said Maya, at large; and I wondered what she meant.

It was the Stewarts actually who suffered from her reign the most, when, at the end of her first term, she must have decided that to meet her Chapter equally, she herself must be Head of a House. Until then, what had been Miss Grant's own private house was actually the smaller half of the Stewarts. Continuation of the long low Scots dwelling, old and flagged and gracious; and now we had to lose it, move away along the playing-fields to St Rule East, into half one of those high stone barracks that might just as well have been built for workhouses, or sanatoria or even prisons, as for girls.

I forget who we replaced – an elderly House Mistress who had retired in dudgeon, I think. Very resentfully, in the first term of my last year we assembled there, a resentment, for all her dry control, I could see that Miss Stewart shared; and indeed it was a change to affect the least sensitive, for there was 'good magic' about that old house, where for half a generation, she had shaped her House, its work, the particular quality of its tradition, its pre-eminence in games.

In days when central heating was unknown, the Stewarts had been shut away from the wind, the Abbey walls embracing it. We had only one fire in the schoolroom; only one armchair beside it for the Head Girl of the House. Down its long walls, only the girls in the Upper School had each a separate desk, where they could have their own pictures, their own ornaments. The younger girls all worked at long tables, well out of reach of the fire. Our dormitories were as unwarmed as the corridors; this, with cold baths all the year round and ever open windows, a punishing treatment for girls, whose bodies on occasions have a very real need for warmth.

A hardening system (we were by regulation very warmly clad) very wholesome for girls from soft or over-fond homes; but certainly in some ways augmented in a manner that was not necessary at all.

Our matron – let her name be forgotten – was a sick woman. The climate told on a wretched constitution, the strain of her supposed care for the well-being of over forty girls. Actually, she sat in her little warm room opposite the lockers and devised ways of making life disagreeable for us. I have never understood why Miss Stewart allowed her such authority. At her job of keeping tabs on our outfits she was capable enough; for keeping, even in epidemics, any kind of efficient guard over our health, of stupidity that was little short of deadly. A thing we all feared, dreading her peevish disbelief, was to report sick. To be ordered over to School with a snub against malingering. To be sent back, an hour later, with a sky-rocketing temperature, by a mistress justly annoyed that infection should be spread. Often to be accused again of malingering, hours before anything was done.

She had her favourites too, girls, heaven bless them, who could wangle leave to stay over for the day in the House, with the schoolroom fire to themselves. I never could. Not even for the septic throats that drained my vitality, which, I believe, it was only a spell of happiness, long after, left to myself to do the work I liked, ever cured.

She would not allow us hot-water bottles – not with hot water in them. She also stopped our toasting for tea of the stale bread and butter piled up in the schoolroom after play, before going over to the long hours of evening preparation. Remember, we had all been playing games for two or three hours, and in that cold and at our ages something hot and buttery and good to bite on tasted like heaven. But, after a time, that too was forbidden, except on Saturdays. Ostensibly because we made more crumbs. Really because she was one of those people who, sick themselves and probably disappointed with life, find pleasure in denying it to others. And Miss Stewart was essentially an easy-going woman. Her business was out on the playing-fields – she was Senior Games Mistress and Coach to the whole School – and the little yellow woman like a sick monkey managed our clothes all right. Also it was against the tradition to spoil girls.

Warm. For all the circulation of youth and its flying energy, that word was at the back of all our thoughts. Warm, and we wouldn't be warm – at the beginning of each term, no chance of that till we got home again. Not curled-up warm. Hot with running, hot with playing games, but never warm except in bed, and only then, however tired you were, after a long time. I remember once leaving Salterns one January with a heavy cold. So heavy that the night before my stepfather had put me to bed with lemon and hot water and rum; so heavy that even Matron said my family had no business to let me travel at all. Hot with cold and cold with cold, but knowing I should never, not for months, be warm. Sitting in the train, on a raw Dorset morning, telling myself what it would be like, every mile the train was going further into more and more cold. With only one desire, to lie quite still and warm, like it used to be in the nursery when one was little, with the fire winking on the walls and a soft rain on the windows outside.

So that, in the end, I invented a person, or rather got the idea out of book. A book by E. Nesbit about a child who had a horrid nurse, who dressed her always in things too cold when it was cold, too hot when it was hot (a great tragedy for a child) and tight, scratchy, starched underthings. A child who got out of a magic a 'kind cuddly nurse, who dressed her in a frock soft as birds' breasts'. Very secretly to myself I used to pretend that I had someone like that, who, when every one was asleep, used to come into my cubicle and make up for all the beastly things that had happened in the day.

The story of Sredni Vashtar; Sredni Vashtar the Beautiful, had not yet been written. Which perhaps was just as well.

It is not often understood how children are aware of neurotics, notice something they do not like the feel of, get uncomfortable, *swerve*. Cannot, of course, explain, but can be aroused to a feeling of fear and disgust; and when such persons are in any sort of authority, fear predominates, with incalculable results.

With our matron it was not so much fear, who was after all no more than an upper servant, allowed a great deal too much authority by a Head busy with other things. By her augmenting of our comfortless life it was to our health that she did most harm. Over in school it could be otherwise.

There, on looking back, it cannot but seem to me that in my time there was certainly one woman who should never have been allowed to teach. Not for incompetence but, apart from the mathematics mistress of whom I have spoken, there was one certainly as feared as the one whose name I do not give, but for very different reasons. Fear touched, not with pride and a very real glory, but with something very like disgust.

A Senior Mistress, one of the ancient staff, who had in her what on long reflection I must believe was a touch of sadism in relation to her pupils. Dark, heavy, very stout (she has long left the School and, an elderly woman then, I doubt whether she still lives) she used to make me think of some primeval beast lumbering the corridors, and in class dropping slow words of contempt over the most eager, the most intelligent head. Bad enough if you were good at her subject, her effect on the inaccurate or the nervous was a very real fear over the whole of the Upper School. This I remember certainly.

We dreaded her lessons, whom it was impossible to please – I have been sent out of the room to fetch some papers and, returning, seen row upon row of white strained faces; and on me she had the direct and immediate effect of ruining the subject I had come there passionately anxious to learn well.

Perhaps she was a woman staled by years of teaching; or again, as my friend with the rouge-pot said: 'It must be pretty awful going through life having to look like that.' All the same, there was something sinister about her. Sinister and brutal. I remember at what was called the Episcopalian Church, that grim Victorian-Gothic barn, whose glass was more dreadful than any I have seen before or since, that half the School attended on Sundays, and her treatment of the new curate there. Poor young man – he was English, I think, the perfect type of Thesiger's curate, and he must have tried to relieve the aridity of Vicar's sermons by vague emotional addresses. Which seemed to me then, as to all of us, the silliest stuff we had ever heard. Children are joyful and pitiless; even I can still fake a discourse in his manner. Our preceptress however took a different line. As he mounted the pulpit, instead of settling back in her pew, she would fall, ponderously, forward on her knees, ostentatiously busying herself with devotion, until such time as the foolish, disconnected phrases came, not to their end, but to some kind of arbitrary stop.

This she did, Sunday after Sunday, term in and out. Until even we were a little sorry for him.

I had a bad pain in my inside. At home Mother might say: 'Stick your toes up by the library fire, and here's a new Conan Doyle. No, I shouldn't go out for long in this wind. A brisk turn with me perhaps, in the woods after lunch.' It would be all warm till lunch-time, lunch in our dining-room, with beautiful things all round you; and because you were looking pale, a glass of Daddy's port. And sometimes my stepfather would smile very kindly. Or Mother might say: 'We must take care of her now, Freddy, she's growing up.'

Instead, instead, I'd got my work wrong again. Stupid mistakes some of them were, I could see that now. Only I'd had to do it late, when the pain was starting, and I'd only wanted to go to sleep. Sleep and sleep and sleep for ever, because, when I was asleep, I used to go away – I knew I did. Even when I could not remember when I woke – only the marvellous feeling all over my mind. Away in the place of the choruses of 'Hellas'; where you heard the Orphic thunder, woke sometimes with it in your ears. Walked too upon mountains with men and women who were the ancient heroes; among pines when the wind rose and shook 'the clinging music from their boughs'. Then together we would go down and cross quiet seas in boats. To the shore and up the beaches of 'that bee-pasturing isle, Green Erobinthus'. In a world ten thousand times ten thousand more real than the one that came with day. The sanctuary of Hellas.

> *Around mountains and islands inviolably*
> *Pranked on the sapphire sea.*

All this made sleep a bad preparation for the day. Waking to the iron bell, the rough maids crashing through the dormitories with their little cans of hot water to temper the icy pans on our cubicle floors. With

> *Swift as the radiant shapes of sleep*
> *From one, whose dreams are Paradise*

ringing only too clearly in one's head. Now there were ugly comments in red ink down the side of my work, and contemptuous references made, before the whole class, about my ambition to go to Cambridge. Only, with this one mistress, we all suffered alike, whom no one could please; and with something of childhood's justice, the class often ranged itself on the side of her victims; with children's philosophy, accepting her as a dreadfulness sent by fate.

Only not quite as we accepted the run of such things. Somehow it was felt that there was something special about it, a shrinking not from blame, but from *her* blame; not from difficult lessons, but from *her* difficult lessons; not from an unpopular mistress, but from – I have never decided actually from what.

In my last year, our transit from the old Stewarts to St Rule East was a moral as well as a physical change. How far the others felt it I cannot tell – school children grumble like soldiers – but certainly a rhythm was broken, of which all of us were aware. Transit from a living house to an institution, a barrack built to house forty to fifty girls. It had never been used for anything else. It seemed to make life at once more painful and less real, uplifted as it was, four square, to the icy winds of Fife. True that in the next block Miss Saunders was said to keep her House warm as a hive. Made friends with her girls, even keeping them over from school when they had a pain, lending them thrilling new books, *petting* them! How we envied; how out of a not too stupid loyalty, we pretended to despise. Indeed her House responded to treatment; brilliant, as I remember, at most things, and particularly at School concerts, and music and singing and getting up plays and at fancy dress. Why, she was actually seen talking to them in the playground, arm-in-arm with a prefect, making jokes. Asking them what they *liked*, what they *thought*. A stout, handsome woman, elegantly dressed and brilliant with femininity. A superb teacher of history. By ill-luck I had only one lesson with her, but one – it was on the Plantagenets – I shall never forget.

Perhaps girls are more imitative than boys, but it was curious to notice, on reflection, how each House took on a certain colouring from the demeanour of its Head. The Schermansons at South Abbey Park were under the only foreigner among the mistresses, a rough Scandinavian diamond and Head of the gymnasium. A stout, sturdy, rather comforting, guttural-spoken woman, and her house notable at games, and for a certain sturdy wholesomeness. This with a faint – the faintest – tang of scientific theory, Miss Schermanson representing the cult for Swedish exercises which a few years before, as Axel Münthe tells, had become the latest elixir for all ills of the flesh.

In the same way, the Abernethys – Miss Abernethy was a great friend of Miss Stewart – ran to classical scholarship. Following her attainments, who might be described as a Scottish Pre-Raphaelite, and inclined, to our joy, to drape herself in trailing gowns of peculiar sage-green, the mark in those days of the unfrivolous aesthete, and long chains of beads of semi-precious stones. So I recognized it and giggled.

Only in her House there were pictures of the great statues; and she was said to have her Sixth form up to the drawing-room, and talk to them about art.

A subject which, in all my three years, at so famous a school, in a university town, I never heard mentioned once. It is true that Kubelik came to play for us, and our concerts were excellent; music, though

219

never mentioned, was well taught. But as for the visual arts, it is no exaggeration to say that they might as well not have existed. Drawing was taught and handicrafts – how well I do not know, whose family, all exceptionally gifted in that respect, had long given me up. But when one thinks of the opportunities wasted, of the *civilizing* power they might have exercised upon children counted dull because pure book-work was not the key to unlock their minds – when one thinks of that vast school building naked except for that solitary Hermes, one realizes that there is no protest against infatuation.

So it was that each House reflected in a measure the woman who commanded it. With only one among them that had a bad name – and a quite definitely bad name it was. Last in games, last in work; as though by some queer law the least desirable girls in the School drifted there. It may in part have been a result of the name of the dog – partly, but not altogether. When we said: 'Oh, she's an X – ' we meant something instantly and disagreeably distinct from a Stewart or an Abernethy, or even some young Scots rough from the Sandys. With some valiant exceptions, the girls were something more positive than undistinguished, or young cats with bad names. The House of that mistress who so filled us with repulsion and fear: who so snubbed the curate: whose looks so oddly repelled us. Considering it as a child, I wondered if like had found like, by magic. Or else, also by something like magic, she cast a kind of blight over them.

Almost wholly out of touch with the School as I have been since the day I left, I know nothing more than this. This may have been seen, as in a distorting glass, wholly out of perspective. Only I do not think so.

Quiet in the playground, along an arm of one of the Abbey's inner walls, between the hard tennis-courts and the nets. Grass ran along the foot of it, grass planted with young plane trees; and at the outer end was the tower you could climb, and at the other, some way off, our House.

Quiet in the playground, on a still evening, when I first came there. So still, even the sea was quiet, the air like a crystal cup filled with mist. Mist lacing your hair and your cloak in a diamond gauze, as you walked there alone in the blessed grace of a Saturday half holiday. 'After Dark in the Playing Fields' was not written then, but it wasn't Dr James's potencies one feared or expected there. They would have been quite a different set in St Andrews, in Fifeshire, in Scotland. After dark

220

in our playing-fields quite a different sort of bogle-work. There were no owls, and the small people out of the green wood and out of Shakespeare have never come to Scotland.

Quiet in the playing-fields – I had made myself a little rosary, of nutmegs and tiny macrocarpa cones, carved beads from the east and pierced tonquin beans the Salterns drawing-room used to smell of, and one or two ivory knobs. All strung together, with a queer Russian cross attached, four equal arms engraved with stiff, hieratic figures. I used to say my prayers on it. A mixed lot, pagan and Christian and one or two I had made up. A 'Hail Mary' and the Magnificat, and something God wouldn't mind that Socrates had said, sitting by a stream outside Athens: 'Belovèd Pan and all ye nymphs that haunt this place.' True, there weren't any there, but I knew places where they were. And should find them.

Quiet in the playing-fields. Good to be out alone, away from the schoolroom clatter, on a winter night when the earth was full of rich smells. And it was on one of those evenings that I had a 'seeing' which comforted me. Just as it was quite dark, out of the chill and the stones and the grimness, out of Scots magic which is quite different from English magic, out of the hardness and grimness, out of all that is Scotland and not England or France or Spain, out of a world that seemed the very opposite of a fairy-tale – or was perhaps its own unique fairy-tale – it came.

On the long grass court, between my walk and the outer Abbey wall, turf used in winter for lacrosse and in summer for nets, from somewhere out in the middle of it I heard a voice say: 'Round the stem of the fairy tree'. That, I remembered, came from a song old Andrew Lang, who sometimes you saw out walking on the Links, had made up. About the Garden of the Hesperides. Then I looked, and out on the grass where the voice came from there was a tree. Not the Hesperidean, but a young slight one, a birch I think, with something gold as oranges glimmering in its branches, only more golden. A tree with a delicate air. Sprung up there just by itself, for comfort. What the Bible called a remembrancer. A magic thing to remind me that all the inside things were true.

Not to be looked for again. Or asked for. Only to be remembered. I stood still, adoring it. I never saw it again. Only, years later, came upon something that was not an echo of it, but its identity – the bark of her sons' hats in 'The Wife of Usher's Well'.

29
Origin of Species

In my day – I believe it has been brilliantly altered since – the School library was pretty bad. A long low room with French windows giving on to a court by the School gates, there were few of the discoveries to be made in it that are among the best adventures of youth. Later I was to contrast it with Eton, where fine architecture houses the living literature of our race. Nowhere even to read in it, where at Eton, in deep chairs and at cunningly lit desks, 'after dark in the playing-fields', my brother could go to read Hardy and Conrad. Carry them back to his own room, where no one but the Head or his Housemaster could enter unbid. Reminding one later of what Mrs Inchbald said, when she warned girls that, should they be brave enough to acquire knowledge, they must hide it as the Spartan boy did his fox.

In all it was a poor collection. With some protest I was allowed to take out *The Light that Failed*. Story again, as I saw, of the Wounded Prince, only I could not forgive Kipling his contempt for the woman who wanted to be a painter. He, an idol, only one less sacrosanct than Shelley, wrote of women as though they were not quite human beings, creatures only of the flesh, the flesh touched with a kind of bad magic; creatures always, in their essence, inferior to men. That was woe. It wasn't, it couldn't, it shouldn't be true; and horrible to think of one's idol telling one that one had no business to learn things and become a writer. That it wasn't even any use trying, because one couldn't.

Sturdily I threw it away from me. It was going to be true. For me anyhow, and Kipling and Co. would have to put up with it. Yet, in the dreadful story of the Gadsbys, a story which sickened me even as a child, I learned something, as the most unlikely, the most protesting persons *do* learn from Kipling, a warning about my sex I was never to forget.

The one other book there, which I found in a corner, untouched since its bestowal, was the *Origin of Species*. I knew little about science. Work in the School laboratory, for me as for many, was confined to the strong hope that one day our teacher would blow herself up.

One day she did. 'Whiz-bang' went something in a flask and a column of fire, water and broken glass spouted to the ceiling. Incidentally, the lesson given was one in pure psychology, an insight into the workings of the human mind I fully appreciated and was never to forget. For, as the shower decended again in a glorious wet ruin, our preceptress, who had hidden her face in her arms, cried out: 'Its all right, girls. I'm not hurt.' To meet a sea of faces, expressive of unadulterated delight; and the pious hope, as we helped to mop up, that it might happen again – many, many times.

Sancta simplicitas: 'It's all right, girls. I'm not hurt.'

Indeed, whether Kipling would have approved or not, I had already had one article published. In the weekly *Outlook*; but pride in the event equally mixed with bewilderment, because of what happened at home. I had written it one holidays, in the middle of my St Andrews years, a short essay, on hymns and how awful some of them were. Showed it to my aunt, and it was she who typed it for me and sent it in.

When it was accepted, with a cheque for two guineas, our joy knew no bounds. I tore home through the potteries. There would be a present for Aunt Ada and a present for Mother, and a Classical Dictionary for me. Till then I had kept it a secret, hoping to surprise my mother. And she was furious. How could I have been so unkind, so secretive (the implication was almost – so underhand) as not to have told her before?

I could not see it. I have never been able to see it to this day. Who had, as I thought, prepared a joyful surprise. It was not as though Mother was interested in my ambitions. With my aunt, who had published several books (and only the bitter complex of circumstances that pursued the Victorian woman of lofty character prevented her from becoming a most distinguished writer) it was our common and not in the least secret enthusiasm.

So, on the whole, my first effort brought me more grief than anything else. What was worse perhaps, more and more confirmed me in the belief that from the majority of grown-up people I should get no help. From my mother least of all.

Yet it is an episode with which she has not ceased to reproach me to this day.

Origin of Species began a new epoch in my life. A book I do not suppose anyone had taken out since it was first presented to the library. An early edition, a fat, squat, green book, dull in bits and interesting in bits, but mostly interesting because of what it all meant. That we were descended from and so had kinship with all the beasts; not with the apes only, but with tigers and panthers and deer and guillemots, and rabbits; with the small birds and the large birds, in spite of their laying eggs; with the great auk and the missel-thrush, the puffin and the condors. That I felt was how it should be. Something too that you felt inside. Why should it make God's glory less? Moderately high church as we were at home, I was still a Protestant child, with its relics of literal Bible-worship, its lack of instruction in theology of any kind. So far as instruction went, belief was still based on Genesis. On the literal, clumsiest interpretations of those first chapters, faiths were made or unmade. There was no one to suggest even that, however true some such theory of our physical descent might be, the point was that at some instant, not too far distant, man became possessed of a rational soul.

A point I arrived at quickly for myself, my faith in God still unshaken. Meanwhile it was rather fun to see how science must upset – well, the parsons and the people who said woman's place was in the home.

Exceedingly moved also by the idea of natural processes, now revealed in all their grandeur and all their diversity. And though – Scotland be thanked! – no one tried to prevent my reading it, there hung over it a slight delicious flavour of contraband. I read it too in a queer place, in the remotest corner of the playing-fields, on a stone outside the dovecot tower. Its innumerable niches now empty but for starlings; dandelions and savage rank grass growing at the walls' feet. The walls and in their angle the red drum of the gasometer that lit the School. Sometimes it was up in air, sometimes it sank; and about half the time reeked of gas, as far as the remotest class-rooms of the School House.

There, gas or no, I would sit on a stone beside a tower that had been full of birds when Mary Queen of Scots was Queen.

Read in it about lovely things; about the orchid that, to get itself fertilized, gave the bees a bath. A ball of honeyed water – as they came creeping for honey, a trap that tipped them up and shot them in. So that they crawled out leaving an alien pollen behind. Or the sundew on our heath I had fed so often with flies. How could any of this make God less true?

At the same time, I began to go to church less. The visible world was opening, and that church had nothing to say about the things that were happening outside. Also the affection of my knee, carelessly treated both at home and at school – such injuries were very little understood then – made it difficult to kneel. I could have been cured. When, a few years later, my brother developed the same trouble, all the resources of modern treatment were brought to bear; and he was cured, but mine had gone too far. A point that hurt a little.

Meanwhile my constant lameness gave me leisure – leisure to spend in solitude. Which again had its own disadvantages. For it is dangerous for a developing organism to find itself even partly cut off from activities of the body. My own temperament saw me quite far enough along that way. Also it ruined my dancing of which I was passionately fond, dancing and swimming; above all, made me nervous of my balance on the decks of sailing boats; the only sports at which I could have excelled.

I came back from my walk along the East Cliffs where I had walked into a ghost. It was the end of term – in two days I should have left St Andrews for ever.

That was over. I was going to be grown-up. Odd! Miss Stewart had met me in the playground, stopped and spoken to me almost as though I were a different kind of person. In a few years I should even have a little money of my own. (Mother didn't want me to have it, but I didn't see how she would be able to take it away. I would give her beautiful presents, and then perhaps she would be kind about it.) Mother had sent me a pretty hat of coarse blue straw with a green ribbon. I looked quite different in it.

It was true I hadn't got to Cambridge and the School would be glad to be rid of me and home not too wildly pleased to have me back; but I could try again. If I could get hold of someone to *explain* the difficulties, I could pass that exam all right. Aunt Ada would help.

I was very tired. Queer to feel so tired; and I kept having a dream – I had it for years – that Mother had forgotten to give the term's notice, which meant she would have to pay for the term I wasn't going to have; so she made me go back. Thanks largely to her care of such things, I had suffered very little from the spots and blotches of adolescence, but just before I left I had one. On the side of my nose, an ugly place; I have never had one like it before or since. A kind of flat boil – I was frightened by it. As though something impure had got inside my body and showed. An ugly mark, just in the flare of my nostril, the small absurd Butts nose my family teased me about. Mother would be disgusted if I turned up at home like that. Only I knew somehow it had come out of being tired, because everything for so long had gone against – against the way one wanted to grow. The thing one cannot help. Three years ago I had come there, all in one piece. Now it felt as though I was in several bits, and none of them fitted into the other. And all the bits inside that didn't fit had distilled into something that made the place on my cheek.

Though I'd fined down all right. No one could say that I was fat any more.

I would wear that hat to go away. No need to put on a School hat any more.

'The Spring comes slowly up this way' – as I remember, that last term was as if it were winter. Winter spaced with flashes of sunshine, when only if you were out of the wind could you feel the sun strike warm. Only you never were out of the wind. It blew that June like a beast sprung off the sea, wind that blew from places like Spitzbergen, or from the dreadful mouth of the Baltic, where the whirlpool is at the mouth of a sea like a sack. And the air was white, and dark with trees that had never put on a whole new dress.

When I got south, I should have missed the spring. It would be high summer and the rose garden in glory, and Mother would have interesting new garden plans.

Only they would be asking themselves what they were to do with me. My stepfather was so often ill now, and never gay like he used to be. But there would be Tony. Tony and the warm woods and one's own rooms and some pretty clothes at last.

The tiredness would go away. Lots of us were leaving too, and minding, minding it very much. I looked inside my mind. Was there somewhere a bit of me that did? I wanted to find it, but I couldn't. I mustn't tell lies to myself. The most I should do was to catch a little of the real feeling that was going about. Or think that it might fun some day to come back when you were quite grown up and really famous. If you were the right kind of famous. Visit the School; but anyhow explore the town – all the parts that had been out of bounds all these years. All the ancient, fascinating, smelly, parts, where I had scarcely set foot.

(It shows how obedient one was, that those last days, when any infection we might have caught could not have affected the School, that it still never occurred to me to break those bounds.)

Instead, I went to the top of the wide street where John Knox's house stands, street of a part of the University, for some reason forbidden, and looked down it longingly.

Saying to myself: 'Some day I shall come back and explore all this; go down to the port and the most ancient cobb, and talk to the fishwives and do every single thing we were never allowed to do.'

The old cobb at St Andrews must be one of the oldest in the world, and over it in winter the awful grey waves sweep – the grey seas of St Andrews, the most awful hungry waves I have ever seen. Un-magic sea. Without the Channel or the Atlantic or the Mediterranean magic. Or perhaps with their own magic of which Ran is mistress alone. Ravenous water, driven down from the Pole, that never warms even in summer. Seas that one winter, in such a northerly storm as I have never seen, bit great pieces out of the cliffs below the Scoves where St Andrews Castle with its bloody history stands.

So that, when we passed next day, the cliff had a different face; and people said that another would hurl the castle itself down into the tide-gulf.

The Castle stands on a buttress of cliff, on the northside of the bay, looking across the great beaches to Dundee. A ruin, built squat against the storms, of squat stones packed tight for strength, with little hint of past grandeur or history or architecture. An image only of the evil tales told of it. I used to compare it with our great ruin, with Corfe –

> *. . . hub of a wheel*
> *Where the green down-spokes, turning,*
> *Embrace a cup of smoke and ghosts and stone. . .*
> *Equivocal, adored.*

As bloody a place, but its end a story of incomparable heroism, one of those defeats that are larger than victory; whose ruin was the foundation of a great house.

Here a Scots municipality allowed entrance through a turnstile, and we were allowed to scramble there; and near to it, between it and the Cathedral skeleton – a curious lesson in time – stood a mean and detestable structure of corrugated iron, the Roman Catholic Church.

In the South you would have thought it the tin shed of some little Bethel. Heaven knows how it stood in the inhabitants of St Andrews eyes. It was on one of those last days that I went inside it – with a Yorkshire girl. (Whom I blush to remember. For once, years later, I met her in London and asked her to dinner in the studio where I was living on apples and high thoughts. Forgot she was coming and fed her casually on eggs. Shall never forget her pearls and black ospreys – her father was making money in the war. Nor her face at that meal.)

It was a Saturday. We went in together, with the curiosity of adolescence, starved on the bleak rigidities of the Scots Episcopalian Church. Feeling we were rather daring; saying a Pater and a Magnificat; and rather sorry for them because this church was as poor inside as out – the Church, as we felt, of all Churches with a need and a right to lovely things.

Thought of the Abbey walls and the bones of the Cathedral, of John Knox's house and of Scots history; and how this place was probably called in the town the Scarlet Woman, whatever that meant. Like a poor little tree trying to grow again after a forest has been cut down. After worse than a storm. After something like Fimbul winter, still my most secret nightmare when, as the Edda says, the spring will not come back and winter-dark will last for three years; and at the end of that, Fenrir will break his chain, when Surt and the Sons of Fire come riding down the sky. Then the World-Snake will lift his body out of the sea; Heimdall will run up Bifröst and blow his horn for the last time. The Rainbow Bridge will break, Loki come out of Hell.

And the Aesir will gather for the last time. For the Götterdammerung – 'when Odin goes to meet the Wolf'.

'Will ye see further or not?', so the Norn asked. And I always said 'yes'. From my heart. Who had been given Delphi and the rational mind. And all that which 'incessabili voce proclamant "Sanctus, sanctus, sanctus".'

I knelt there, saying the Te Deum. Perhaps Scotland, when she backed John Knox, in her heart of hearts had gone back to something that was older, something behind and before the monks of Iona came to teach her. Teaching perhaps she had never really liked, hurling herself on it to destroy it, once she had the chance. Out along the Crail road, seven miles away and one of our best walks in the level lands towards Cupar, there was a cairn in the wood. In black pine-woods – not an old planting – a cairn of pink granite, hideous and not like a Christian thing, to the memory of Archbishop Sharp. The Scots had waylaid him there, and not shot or stabbed but torn him in pieces, more vilely than Viking pirates with their mutton bones. The man their King had sent to make them have bishops; and even today bishops didn't matter in Scotland. Only allowed so long as they behaved themselves – not

Scarlet Women, but a kind of Pale Pink.

There was something much more horrible about it than the murder of Thomas à Becket. A viler death and no saint came out of it or any glory of repentance. Only that hideous monument hidden away in the woods; so ugly that it was like a last insult to a man of the seventeenth century who wouldn't have known what ugliness meant, least of all in stone.

Then, as I found out later, the Scots had begun to pretend: that their Reformation was according to the mind of the monks of Iona. Enough to make St Columba leave his grave. Perhaps truth had taken a subtler revenge – the reason why there has never been a great historian in Scotland.

Here was this poor little tin thing, hanging on near the castle to the edge of the Scoves cliff. Near where the sea had taken its great bite, near where the Castle walls were crumbling down into it, stone by stone. Once a Cathedral, with a great Abbey. Now this.

Which did it mean? With some such thoughts dimly in our minds, on another day we returned. Both times the priest saw us; on the second treating us to one of those exhibitions of adult tactlessness, want of perception which sometimes are so freighted with consequences.

He might have talked to us about the weather; he might have talked to us about us; he might have talked about theology or presented us with a copy of St Thomas Aquinas. Instead he gave us a tract, written for the illiterate and, pointing to the ciborium, asked us if we knew what it was.

He had seen us kneel and pray – so daring as even to cross ourselves. He could see where we came from, in the colours of the School's proudest House. Our hair up, which meant that we were in the Sixth.

And he asked us coldly if we knew what was on the Altar. It was Grown Up People again. We never went back.

The last night. A trembling running through St Rule East. Friends weeping together, whose homes lay far apart, the desolation of the first separation of youth. Phyllis Guillemard was not crying, only looking eager and grave. She was laying down great responsibilities, her captaincy, the highest traditions of the House, to a young sister, whom she must train though she could trust her. To her the School had been a place of perfect rhythm for the first exercise of all her gifts. It had adored her and she had adorned it. Gravely the young athlete laid down her maiden-bow for a stronger. Young Artemis, who was to go up to Olympus sooner than she could dream.

One or two were sad, because, all said and done, they had not much to look forward to at home. One with dread, because she had to face a house full of sisters, prettier than she was, greedier for life and better able to satisfy that greed. I knew one of those sisters, like a handsome dark ferret. (A girl who some years later killed herself.)

One was full of grave content, because she had passed for Cambridge most brilliantly. More than one was well pleased because they were going there. Many more than one that, at last, there would be parties and frocks, and with any luck, next year come round, they would be maids no longer.

So through the foursquare stone barrack passed the trembling, at the end of the term they called summer, of so many young things standing with timidity or relief, doubt or delight, at the door of the world.

When the others returned the earth would have made her gifts, in the brilliant Scots autumn where the winds of the equinox, which in the south marked the turn of the year, were there only an interlude.

When descends on the Atlantic
The gigantic
Storm-wind of the equinox . . .

Up here in the north, the year-dance was set to a very different tune.

Tune I hoped then never to hear again, like a music that had hurt from the first, or a dance whose step I could not pick up. Song out of tune to the tune of my blood, pattern I had only been forced to follow, learned with the mind, not the nerves. Had not lived; could not like. But having learned, in those last hours, began to admire.

Had first admired ignorantly, seeking something the fierce needs in my father's blood and its capability for detached scrutiny told me I must learn. Like a bitter herb, needed to purge and restrain, in the direction of a kind of cool steadfastness; also to an admiration for all I could not be. For a warning also. The dark romance I had sought I had not found, nor my own peers for friends. I should have a long way to go for friends yet. That also I now understood.

Foursquare the alien culture stood up before my mind, sure and strong and self-sufficient and self-content. No one had wanted to help me there, except one who bestowed her blessings on all alike. It was not out of conceit I had refused what they told me to take. Not that, as they certainly thought, but because life had made me to do other things.

Instead, they had taught me to stand alone.

That had been their gift. Not a golden apple off the Tree of Life: I must find my own way to the Garden of the Hesperides. Rather, something done up in brown paper, more like a pair of strong shoes, in which to go off walking, all weathers, dry-shod.

'The woman ye met by the Scottish sea' – she had brought a king death, and I had come off better. When the worst came to the worst, I should now be able to live alone.

We went over to School Singing – on the last night of each term, the School's one concession to sentiment. Nine times I had joined that chorus, never once wholly able to give myself to it if only by reason of the painful nature of the words we sang, the verbal horrors of such lyrics as 'When you and I were new'.

Tonight we should end as usual, with the one that went to the Eton Boating-Song. (Why had we to steal another school's tunes and often parody its words? Why couldn't we invent a decent song, a decent tune of our own?)

How did it go?

> *As scholar, mother and wi-i-ife*
> *Bravely their fate have met*

I'd meant to be the first and hadn't brought it off. Did not care tuppence whether I should manage the other two.

Tomorrow none of this would ever happen again.

Tomorrow none of this would matter any more.

Tomorrow I had seen all these people for the last time. Not yet old enough to see the pity of it. Not the exquisite Nancy Shelmerdine even, or Maia, who'd be married in a minute. Not Enid Duff who knew what Greek was, and whom I had never known how to make like me.

Not Doria – Doria planning a lordly trip in her brother's first car.

Not the Guillemards – though I little guessed the curious link that, indirectly, would unite us again.

Tears, sighs and laughter all through St Rule East. Pairs of voices, whispering; here and there in dormitories, the catch of a sob – light rain 'à l'ombre des jeunes filles en fleurs'. Our Cambridge pride was sitting at her desk, with a kind of mathematical elegance piling her books. Her name would be up in gilt letters sure enough on the hideous varnished boards. (Always to my mind the most dreadful record of excellence ever devised by man. Record of School triumphs, which actually helped sap my ambition. Who could want to be commemorated on pitch-pine, in vulgar-lettered gilt?)

Anyhow, mine would never be there.

But she, our House-triumph – she would not mind. She had done what I had not been able to do. She had come to St Andrews to learn what she wanted to learn, do what for her was music. A fine content softened her coldly chiselled young head.

Night, lowering itself like that gasometer on St Rule East. Tomorrow I should go away, a very long way to a place where, on the whole, I was a sort of embarrassment. Just that. There I should have to go on finding my way – a way I had lost rather considerably since they had sent me here. Something to look forward to – surely there was something to look forward to? I could see nothing, but no one at eighteen supposes it is not there.

Should I find it there – in a place that a tide was cutting off?

I must not be cut off by that tide? Was I? Should I be? Nonsense, nonsense, I gentled myself, lying in my bed in a flood of cold moonlight. Something floated into my mind. A light thing like a balloon, bumping about inside, as though my head were hollow; trying to catch on some point where it would break and let out what was in it.

It was always like that, the moments before something important got clear. In our small square dormitory, the breath of three maiden sleepers rose. I only was awake. Three maids asleep under the moon. Turned on my side I bathed in it too. It did not warm you; it did not chill you. Only you could feel it seeping in, and that if you lay in it long enough, longer than the moon ever stayed, something strange would happen to you.

It was then that the bubble, nosing its way about my mind, broke. Broke – and it did not surprise me – on the edge of sleep, not with a vision, but with a fact: that somehow, some way – I didn't know how, but I could comfortably leave it – the lessons that one woman had taught us, the lessons I have said so much about, would show me the way. Like a pair of sound shoes no tramping could wear out, or a knapsack of provisions you'd sling on your back and forget, unpack far later when you were hungry – they would see me through. ('The way to the Stone that is in the Stone' I should have said, if that book had yet been written.)

Falling asleep, I understood, quite comfortably, that all those years she had been packing the basket with the foods I should need. The First Isaiah and the Second, Edmund Spenser; Amos the Shepherd, John Milton and King Arthur and his and Aristotle's magnificence. Colin Clout (who might be me), Ezekiel, the great noble in Babylon. The Diamond Shield and Queen Elizabeth, who was England, who was Britomartis. And Britomart came from Crete, and from Crete you stepped like the legs of a compass to Egypt, and from Egypt round again to Cambyses, between Darius and Cyrus the Persians.

All parts of a pattern, the web on which the world is strung. My seeings were part of it, and you had to go on filling in the pattern as she had taught us to do.

All the way round, like the plunkerty song in Kipling: 'From Delos up to Limerick and back'.

I slept.

The slip coach along the branch line to Dundee drew slowly out along the low-lying lands behind the Links. All the way to the river it skirted them. On the Championship Course a few figures were still moving in the evening light. I stood by the carriage window and stared across them at the grey town I was seeing for the last time. Stared and stared. Suddenly it was lit; lit and showed glaring by a light I felt risen behind me. So I turned to the other window and looked out again across Fife. A curve of the line showed me the town and the source of the light that was over it, its walls, roofs and towers dipped and dyed. By a sunset such as I have never seen, before or since. Between swollen clouds the sun was sinking – into such a redness for which I can find no comparison, a fury of blood. Blood-hot rods shot out between barrels and rollers of grease-dark smoke. I was horribly moved by it. Like a hideous eye the sun glared, over the living city and the bones of its past, on small figures playing on emerald a last round before night. On a walled sea marching in where Ran fished. Polyphemus' burnt out eye – what did it mean, that bloody look?

For it had a meaning, I knew, as I shuddered, glared down by it.

The great train gathered speed on its run through Scotland, across the Scottish hills, into the north of England, a country far less kind once the Border is crossed. Thud and spring; thud and spring, and the continuous humming overtone the voice of the Flying Scotsman in his stride.

> *To Lancashire, to Lancashire*
> *To get a pocket handkercher –*

It had said that when we were little. Now it said whatever you liked to make it. Though 'penalty for improper use, £5' takes some doing, as later Aldous Huxley said. At Edinburgh the darling guard, who knew us all, took care of me. An enormous man with a square beard – beard, voice and eyes that all matched in one kindness, the kindest kindness in all my three years there I had ever met. I must tip him properly; I was grown-up now, and Tiger-Tiger was very particular about that. Said women were likely to be mean. Anything was better than being mean. Would half-a-crown do, or ought it to be five shillings? 'Ye'll no be coming this way again?' I shook my head. He'd seen by my hat that I was grown-up.

I bought all the magazines I could think of. Then, as though he understood *everything*, he shut me up in a carriage by myself; said he would bring me tea, and a porter at King's Cross. Suppose there were lots of people who were kind like that.

The train roared on. Soon we should be at what they used to call 'merry Carlisle' only it did not look it now. Roared and leaped and gathered, and I sorted out its song. Now we were really away; now we were right into England, crossing great desolate places where by day there were fewer people than I had ever seen before – the Flying Scotsman with the bit between his teeth. Now he had got away, now he wasn't singing any more – he was shouting. Now – thud, leap, thud, leap – he was shouting a bit of his mind, one last piece of advice for me: thud – leap, thud – leap. We rocketted over points. 'Forget it, forget it, forget it'. Now we were in the straight again, more solemnly. 'Forget. Forget. Forget.'

30
Crystal Cabinet

'FIFTY mad elephants with the voices of devils' was what my stepfather said of his stepchildren, when he realized the presence of Tony and me about the House, all one summer long. Words which, oddly enough, felt the nearest to real welcome that met me on my return.

Summer was half-over. What seemed to occupy my mother most was a desire that I should now consider seriously what I looked like; and according to her, I did not. As often happened, she was wrong and right. It was not that I did not care. Only, again as usual, I wanted leading up to my fences; as had become habitual, I did not know how to explain to grown-up people and was inclined to distrust them whatever they did. I can see now the distressing, dismaying object I must have presented, still half-raw schoolgirl, with my passion for learning things unaltered, high-minded, silently emotional, insufferable with naïve cynicism and naïve beliefs, with a kind of contemptuous shrewdness dawning on top of it.

All was not well at Salterns. I was aware at once of an internal fret, a silent ill-being distilling there. My stepfather had been ill – as I was told, the effect of an old hunting accident. An internal hurt – the pain of which affected his temper. I must be patient and take no notice. I was perfectly willing to be patient and take no notice, but I did not like the feel of it. The sense of something irremediable – of a worst coming to its worst.

Indeed I can only apologize to those who remember those days for the unhappy spectacle of shy egoism I presented, free, to my elders then. I did not know what I wanted but, like the men in Frank Reynold's book, 'I wanted it devilish bad'. Only with my brother I forgot it all; the knots untied themselves, the sails filled to the breeze; because I loved him, I turned into myself; man and child as he was to me, in one. As with my aunt I could forget in another fashion, become what *she* wanted, as she understood it, the young seeker after truth. And, as I have said before, the debt I owe her is past statement, let alone return.

Indeed I would have sought how to be of use to my mother and my stepfather, but the heart of our trouble was that by nature they had no use for me. For the kind of child I was, still less for the kind of woman I might become. I know now what it was they wanted; in a way I knew it then. Only, and it was a dreadful thing to know, that I could only give it to them – to my mother, at least – at the cost of my own life. By nature, she was one of those women who find it impossible to deal with an equal of her own sex. In her vigorous activities all over East Dorset, she had only clients and assistants; she had no women friends. To be a daughter to her I could not use the life now rising within me, make it coherent, put an edge on to it, without leaving my own being to waste away. Already I had been through so much sheer pain. From her – and from him – I wanted the mother's function and the father's, comfort and understanding, opportunites and intellectual light. I might as well, or better, have asked them to make a duchess of me.

Like a little brook my forces were gathering, and my wild garden, which already knew drought, needed the last drop of it. Digging there had begun, and the planting of roots they did not know the name of. Who, outside the garden, were suspicious of new plants.

All of which led to one last deplorable result, that I ignored or suspected or refused such advantages, such opportunites, as they might have given me. And here again accident led my mother into a new and particularly fatal mistake.

Shortly after my return I was in London, and she wrote to tell me that some old and rather amusing friends of our family would be asking me to their house for lunch. Would I be sure to go, answer at once and be sure to make the best of myself.

I remembered them. They had been rather fun – husband awfully gay: and they knew lots of Interesting People and to meet such at that time I would have walked to the ends of the earth. What I did not know was that the husband had recently become a man with whom neither girl nor woman could be left alone.

Then, after a gay lunch, too gay for so old a man, gayer even than he used to be, he asked me down to his library to see his books. Timid and terrified, as I suddenly saw, his wife tried to stop him, but he pulled me aside, and into the library together we went. For a few seconds it was dreadful. Somehow I tore myself away, utterly bewildered, troubled, alarmed, contemptuous – I hardly knew at what. When after I told my mother, she was sorry, but evasive, and with the brutal justice of youth I thought it out. If she'd known it could have been like that, why did she let me go? If she didn't know, well, on her own showing, all her talk of how dreadfully careful girls must be, she ought to. It hadn't been fair.

Slowly I thought it out. I mustn't let the memory of it make a sore place. He had been, as I remembered, a very brilliant, excitable man; and somewhere I'd read in a book that things like that happened to men when they were old. Science explained it. It was that. Science, the great antiseptic, cleaned it up. (He died soon after. 'A good thing too,' I said at Salterns, at lunch. Again my mother looked uncomfortable and was silent.)

Only, again, the effect was to deepen my under-appreciation and instinct of such things as they had to give. If I were to do the things they wanted, was that sort of thing to be my reward?

I was seeing my mind as though it were a cabinet, furnished with all sorts of shelves and cupboards and drawers. Secret cupboards too and secret drawers. Lots of the others were empty yet and I longed to fill them; there were more in the secret places, some of whose springs, from time to time, I would forget. Places where the memory was kept of the tree in the grass-court at St Andrews, under the Abbey wall. The Tree and the Evil Hero and the Wounded Prince, the gifts of my father's spirit to me.

Yet still on the whole an empty cabinet, a crystal cabinet like the one Blake wanted to live inside and outside of at once. Perhaps that was what learning to live meant, really learning. Not the half-learning, which seemed as much as most people learned. Anyone can live outside it, and a very few, like the duller saints, altogether inside. But to do what Blake said – and be inside and outside the cabinet at once? Wasn't that what someone called the 'same thing and simultaneous possession of eternal life'? Wasn't that what Delphi had tried to show the ancient world?

Meanwhile what exactly had I undergone at that house? What had happened to me? (And I'd run away and behaved like a schoolgirl, not like the perfect, poised women I knew my stepfather admired. More than he admired Mother. Women like Kipling's Mrs Hauksbee, he'd known as a live woman in India.)

What was it? It was then, for the first time, the little pack of real knowledge, which one woman at St Andrews had put up and sent me out with into the world, came into use.

What was it *like*? Had anything been written about it? In true psychoanalysis fashion, I saw a white and red hat-band. The day-girls' ribbon, and, underneath its pale straw halo, a very plain Scots face. Little green eyes and a sulky mouth and the same Christian name as mine. The form-room of the Fifth. Then the rest came back. The Seven Deadly Sins in Spenser; the one we had been told *not* to write a description of and she, by accident of absence, had, and been reproved.

Lust – that was what it was. The thing that went with love and, if it went too much, spoiled it. Lust, that time, all by itself. I cheered up and forgot the whole business.

Only with the proviso that it was my own people who had let me in for that.

Remember, at this time, girls still went chaperoned. An incredible ignorance was supposed of them along with an equally (to me at least) incredible, unacknowledged curiosity. At eighteen I knew as much about sex as a boy of eight and probably cared less. I think my mother must have realized this, for her efforts soon ceased to curtail my walks, and I tumbled about the place and across the countryside with my brother, careless of everything so long as he was with me. Careless of being grown-up or not being grown-up, of knowing or not knowing; careless of the future, caring only of being with him, in the unexamined, inarticulate serenity of love.

Then, suddenly, the question of my further education solved itself. It was my beloved Miss Hill at Sandecotes who suggested to my mother that I might go where she had been. To Westfield College, part of the University of London, and there read for a degree, as I chose, or not. To me she advised privately: 'Mary, I shouldn't. You don't need to teach. Go and read what you like.' Adding something to the effect that she did not think I was going to be a woman to whom academic distinction would mean much; and I, who at the time believed that to write M.A. after her name, was, for a woman, the sum of earthly ambition, felt inwardly indignant.

All this is vague and rather mysterious to me now. Why did my mother consent so readily? What part did my aunt play? I can guess at some of the answers. At least, Miss Hill was right in not thrusting any more examinations upon me.

'You can sit for your degree preliminary next year if you like. Meanwhile you'll be doing the work.'

It seemed all settled in an instant. No need to explain or beg or defend one's point of view, keeping back all the time a blind desire to

cry. Nor to be restrained and sensible and fightly shrewdly
heart's desire.

It was not in the least like that. In a way I did not unde
was hustled off to London at the beginning of the Michaelmas

With sufficient sense to take it and be thankful. After all,
be at a university and there would be a room, no, two rooms, to
It was right up a hill called Hampstead, a great red building
large garden. A town-garden – I sniffed – but a splendid library;
the bottom of the hill there was the whole city of London. I co
there, all by myself, when I liked. Indeed my mother had n
faintest idea of the liberty we were allowed. Only, again, Miss Hil
'You will be happy there, I think.'

I was. At the time it sounded like a miracle; and served, how
little my home, apart from my aunts, reinforced it, for a very
transit out of girlhood. If the alternations had not been so sharp, in
perfect one. If there had been any link between the terms and
vacations. But there was none. There I learned – a great many thin
every one of which has served me to this day. Came into contact w
life in a score of unknown aspects, intellectual, social, cultural.
return home as across a gulf spanned only by a railway train, and I
nothing else on earth.

Ever since I had done what the train had told me, and St Andrew
passed clean out of my mind. With a completeness that was almost
pathological. Except for that one dream, and for the little pack for
secret emergencies I was not to need again for a long time to come. Nor
is it here the place to write much of my life at Westfield – happiness has
often not much story to it, nor the discoveries of immaturity. It was at
Salterns that the important things happened; and the proper end of this
book a little after the end of my university life.

A first year of almost incredible release. A year when no one
scolded, no one sneered, but the students of my year, the dons and the
lecturers alike, treated me as a gay young friend. A college that was the
product, possibly the last vital product, of the old school of Evangelical
Christianity. 'Simeon's lot' a century before, as Mr Worby, the verger,
said to Mr Lake. Pious, it did not insist that you should be pious; in
effect a place where all the world appeared as friends.

As for work, even those Scottish lessons were forgotten. Seeming
fulfilled in such plenitude. And there I was entirely mistaken. Except
for Homer, some Sophocles, some Plato and a thorough, end to end
drilling in the elements of the whole range of our literature, this and the

way to handle such material as springs from *The Golden Bough*, I remember little that I learned there. That there I learned more *how* to learn, I do not doubt; but the supreme good of that life, for the first two years (after which other problems of growth came up in their course and were badly solved), was its release.

I remember, one morning in my second term, running down a passage laughing. In a pretty dress, my Plato under my arm, stopping at a window in the sun, shaking my curls over my face in a kind of rapture – until something caught me up short, and made me wonder why I could never remember laughing like this before. Made me look at myself, and all I could see was that I had happened into a world where no one was angry; where in seminar no one snubbed your questions – where intelligent questions were welcomed; and wise and sometimes even lovely women – one or two of the dons absorbed my young capacity for hero-worship – asked no better than to help you to the understanding of your own mind. Women who had fought for knowledge and won it. (We had a most distinguished staff. Indeed, on looking back, one might say that, in many ways, Tennyson's *Princess* had come alive and ceased to be ridiculous in those Victorian red brick quadrangles, perched on the top of Hampstead Hill.)

Making up for lost time, I grew flights of growth in a week. Worked hard, picked up new ideas, played with them and forgot them. Minded my books in the blessed freedom of which long before, before the days when they had sent me to school in the north, I had dreamed. Explored London, but very tentatively. Remembered to remember the poor.

Did everything in fact that a serious-minded, healthy-minded, child-woman did in the years before the war. Put on pretty clothes, powdered my nose and waved my puff in the face of the more serious undergraduates. Made my rooms pleasant in a wholly traditional way, decent china and pictures and books. Wrote poems, sampled various new ways of going to church. Above all, made friends.

Friends that again were to be a source of trouble at home. I was suffering a common and violent reaction from the extreme class distinctions in which I had been brought up; sick to my very soul of people you could know and people you could not know, irrespective of what they were like. A set of taboos almost inconceivable today, in a world that had better invent some new ones if it wants to have any peace.

With the natural result that, granted wits and some physical

distinction, the further a girl was from those of my own kind the better I liked her. Nor had my people in any way realized my three years' starvation up north from companionship of any kind.

The result was friction – for at first I would try to being them back to Salterns in the vacations; to be sometimes vehemently reproached. Not shown or gently persuaded or offered alternatives. With the natural result of setting me in my obstinacy.

Actually, a transition-phase which needed careful handling. For my experience in Scotland, by checking my growth, had left me still capable of *schwärmerei*, and I was like a starved puppy at its first warm meal, blissfully lapping, when I found that people would be friends with me. Then my home, by making it chiefly a matter of social status, roused me to a kind of savage loyalty.

Yet there were times when my mother would try and show interest. Only, as I knew, as I had long known, directly we got down to the heart of things, directly our discussions got beneath conventional appraisings – to my impatient youth began to mean anything at all – she was shocked. Fell back on the Bible, or 'what people say'; on proverbs, quotations and misquotations and free use of the will of God. Let aside her own native shrewdness. It was that I liked about her best.

Foolish undergraduate talk – yet an entire necessity for the young mind; like a butterfly drying out its just-hatched wings, getting the feel of the air.

Only the youth who cannot play it at home will go off all the more and play it with its peers. And if those peers are not welcomed, like the puppy it will go after its food where it can, bury its bones under the ash-pit if no better place affords.

Mother was often bored, often shocked. My aunt most nobly played up.

I must go on alone. After my first year's release I very soon saw that. Better armed I was now, for flying or running or walking; I remember the night at Salterns when I saw that again.

It was as though something out of the past, something which I thought had let me go, had come out of a dark and was upon me again. Like a traveller by night in a forest, with a beast on his track that had followed him a long way, and he thought he had given it the slip, and now, much further on, he hears behind him its feet and its breath.

It had let me go for a little while, the beast of being alone. The beast which all my life would hunt me into waste places where very few other people went. Like Bellerophon, who, although he was a hero,

241

'even he became hated of the gods and went away . . . eating out his heart'. Poor Bellerophon. Although he had killed the Chimaera and saved his city.

I sat at my table, looking out through the winter branches, into the dark that held the Harbour with the living tide for bloodstream and pulse. One of those hours – I used to have them – when something of my future and my past seemed to meet, in a present that was more than present, and with it went the sense of a vast fate, waiting for the world and for me round the next corner in space. (For, like the man in *The Moon Endureth*, space always seemed to be full of paths and corridors, loops and pools and depths and heights – that birds perhaps and cats had more knowledge of than we.)

Unconsciously I was looking for the pack. What was it she had said in our last lesson – our very last lesson with her? I remembered. It was how a prophet ended up. A kind of farewell to those people in Babylon, when they had begun to see that some day they would get back to Jerusalem. And, comfortably settled in Babylon, had rather funked it.

What had he told them? What had she said? Out it came. A promise: 'they shall mount up with wings as eagles' – they could fly whenever they wanted; 'run, and not be weary'. Then, last of all and the best of all, for the first two came easier: 'they shall walk, and not faint'.

That was what Isaiah said and she had said; that the best of the first two was in the last.

Once more, I was comforted.

31
The Weeping Babe

MY mother, my stepfather and I were of one mind, at least, about one thing. That was the menace of the Tide, which, the years I had been in Scotland, had gone on rising, for a human tide, very fast indeed. Already if you climbed Bryant's Hill you could see the edge of it, not more than two miles away across the Sandecotes woods and the far valley, on the crest of the rising land towards Branksome Park. And nearer to us, still hidden in the School woods, penetrating them like a herd of jungle-swine, the houses were going up. Houses there of fair size, for gentry and un-gentry, planless and scattered, but in all that part also the woods were crashing. The grove of silver birches on the far side of Sandecotes – it was hard to forgive even our dear Doctor Brett, who had brought Tony into the world, for building his fine new house in the ruins of that grove.

'They've called it "Queenwood",' said my mother and groaned. Next door there was a more forgivable invasion. The father, a handsome man, retired from the post he had held on the other side of the tide, brought with him his youngest daughter who was simply the most beautiful girl that any one of us had ever seen. The sheer, the knock-down beauty, that has no necessary relation to disposition or to character. I don't suppose anyone ever bothered, poor lass, to ask, with that splendour staring them in the face. All my life I had watched her beauty grow. As a child, walking through the Swanage streets, I saw a whole string of passers-by turned and checked and staring after her. At night-blue eyes and dark, bee-gold lashes laid down her cheek, at her lips' pure scarlet, and a body as lithe as it was strong. And from the young stately head, hair like a fountain of gold bubbles, a Danaë shower of curls. A Perfectness. Everything the Tudor poet ever said about his mistress or a Pre-Raphaelite painted for the head of the Beloved. The type to which in England all others approximate or set off.

Only Mother said: 'I wouldn't be her. No man wants to go on having his breath taken away.'

When the war came, many seemed to chance it, and one succeeded. A story whose end I have never learned.

Yet it is always of importance in one's life, the meetings of high beauty in the flesh.

The point about that family was that they came from the other side of the Tide, the sundering flood that was cutting off this part of the land from its roots. From a village set in deep woods. Woods and water-meadows, not far from Wimborne. Wimborne, the ancient city, still untouched; with the two roads that run out of it to the north and the west, to Crichel and to Kingston Lacy.

The uncorrupted world neither Poole could touch nor Parkstone nor Bournemouth, already linking up as far as Christchurch, principally, it seemed, to make in England a City of Dreadful Joy.

Salterns was cut off. Perhaps the first adult judgement bitten into me as if with acid. On all sides, even the wild wooded cliffs between Sandbanks and Branksome Chine broken into; the Sandbanks themselves patched with toy bungalows, dished up for summer visitors with a lick of paint; in winter a dreariness beyond description; the puffins long gone, the rabbits even had abandoned.

On all sides but one – the Harbour side. A flowing world, flood and ebb, ribbons of the tides' pure silver, the green weed-knots at ebb. Defined by barrels stuck on posts, each with a cormorant for crest. Bar of Brownsea woods and, along the horizon, the body of the Purbeck Hills. Laid like a god, sleeping; like the woman in Blake's *Pity*, to receive the child from the seraph lying under a terrible sky.

That was the way out. On foot to the Harbour mouth. Then across in the ferry – I used to think that, even if my smashed knee had let me become a strong swimmer, I could never cross by myself that deep-flowing race, where a hundred miles of water, thrust into a bottleneck, swirled and drove and pulled in and out, tide against tide, and tide against river, wind and tide and river disputing, lifting their voices in the urgency of their business, under the invisible hands of the moon.

On the other side you were through. Through, in a world that had its visible being in the orders of the created universe. A second order that you had visited. Not only in sleep.

Your back turned to your own place the evil tide had cut off, your face to a world which, as the Sea with its voiceless children is called the Pure, so was its grass. Grass of meadow and water meadow – fields near Wool where my nurse came from. Grass of lawns, muttering grass of the sand dunes; above all, grass of the chalk, the short, curled, pale, sea-shelled, thyme-and-violet-patched turf of the downs.

Places too far to walk, too far even for a bicycle, now made possible because of the car.

As good a car as in those days could be got, a high-powered Renault; and my stepfather, with his fine sense of justice, sent our young coachman, a most intelligent man, to London, to learn how to handle it. Where, I believe, as was the custom then, he first practised on a taxi.

To return, in those days with all the authority of the chauffeur; and again it seems to me, with regard to any car I have known since, we got our money's worth.

My mother, as I returned to find, had flung herself into politics. Not the mild Primrose Leaguing of my childhood, but the full-grown Women's Conservative Committee, with meetings all over East Dorset, consultations with agents, concerts, house-to-house canvassing; arrangements of meetings, entertainment of speakers, lendings of the House, the fields – even the garden. A whirl of activity by a nature-born organizer; and with it bribery and corruption under every form within the Act.

The change made possible, as I dimly discerned, by cars annihilating our distances, but even more by the Tide. The Tide with its influx of people, upsetting the balance of an old rural constituency.

The whole change, had I known it, had I dared admit what I felt, more than symbolized – given us in the flesh. The flesh of an ageing naval officer of rather equivocal rank, who had been a political agent, with a wife he kept very firmly in the background in their villa on the edge of the Tide. A grizzled, jovial, hard-drinking man, I found him penetrated to the heart of Salterns – if he were not to be agent for East Dorset, very determined to be agent for our family affairs.

Little ladies took life very much more for granted than they do now. In so far as I puzzled it out, I could make nothing of it. He was not amusing or particularly kind. He was not handsome or debonair. Hard-bitten, with, as it were, something ugly *behind* him, he knew nothing – though I had given that up as hopeless – about Interesting Things. He was not a gentleman. He detested me and concealed it. He deeply admired my mother and had got her taped. He was always living up to the bluff sailor, flattering my mother – and where did Tiger-Tiger come in?

Tiger-Tiger was very ill. Time, which could not destroy his beauty, had thinned, thinned and refined it to a death-mask of itself. Tall as ever, groomed and scrupulous as ever, he had wasted to a transparency, his moustache white, his hair a black and silver enamel cap.

One might have thought of the soldier-saints, who 'burn upward each to his point of bliss'; yet it was not like that. A wasting, not a burning. Yet there was a flame there. Then, as I guessed, a flame he was ever shielding to keep secret from us. From my mother particularly. Keep un-blown on; keep for his very own.

I wish now as I wished then that I knew more. As I might have known; but, as I shall have to tell later, in one of those terrible scenes of which she had the secret, outraging alike my modesty and my innocence, it was my mother who insured that for the future we should have little to say to one another. A pity as well as a cruelty, for we each had need of one another. My young strength in alliance with his knowledge of the world might have made it harder for that man who came with the Tide to have all his own way with us.

My mother would not have it so. Also, it is one of the charms and one of the extreme dangers of gently-raised youth that it does not easily realize the existence of persons out for what they can get. Now, with appalling clearness, I see the part he played in our lives, and how from the first my instincts warned me against him. Again, that his dislike of me was instinctive on his part; that, set as I was, I should in time find him out; that it was to his advantage for division to exist between me and my family.

That man is dead. It may be that I wrong his memory. But I do not think so.

To make matters easier at home, all that I knew about my mother's politics was that they were wrong. And indeed, then, and, I do not doubt, now, a by-election in a half-rural, half-new slum-and-suburb constituency was a particularly shame-making affair. As an introduction to public life, an infamy. Indeed, in the days before the Reform Bill, in the days of Old Sarum and the rotten boroughs, one would not be surprised to find less essential dishonesty. When nobody ever thought about it, or 'fair play' or 'the game' or any of our current catch-words. Or in the days my father used to talk of with a grin, when he used to walk down Poole High Street, his hand behind his back and a series of half crowns in the palm. At least they gave us government no whit inferior to any we can show today.

East Dorset was Liberal, and had become so since the days when the great Wimborne family had 'ratted'. Cornelia, Lady Wimborne, was Winston Churchill's aunt, and, as people admitted, had her nephew's career to consider. They carried the voters with them, and it then became my mother's business to work up the opposition in our more populated district, and be of general use to the great Conservative families, the Shaftesburys and, nearer home, the Alingtons of Crichel. They, bless them, still lived out of it all, still in the pure green world. Votes round them were blue and secure. It was Poole, Poole and Parkstone and Upper Parkstone where the election was fought, the depths and the fringes of the Tide.

Then women were voteless and of immence influence. Of ignorance so colossal, of convictions as stable as they were baseless – a miracle! Of consciencelessness so remarkable (when you consider their scruples as private individuals) as to point once more the old morality of the division between private life and public. Also, the whole business thrilled my mother as well as amused her, unleashed her sentiment, her desire for power, while giving scope to her immense gifts as an organizer.

But to the eyes of eighteen, still saturated in the principles of Godwin's *Political Justice*, it was something very like, had there been one, the work of the devil.

Such things must be. As the little devil I still tried to call Doubt, already whispered in my ear. Yet, I will still swear, never was there such an illustration of man's capacity, in collective action, to lose his values, his experience, his sense of fair and unfair; and in his capacity as Voice of the People do such things as, man to man, he would repudiate with disgust.

Again, if women, and women only, were allowed to vote, would they exert greater influence than those voteless young dowagers, in their ravishing clothes and sweet persuasions and personalities? (Unconnected with the least real interest, let alone information or understanding, as to what they were asking their overwhelmed audiences to vote about.)

'That's my fifth pair. Why can't they invent one people don't come off on – an election glove?' I gigggled and forgot to be indignant, watching Lady Alington, stripping her splendid arms to draw on

247

another pair. She was trying to calculate how many handshakes went to a vote. One each seemed to be the answer, as you watched her in the splendour of her beauty – beauty of a flawless, bee-stung, dark red rose. The ease of her, the drawling, husky voice, rich with vibration, permeating her dignity. To each workman whose hand she touched, sharing something of herself, in perfect proportion the great lady and the woman, a lovely separate gift.

One of the great Edwardian beauties, of an age that demanded its beauty sumptuous, displayed, depending on carriage and *tenue*. Not the stripped, light, 'gamine', 'take it or leave it' loveliness of today, but a glory, set apart, prepared. For whom Milton wrote his comparison, depending not on age or time or place:

> *Comes this way sailing*
> *Like a stately ship*
> *Of Tarsus, bound for th' isles . . .*
> *With all her bravery on, and tackle trim,*
> *Sails fill'd, and streamers waving,*
> *Courted by all the winds that hold them play,*
> *An amber scent of odorous perfume . . .*

Only it was more than amber. Amber and two flowers, the magnolia and the red rose.

> *Oh, no man knows*
> *Through what wild centuries*
> *Roves back the rose.*

Shelley too would have to put up with it. Only if I was to be his kind of woman, I shouldn't be that. Anyhow I couldn't be, as I grinned acknowledgement. To begin with I hadn't the body. Let alone Crichel for background. It was her business to be beautiful like that, give men the eternal presence of beauty, and the King a good time when he went there. If fierce bits of you asked questions, and believed them pretty hard when Mother wouldn't consider them, on the rights and wrong of great ownership of property, the answer was in herself. As one had just sufficient sense to recognize.

Beauty one admired as only the young admire, as a child with its face to bars it cannot pass, its nose flattened against a window that will not open. 'Then why on earth, if you admire her so, do you come down looking like that?' Mother would say, with every possible reason on her side. Yet, after I left school, it took me a year and more to fall in love with my clothes, sit at my dressing-table to groom myself, come down all of a piece. For reasons, good and bad, that with pitiful plainness, I now see.

Again, I could never – it was my father's blood working in me, teaching me the orders of style – I could never look like that sort of woman. He had given me a passion for perfection, and that order of perfection was not for me. I could never put that face on the world. It needed another temperament; also resources no little Dorset squire's daughter could command. Like an art you'd no gift for, it was no good to practise it. A little gift was all you had, a small garden of good looks and make what you could of it – with a little perfume and no draggled flowers. But not in imitation of the glories of those women in whom all beauty walks. Too much of a life's job, and I had other things to do. A mind to garden, that was still mostly unbroken heath.

Besides, besides – as I looked round me before my twentieth year, before the war had broken, perhaps those were the only days when I was filled with something close to despair. That one was due to have such pains – that I learned from books and the knowledge helped; but now all life appeared as it were in two dreadful categories. In one, life as nature made it, and, with regard to man, as great spirits had shaped and liberated and handled it. The other what man made of it left to himself. Great good-fortune, happy accidents and some greatness of spirit had made Salterns lovely and Crichel glorious. Crichel and Kingston Lacy and Wimborne Minster and Brownsea Castle; Wolverton and Grange. Yet, as a voice cried out in me and still cries, were any of us getting the best out of our heritage? All the different bests? It was clear enough that we were not. Yet when I even tried, I was almost hated for it. Distrusted. Almost feared, and perpetually reproached. How could I learn with everyone's hand against me? I did not want to do bad things, but the things that would make them proud of me. Yet my home did not fail to tell me that I was becoming a disgrace to them, that people would soon not want to know me. Increasing my natural timidity so that, nonsense as it was, for years I shrank away from everyone I had known when I was young.

Nor was I happily situated for any outside help to show me what my life might be. Very little of that essential food of youth, contact with the living mind of its age, had penetrated to East Dorset. A victim, the lamb of the green earth, its throat arched to the knife. Sacrificed to what we politely call 'the play of free change' in a world hurling itself into new forms, controlled neither by mind or love but by every instinct, crude or base, racing, unchecked towards the conditions we are now beginning to see in all their horror, their potentiality for evil. A catastrophe of which the war was but an incident.

'If ever it occurs to people to value the honour of the mind equally with the honour of the body, we shall get a social revolution of a quite unparalleled sort – and very different from the kind that is being made at this moment.'

It did not occur, in the country-house any more than in the villas of the Tide, or the slums where the new work-people slept.

With the eternal exception of my aunt, and, at that time, of her most gifted sister, there was no one with whom one could even begin to talk about such things. But no one generation can supply life to the next. I had a long way to go before I could so much as realize their quality; and thank them as I might, I knew I should soon have to set out alone.

Apart from them – and it was here that the dreariness became sharp and sudden, like a sinister knife there seemed all round one to be more than ignorance – contempt. For the things of the mind and the things of the spirit, once you began to take them out of their wrappings, the pink cottonwool in which those people sunk their jewels of crystal and steel. And where there was beauty, there was no knowledge; where there was kindness, there was no understanding. Where there was knowledge, it served only convention. And when there was no beauty, there was triumph because there was none; and where there was faith, it was timid, or, as I guessed when Canon Adderley came to Parkstone, mixed with despair.

When Canon Adderley came as Vicar, he told the ladies of Parkstone, from the pulpit, that they were damned cats. Maybe that did not apply to us at the Holy Angels, but in the civilities that attended the coming of a well-known churchman, I saw at once that, as a unit, he disliked us; and it was made hard for me to accept the brusque kindness he would have shown me.

Salterns, whose beauty then was at its height. Deep in its woods, a pool of loveliness, its face to the hills and the sea. Beauty and ignorance of the source of beauty, an ignorance which I felt was doing the beauty no good.

Indeed I knew *what* had happened, though not what it meant. It was like when you played with the Stump, years ago when I was little. You had so many exciting things to go with it that you tried to use them all at once, and the result was not a pattern but a muddle. Something the same was happening at home. Never had Salterns, inside and out, been given so many beautiful things. And if that went on, very soon you would be seeing them, not it. Not the place but its adornments.

Yet this again was only a way of saying something that I did not understand in the least. Sure of this only that, into even our temenos, something had got in. Something in disguise, that escaped definition, yet was feeding the place on something unwholesome, on something false.

Something that came over from the uplands, with the Tide? The way that sailor dog-of-all-work used to come, on Mother's errands? Something that winnowed Tiger-Tiger to an even greater transparency and withdrawal. (It wasn't 'fifty mad elephants, with the voices of devils' when Tony and I made a noise now, but sudden turns of rage and occasional ugly abuse. Once I was utterly terrified, and my mother, who had heard, raved at us with taunts and abuse which were more dreadful than anything he could do and say.)

Later, when the war came, and the great trees were cut down, and so many things added that could as easily be taken away, it seems to me now that the answer to those sums was already implicit – that within ten years the Tide would have broken in, and Salterns, house and gardens, woods and orchard, meadows and the moor should be blotted out. Under scurf of bungalows, like the one on the Cornish cliffs I am at present inhabiting, as utterly, but not as blessedly, as if the sea flowed over it.

I see now that I knew all this. As E. F. Benson says, it is exceedingly difficult to know when, *in actual truth*, an action takes place. I also thought of it as hopeless. Or, more exactly, relying on my brother when he came to manhood, if only in despair. After all, Salterns was his business. He could do what he liked with our mother. It had not yet occurred to me to ask what exactly Tony would like.

I could only save myself, I said. Save myself first, and I did not know how. Only that I was in some form of peril. In agonies of growth and awakening powers thwarted, under and over-nourished by solitude, by learning, by ignorance, by extreme innocence and equal pride, and an imagination saturated by gay dreams of what life might be.

There were moments when I thought to begin all over again, sit for my degree, hope ultimately for a Fellowship, and in the decencies of the Senior Common Room give up my life to the pure learning which, as I had seen, for what it was, never let you down. Today I might have done so. But those were the days of 'Plain Jane and evening clothes to stand the rain', so that even in that garden enclosed there was something that repelled. Stuffy and even a little grubby, narrow with its own special narrowness, with its own special unkindnesses, unkind. I had other things to do as well. I had red hair, and what was I going to do with that? Or rather, what was that going to do with me? That would keep, but it wouldn't keep for ever. When its turn came, I should have to obey it.

Besides, in my third year, Westfield and I had parted, none too kindly, because of my intention to get to the Derby. Accident, not virtue, had prevented me at the last moment, nor had it so much as occurred to me to hold my tongue. All of which had given a charming, jealous, elderly don, to whom I owed much, a chance for a little exasperated intrigue. It was all very silly, and mercifully not a crime for which my family would reproach me. Only once again it seemed my elders had let me down.

I had made many friends there. But only one who was to last me all my life. The femininity of their minds irked me – nine out of ten only wanted to get married – whose need was growing for the companionship of mature and powerful men. Besides, as I have said, more on instinct than on anything else, though it was counted to me for perversity, I chose them with complete disregard whether or not they were the kind of young women whose existence my family would admit.

(And here my family have my heartiest sympathies; more than one young female dumped on them, brought to Salterns with no other recommendation than that they were sure of a First in History or that their parents lived in a mountain village and for preference spoke only Welsh.)

Sympathy that perhaps is overdone. For I very soon learned not to repeat the experiment.

Indeed it takes a very wise family to be patient with their children's first blind experiments in friendship. Learning so vital to them, so tedious for those who have already selected their companions out of the world.

Yet no child ever more needed guidance. After so solitary a childhood, after my school loneliness, I was making up for lost time, behind many younger creatures in judgement. What I was looking for, I did not know. Only that when I found it, I should know it. High spirits and ingenuous confidence would mount me, as on a high horse. To throw me as the pace quickened; and there was something in my callow enthusiasms that brought down my mother's anger, her often just impatience, her not so just contempt. Out of that would come fear, fear and new desolation, a queer sense that behind all our lives at Salterns there was some strange inability, as though we were no more than shadows in a mirror-world. In our glass, what lay round the innocent corner of Alice's garden? Some horror, real and unreal? Some day I should do what children dream of doing, step through the mirror round the angle of reflection and meet it. If I did that, so the dream went, whatever it was, that lived in our Waste Land, it would have no power over Tony. Not yet understanding that you cannot go to the Dark Tower for anyone else.

All this apart, another spirit in me, clear and vigorous, the strength and sap of my youth, told me that I must go away. Get out. Go off on my own life. Into what world? There must be a world somewhere, of the arts and the mind and one's work – where nothing counted but these. How was it to be found? And how was I to serve my kind, as also I longed to?

It did not occur to my family to help me to look. I quite see now why it whould not have seemed necessary to them. A presentation at Court they would have given me or even a London season; but with the priggishness which, it seems, must go with these shapings, I would have none of it. It was gilt, I said to myself, and I wanted gingerbread. All round me were the people of the place, the middle-aged ladies who expressed surprise at me so much as to drive my mother to my defence. People you had to hear saying: 'Of course there were none of these ideas of education going about when we were young. Do you really find it makes her any happier?' Indeed my mother could not, who, knowing none of the joy, saw only the discontents. And what they meant was: 'Do you think you'll ever find a husband for her?' There were the facetious old men and the scornful; and others who, as was pointed out, I would alarm and disconcert, and so they would never be friends with me. Men would not like me – and that would be my lot in life. A dreadful lot, as I could well believe. Only I didn't quite believe it.

Always to the tune: 'Whatever you know, don't let men know you know.' As though knowlege was shameful. To which song went the accompaniment: 'How will you get, let alone keep, a husband out of this?'

Oh, those old ladies! I used to see them as the Graiae, passing that song, one to the other, as they used their single tooth.

I was taking no interest in husbands then, already aware that, as husbands, husbands would not be the first things in my life. Mercifully, the current feminist literature did nothing to pervert a dawning judgement of men; nor even the dislocation of my mother's two marriages. (Indeed I might have learned more from it than I did.) Rather I dreamed of a marriage of two minds, minds and bodies, without distinction of race or class. Body and spirit, take and give; coming to that part of my life with all wisdom and with none.

I said I was a Socialist – at first very much in the spirit in which a new convert must 'testify to the Lord'. What it was, I did not know. Only that my people knew less than I, which made it safe for the moment: but someday, nagged at by my respect for facts, I knew I should have to find out.

What it did not mean, I knew quite well. It did not mean William Morris, art serge and lumps of amber round the neck; nor leadless pottery, painted in brushwork, nor being a vegetarian or a fruitarian, or any of the particular complex of living that, at that moment, passed for 'advanced thought'. All that was sanest in my training had taught me to laugh at cliques and fads and rejections of common good. Patterns of living – *fabriqués*, detached, without essential rhythm or structure – my father's laugh still echoed in the corridors of Salterns, exorcizing such phantoms. A laugh which, in the world as I should find it, was a great grace to me.

Oddly enough, I believe my mother would have been happier if I had adopted some obvious cult, or gone about, at least away from home, dressed in sandals and beads. I remember she said once: 'I would not mind your going about London alone if you looked like those people. But turned out in the pretty clothes I have chosen for you – it can't be safe. Heaven knows what people will think.'

'It is not what people think, but how I behave,' I would say, trying to be respectful and reassuring. 'Besides, to have both is half the fun.' And indeed I had learned so to carry myself that I was never once troubled in the streets. A thing my people could not understand, who could not see that a child, saying to herself an Antigone chorus, is pretty safe anywhere, however smart her hat.

But my mother could never make up her mind whether to trust to my modesty or not. On the whole, not, but more, through her belief, common to women of her time, of man as a raging satyr, leaping on the unprotected damsel almost as a matter of form. A possibility about which I share, and still share, the scepticism of Queen Elizabeth.

I can see now also what a shame it was to tease them with Socialism. In those days a mere bogy-word; 'The Jacquerie is upon us' as the lady in Saki said. (Later, I was to work hard at it and for it – coral and bells as it has been for the tooth-cutting of a generation.) But in a south-country house in 1912, pure devilment; and all that it meant then as a password for escape I soon learned to exploit.

It is a delight of increasing age to see no fair effort wasted. As a training ground (I went on to the London School of Economics) it did its job. Taught me to be friends with the common man, to sit on a box or a pile of stones, try and talk Trades Unionism and soon get on to his family troubles and the way the foreman had behaved. Taught me the study of the philosophy of history. Taught me to see, and to see through, revolutions and barricades and blood, strikes and legislation about this and that, and the meaning of the Marxian apocalypse. To dig at last to the edible root, the nourishing plant of the attainable; with ideals as high as I knew how to shape them, my expectations strictly moderate. The knowledge by what way our desire 'from each his strength, to each his need' may cease to be more than a pious platitude or ring down the curtain of a Communist play. And when and by what reasons the honour of the mind equals the body's honour, then we shall get our revolution – the very different revolution from the one to which, essentially, my land was sacrificed.

The honour of the mind – in the midst of these desolations, egotism which knew itself for egotism, yet knew, for all that, it must live; at the bottom of the burning bitter cup from which some youth must drink – like the frog the old potters set in the depth of the beer mug – there remained the understanding of that honour of the mind. That never fails, that cannot be faked, that sustains always, in its variety and its unity never changed. Agonies or ecstasies came and went, rose so quickly and passed. Or, mixed with some other element, became impure. Only the knowledge gained from them remained, their significance in the fire that was tempering me – the honour of the mind. Facts in their sobriety, and their slow structure into coherence and pattern, little boxes of pure gold, lying about for me to put my jewels in. I had no jewels yet, or very few. Or how even to estimate those I had. Only it was the mind's honour that I should not deceive myself. Let any showy sentence or trick phrase pass without scrutiny, the moral or religious or political catchwords – the dreadful appeals to the emotions, the sentimentalities, which are or used to be made most particularly to girls.

I was to know myself, and remember the counterpoises attached to every action under heaven. I had said I loved the mind. Now I had to trust it. In the hope that, in the end, the mind would come to no dishonour through me.

When I could think like this, I knew I was in my right way. As I learned to think, 'all passion spent'. Then it was I could see my people and my separation from them. Only I was no more than at my beginning, fiery with youth and confidence and trust; innocence and ignorance, as I asked with the pitilessness of youth what honour the mind had among them.

That was the root of our discord – that never was it possible to meet them and talk as equals, making serviceable their knowledge, their experience, because, since my father's death, the mind, at Salterns, was held in no honour at all.

They would not have called themselves unprincipled, yet in effect they were. Reason and knowledge became like a kind of treachery to them – if facts contradicted their passionately held beliefs, so much the worse for facts; and in their hearts, it was not for callow thinking that I was held in anger and derision but for the fact that I was found thinking at all.

Here it was that pure anger rose in me, not for any injury done to myself, but to the certitudes I had begun to learn, standing around us in more than Miltonic ranks. Who were these people to deny them? I at least offered my breast to their crystal spears, the 'terrible crystal' the prophet spoke of. When these people started to run, they would get it in the rear. Who in their lying elections denied every principle of fair choice and reasoned government. (That there was not a pin to choose between either party, I was just about able to admit to myself. But then, at least, English Liberalism was making better promises to the people.) And I remember my mother, clapping her hands because, just before the poll, someone had discovered that it might be possible to discredit their candidate for a boyhood's debt. That might snatch a few votes; the only question being whether it came within the law of libel or not.

In and out of the House there flowed the new people these activities had given the freedom of Salterns. Only one constant – walking over, ever more and more frequently, from his house on the edge of the Tide, as it were a sea-point shifting, to and fro over a tide-bared stretch of sand. The man I have spoken of – disliking me more, as

I, a child, felt I ought not to dislike him. Not much butter on his bread at home and the Salterns' butter spread thick. People to whom it had never occured to be sparing with their butter – it was he who was teaching my mother how elections are won. (Elections we never won, who never regained that seat.) Without him she would never have thought of things like that.

32
The Rings

IT is from Plato that the mind first learns the archetypal construction of the world. Learns to distinguish – that is to say – to pin down an awareness in the invisible to its correspondence in the external world. Thrones, Dominations, Principalities, the 'helmèd cherubim and sworded seraphim'. Whose number is the original Dionysiac Nine. As is said in what Yeats, writing of More, the Cambridge Platonist, calls 'the holiest book of our time'.

Some such knowlege was awakening in me, a 'divine property of first seeing'; and the only name I could find for it, the Intellectual Love of God. *Amor Intellectualis Dei*; perception of a hierarchized universe, awakened by every order in the external world. Tide-pull and up-thrust of trunk and root, of bulb and seed. The down-pouring of light and its scattering, especially on the green fountains, the lifting of branch and leaf against the sky. In the heavens, the night-ballet; in the wind pouring up from Arne, from Corfe with its towers, the hub of the downs-spokes' wheel. The strong wind, visible now, breaking on the white Salterns walls, or in its enclosed gardens trembling like a flock of pigeons upside down in the sky.

'A garden enclosed' – Salterns was that, and the fair green land we and our like had signed with our hand. Land we had thrown open – how long would Salterns remain inviolate? Were we not leaving it open to spoilation, who had blinded our eyes from understanding from the day the earth had closed over my father's head?

It was all part of a process, part of a pattern. That I began most imperfectly to see; and that the measure of our blindness would be exacted from us. Till the spoilers and the spoiled should be identified one with the other.

Walking up the drive, one afternoon, at midsummer, I saw the trees, talking in their crests, like angels, discussing this.

Not mourning, not even their own death, but in contemplation;

258

and suddenly a god shook them with a thunder that turned to laughter, and, as it were, a burning up into inhuman bliss against the profound and absolute blue of the sky.

Standing on the gold drive, I was very afraid, for their joy and their meditation were not in terms of human quality. Yet I was seen as I stood, looked at incuriously. 'This is Dionysos,' I said, trying to stand up to it. Oh, it was remote, what was happening in the tree-tops, and all at once, I knew how Semele died.

Indoors, it was as always cool and fragrant and still; and I was glad to see my stepfather in his green chair; a book on hunting in his frail hands, his old dog at his feet.

I went over to him and kissed the top of his head. What I had just seen had struck me cold with awe. Not for me, only, for an instant I had seen; and I wanted human beings very badly. Just then my mother came in. A little later she turned on me: 'What d'you mean,' she said, 'kissing your stepfather like that?'

To bring this book to a close – it was about then that there happened the two terrible things, part of the series, the first of whose terms I noticed at the burning of my father's books. Where it began, in what part of the Waste Land it was determined, in what obscurities of personality, I shall never know. Twice my mother came into my room, the first time – it was that same evening – to accuse me of a desire to enter into corrupt relations with my stepfather.

I was just old enough, with difficulty, to translate what she meant. And with the cowardice of innocence, of ignorance, of horror, of actual incredulity – what could Mother *mean* – tried to drive the memory of it out. What I could not drive away was her face, my lovely elegant mother, her hair hanging loose, her face greasy from stripped make-up, huddled into an old dressing gown, over a cheap cotton shift. Her eyes small and staring, the stones in her rings burning, incongruous, her mouth in a different shape, snarling, her articulation coarse and shrill and thick.

It haunted me. It still haunts me. I was not brave. I did not cry, but it was somehow like, even in memory, some hideous pain. Like the pain of one's knee, dislocating, going on. Or some unknown pain, deep inside, that one's strong body had never known. I did not think to look into my glass, remember the time of my mother's life, and find part, at least, of an answer there.

Instead I tried to forget it. At the same time, in every subsequent relation with her, it rose, unconscious but implicit, dividing us.

And, like the books' destruction, I knew it was given me for a sign. Implicit – until its repetition.

They cannot be told now. Only the second time I was older – old enough to know of what I had been accused; not old enough to have mercy because I knew why.

Then, one day, at a luncheon-party, I sat next to what I saw had come straight out of the people who went about with Dionysos, the people in Titian's picture. Dionysos when he came down to earth and started having fun with people. Desperately shy, it so quickened my imagination that I felt like the rider on a bolting horse. Besides, before that lunch, my mother had been vexed with me, and weariness added to shyness added to perception left me speechless, only able to take little quick glances at him as he sat on my left.

A sudden humility seized me. His mother, in the splendour of her now legendary beauty, was sitting at the far end of the table, under the Lely, where Louise de Querouaille thrust out her tiny, wicked, foot. Humility because – partly because I should never have anything like that to play with. Any more than I should look like his mother. Because of the bargain I had made.

I was partly wrong. Only such share in it as I was to have came later, and rarely enough and almost always as a treat. Almost always I was to be the child with its nose flattened on that shop-window, not often asked to that party; or invited, allowed to accept.

All because you cannot have it both ways. All because of what I had to go on learning. All because once you have cried 'Heads!' you can't cry 'Tails'. All because of right and left and debit and credit, the eaten or uneaten cake.

All of which I tumbled to during that lunch and after, like a sudden jump into cold water, as I meditated on the first young man I had ever noticed to be one. As the wise woman said, not in love with him, but with what he made me think of. Cheiron, Kourotrophos, and magics. Which magics? Comus or Narcissus? Comus would do or the Afternoon Faun. Superb and lovely and exciting things, all one part of me – the part to that instant I did not know I possessed – they were about to happen. And I should not be there. (You've a long way to go yet.) You'd be able to laugh as you didn't know you could. Laugh the prig out of you; laugh you into the pride of life. (Not yet. Not yet. *Ever?*)

His cheek-bones had a down on them, the red stain of a peach; his dark hair buckled over, picoted with gold. The scarlet of his mouth suddenly terrified me. And again, I was ashamed. Little bread-and-butter-miss, with nothing to say, sitting at his elbow. All my mother's taunts and dismal judgements returned: 'The right sort of man will never have any use for you.'

I tried to remember what Delphi told you to do, before you could get any profit out of the Pythia, and the tiny effort steadied me again. After lunch they went away, and I ran down to the shore. 'Wild sea-banks', the ridge of turf and shingle between the Harbour and the real Salterns, the great marsh. A cool grey summer day, the tide flowed quietly, pure silver. (They might build down to its edge, but they could never touch that.) The land is man's dog, but the sea is like a cat and escapes him ever. Besides, I knew that you were never given, never able to see all that for nothing. If I never set eyes on mother or son again, I had seen what I had seen. I had made my choice, but the pattern would go on happening. Two long ways round we might go, but to the same place. The long way round, which, as I had to take on trust, would be the best way home in the end.

Home? If our homes vanished; if Troy fell (and our fathers had sold the gates) we would get out, not with them but with our lares and penates on our backs. Save our *sacra*. Save Helen.

It was not long after that I found out where, in our land, the door to our city was and the Skaian gate.

More and more I went further afield, often alone on foot from Salterns, across the great heath. Into the Goathorn woods, to the grey apple-orchard set in the open moor, an island in the bee-roar, in the purple tide. Near which are two cones built of sandstone about three feet high. Boundary marks – or the twin pillars of the Cabiri? Probably the first, but they served as remembrancers. Over to Worbarrow under Flower's Barrow and Arish Mell Gap. From Worbarrow Tout, past Gadcliff, up to the stone seat some Bond of Tyneham had placed, high above the sea, before the haunted, broken upland of Tyneham Cap. A 'pass no further' mark that bench, a boundary-stone between man and no man's land.

Below Tyneham Cap to where the Sacred Wood runs in its closed fan to the sea; to the blunt-nosed cliff of Kimmeridge Shale, to the gold rocks and jade pools thrust into an elbow-turn of the outer sea.

Or motoring inland with my mother or walking there alone – one way or another I was seized of those places, the process by which one comes to possess utterly one part of the earth. Possesses and is possessed. The work of my childhood knit up on the edge of my maturity. The one thing my family could not mind, to which they could not – nor did they try to – give any bad interpretation.

Each going there a knot in a pattern; each time, each place, unique in itself. Of incalculable importance for the future, as I knew; yet each perfect only for what it was. 'In my end is my beginning', as Mary of Scotland took for her device. The meaning of everything was there, and would make itself plain in due course. When I was old, or perhaps not till after I was dead, but the pattern was being shown me there, the patterns and the meaning of the pattern. The visible and the invisible world, and the veil between drawn exactly as much as I could bear. Not only such knowledge as Wordsworth drew from lake and hill, but knowledge of house and breed and good and evil men; what spiritual income I had; how to invest it; what bills there were likely to come in; not the time or fashion of their presenting.

Steadying me through, bringing me up to a life which, but for the war, would have found its true shape easily. Which the war deflected, made savage, narrow, insolent, fierce – as it did so many of us, a mask for despair. Repetition as it seemed, on a world-scale, of certain qualities I had already met of prejudice, injustice, cruelty, the dishonour of the mind. My own growth, as it had been before, forced and stunted; till by the end, I was once again all shapes and sizes; but this time a cutting into vital places, a scraping to the bone. As it has taken twenty years to save what was left, make the maimed serve for the sound, the part for the whole, seven fingers work for ten, cut out what was killed and rotting, sterilize the remained. Cut out dead wood. For watching death, and above all, after death; not death in battle, but death after battle, brought me to certain indifferences that are also a form of death.

Something held. Something in my blood and my training that came out of the very stuff of England, the fabric out of which her soul is made. The knowledge I share with my father, that he gave and elucidated in me. A singleness of purpose my aunt did much to establish. For I did not doubt that I should become a writer, and be a lover and see my share of the world and get my pleasure of the arts. Whatever my people said. Over the first, at least, there were no apprehensions, only the swift passion, the agreeable content to learn how it was done.

And not to hurry: to see something of life before I began to talk about it; get my living over as a woman. Then to sit back and deal with what I had learned. All other plans were secondary to that – and if some of them went wrong – 'Where your treasure is . . .'

If, if – if in those days, before the war came, my own people had had any pride in me. Pride or hope, let alone delight. (Cousin Henry had, but there were intrigues and he died; and we are a kinless, dwindling stock.) Instead, on looking back and comparing my own with other bewildered families, I certainly encountered, among the varieties of misunderstanding between parents and children, a curious hostility. One not wholly accountable by any priggishness or wildness on my part; one, so it seems, not fully documented yet.

If it had been otherwise – one is nagged by a grief, especially when one reads such an account as Mr Derek Patmore gives of his ancestor's childhood, and how the father of Coventry Patmore kindled and nourished the spirit in his young son. A grief as at a series of notes played backwards; notes, played the right way round, of a symphony. Instead, the exact reversal of the intelligent pattern; and, rising out of its reversal, certain phases of extreme ugliness.

As, a little later, even it may be in the first months of the war, the second time that my mother came to my room at night. (As she did, the night before my second marriage, for the third time.) This time with no accusations to a child about a dying man. This time I knew what she meant, when she accused me of wishing and attempting to corrupt my brother. This time horror possessed me much less than an exaltation of rage and contempt. The boy who had my heart, for whom I would have been content to live my whole life. Who, bewildered by the obscene evasions of his training, came to me for sense and laughter. Tony, at Eton and already in deep enough waters. Tony, whose capacities I knew, whose weaknesses I sensed, but not enough. Not yet enough. Only the danger of leaving him to what, for such a nature, were my stepfather's futilities, my mother's not quite clean ignorance; and, what again I did not yet understand, to her insensate jealousy and possession of him.

There she was again, mouthing to me in the candle-light. Sick and faint and not shaken, I saw her stripping herself of her maternity. So that I might see her as she was. So, I thought, I will. There was a Shakespeare at my bedside, open at *Macbeth*. 'Unmilked of my mother,'

I said when she had gone. 'By my mother. Now I know.'

I had been bathing, and the pearly sand that fell off on to the carpet from between my toes, I knew for the dust of Salterns I was shaking off my feet.

All these things happened together, one span, before the opening of the war. At the back of my mind, the two night scenes of which I have spoken, scenes of whose significance I should be made progressively aware. Busy writing poems, reading Homer, reading – bless his heart! – Gilbert Murray, whose influence on youth about that time deserves a critical study all to itself. Mr Eliot's cold water is by no means the entire answer. Trying to clear my mind of superstition, of cant; wandering about the woods, arguing with an invisible Bernard Shaw. Or in my room at the top of Salterns, where one window looked out on the fir woods, the other, on to Purbeck. Through the squirrel-beech, I had seen them going to their larder in the hollow of its fork ever since I could remember; and that summer the tree was running with them; another magic seven, chasing each other round and round.

It was late May. My brother had put a jar of hawthorn on the swinging bookcase. Heaven forgive me, I was pleased with a poem I had done.

I had been that day on the Rings. It was my mother, a year or more before, who had suggested our going there. Sir Frederick Treeves, who came from Milbourne St Andrews, a chalk village high up on the Shaftesbury downs, had just published his book on Dorset; and after his description of it she said that we ought to go to Badbury Rings.

In all this, I do not remember the exact sequence. Of that business which included in itself end and beginning and all sequences that run between. All my explorings of my land, asleep or awake, my watching and my seizings, summed up there. A summary that surpassed terms of start and finish, and here this happened and here that. This had to do with Morgan le Fay and that with a secret folk-knowledge; this with Rome and that with Kingston Lacy: this with an ancient battle, and that Dr James knows all about: this with clairvoyance and that with archaeology.

Only that we went there first for a picnic, she and Tony and I; and that soon after I borrowed the car, and went there with my brother alone. Then I went there by myself.

Then, often and often, I walked to Parkstone Station, took a train to Wimborne and, my lunch in my pocket, walked out there. A long way, a dull way, under great trees. All along the park of Kingston Lacy, where, in their splendour another order of power and loveliness, lights at another shrine burned 'to their point of bliss'.

> *Without God there can be no man; without supernature there can be no nature; without philosophy there can be no psychology; without theology there can be no science; without mysticism there can be no commonsense.*

This is truth, and our age has chosen, clause by clause, to reverse it, make the first of each term dependent on the second. With results we are beginning to appreciate, destroying piece by piece such natures as the war has spared. It is no part of this book to tell the secrets of Badbury Rings, yet it is no exaggeration to say that, in after years, it was because of them that I still remained, however uncertainly, critical of that reversal. What *can* be told is that there, once and actually for good, the compaint was stilled, at which man grumbles, of the equivocal nature of the contact between visible and invisible, the natural order and the supernatural. The materialist's argument as catchy as Voltaire's wit; the appeal *ad consensum gentium* has its traps; the appeal to saint and artist weakens if psychology preceeds philosophy. In short, without the Rings, I know what would have happened to me – whirled away on the merry-go-round of the complex and the wish-fulfillment and the conditioned reflex, with Jung and Pavlov, Julian Huxley and Bertrand Russell, in all the consciousness of my group. On those rocking-horses I might have pranced for ever, with the rest of us, in a ring we mounted with zest. At a stall nearby, men were throwing three rings over a crown – was that a reminder, which shot me off, on to the trodden grass and torn papers of our Fair, tired of its Vanities?

In short, and especially in retrospect, so much can be, not explained but explained away. As one half of man's nature longs to as the other longs not – dragging in the wish-fulfillment to disprove the truth of the thing he swears he does not believe in.

Only aware, outside the circle of tents and painted boxes, flares of light and invitations to see humanity at its fattest and its thinnest, its tallest and its smallest, and all its diseases in glass bottles, that it stood, our fiery uproar, as I had seen it in Dorset, from Salterns to Woodbury Hill, inside a tree-ring; that above our lights the travelling moon lay on the ghostly shoulder of a crowned hill.

On that merry-go-round though I might have stayed. Except for that day. That day there, and others, one an agony and one a dreadful warning; but because of that day, one dispute, in essence, forever stilled.

Oh, Roman Britain would have been quite definite about it, and I had just learned enough to follow them; that there we were in a temenos, and a place for initiation. Initiation we had been prepared to receive in the right balance of mana and taboo, a brother and sister ceremonially perfect – but for my father's death.

That afternoon, I was received. Like any candidate for ancient initiations, accepted. Then in essence, but a process that time after time would be perfected in me. Rituals whose objects were knitting up and setting out, and the makings of correspondence, a translation which should be ever valid, between the seen and the unseen. Like any purified, I was put through certain paces; through certain objects, united to do their work, made from the roots of my nature to such refinements of sense-perceptions as I did not know that I possessed, made aware of those correspondences.

'The key to your situation is here', it was said. Its meanings made sensible principally it seemed by repetitions of light, movement and sound in the tops of the grove. Light and flight, in relation to the earth moving and to the triple ring. In its own speech, it was the same at Nemi. Here it was awfully pure.

Here it came with a radiant bliss. Bliss of light, bliss of green, bliss of birds. By means of the boy's pure mind? I think so. He was so very young, server and acolyte. And a child making a bonfire, because people had been there to picnic before us and he said we could not go without leaving the Rings clean.

Then, that night, I went upstairs to my room. Not long before the war. In a bungalow near Java Head, a young Scotsman with an eyeglass, with heavy shoulders and delicate hands was investigating a *poltergeist*. In the verandah, stones flew out of the open sky. Indoors there was a room that was kept shut up. In the grim north of England, a very young man made up his mind to come to London and be a painter, not a musician. In London a pale lad of great beauty determined to turn his back on Whitechapel and on Jewry. In central Europe, his namesake decided to kill a man who would be a king. On a Mediterranean beach, Isadora Duncan saw the man who gave her her last child, rising out of the sea. In Russia, a pageboy with black curls and eyes the colour of green ice, went down to the cellars of his grandmother's house to watch the snakes fed. In the Middle-West of America, a college boy and girl said they would come over and learn all Europe had to teach. Two others said they would come and take all Paris had to give. In Paris, a boy whose beauty was supernatural, was laughing after dinner at a great house. They said: 'Since Voltaire died, there has never been such wit.'

At Salterns, in Dorsetshire, the midsummer night lifted up its arms to the heavens, wavering like a dark fire. So many insects that heat had brought to life that out of pity I closed my window against them.

They crawled outside on the glass panes, iridescent fragilities, swift hatching after swift hatching; moths and a kind of fly I did not know and did not like, with pale bodies and transparent wings. Mosquitoes that went ping, and beetles in armour. Hollow cockchafers and rose beetles in green mail; small beetles, and dying bees from the dark crack under the eave-shoots. Whose roar you could hear by day, whose honey you could smell, night and day.

In the closed room, the hawthorn-jar gave out its sweets, the scent one loved and was told was dangerous; that Nurse had said would kill you if it slept beside you; a magic. I took my Homer and began to read about Helen on the walls of Troy.

Πολυν Χρονον ἀλγεα πασχειν – instead, in a way I can only say, not describe, Nurse was right and the burning scent took me in something that was more than sleep.

Immediately I was back on the Rings; or rather, approaching them fast, in a small car, in winter. *Pendant l'horreur d'une profonde nuit*, but before dawn.

The boy I had sat next to at lunch was driving the car. He vanished and a turn in the dream brought me face to face with the Rings.

Only, and these words are the nearest equivalent, in their actual shape, the nearest equivalent my very partly enlightened mind could conceive. I saw more than I could tell, infinitely more than I could carry. Yet enough when I woke and, like one struggling back from one life into another, flung open the windows, and through a swarm of winged creatures thrust out my head to the night air and the stars, to know that I seen enough, if I could use it, to carry me to this journey's end.

And over. To where, as it is said, I should know as I was known.

It was more than ten years later that I met him again. More than ten years , and the war was behind us. We had been living in that world before it happened, and now we were living in this. In Paris, dancing in the rue de l'Happe. A great many things had happened to both of us: we were now both perfectly grown-up.

More than ten years. We danced together and he said: 'What are two little Dorsetshire rabbits doing in the rue de l'Happe?' And I answered, without thinking, yet as though it was waiting to be said, 'It's because of Badbury Rings', and remember only that he seemed satisfied with the answer.

Mary Butts. Ita perfecit opus.
Sennen 1935-6.

Salterns, c. *1900*

Mrs Sarah Briggs, c. *1900*

Mary Briggs, c. *1889*

The dining-room, 1920

272

Captain J. F. Butts, c. *1860*

Mary Butts with her mother, 1891

269

Mary Butts, her parents and aunt, with the crew of the Vanity

Ada Briggs, c. 1918

Mary Butts, c.

Mary Butts, c. 1900

Anthony Butts, c. 1914

Mary Colville-Hyde, 1914

The terrace of Salterns, 1920

The hall of Salterns, 1920

Mary (Butts) Rodker, 1919

Mrs Sarah Briggs, c. 1900

Mary Briggs, c. 1889

Captain J. F. Butts, c. 1860

Mary Butts with her mother, 1891

Mary Butts, her parents and aunt, with the crew of the Vanity

Mary Butts, c. 1900

Anthony Butts, c. 1914

270

Ada Briggs, c. 1918

Mary Butts, c. 1910

Mary Colville-Hyde, 1914

271

Salterns, c. 1900

The dining-room, 1920

272

Afterword

In a tribute to Mary Butts, Bryher tells of their meeting in Florence in 1923 and of listening in fascination night after night to stories about Butts's childhood. Over a decade later, *The Crystal Cabinet* appeared, the title taken from a poem by William Blake. Describing her childhood world and its loss, which were so crucial to the hard-won childlikeness of her adulthood, the book traces her beginnings as an author. From the many watercolours and temperas by Blake which hung on the walls of Salterns, where Mary Butts was born on 13 December 1890, she learned to see the eternal in time. The gap between the vision art and poetry afford and the way most people live, created a conflict for her, and she nearly despaired until she found her place in the arts and her work, which, she discovered, had everything to do with what she had known as a child.

As it illuminates the making of the artist, *The Crystal Cabinet* also records the 'un-making' of Butts's family and the disfigurement of the land near Salterns by developers, both of which tragedies she associates with her father's death. Captain Butts, who was thirty years older than his wife, introduced Mary to Greek mythology, Dante, Wilde, and Whistler, and shared with her a belief in a God known only through the beauty of things. Mrs Butts was less interested in ideas than in social position, and preferred a God who approved of a young girl's behaving acceptably. The family regularly attended the nearby Chapel of the Holy Angels, built on land given by Mary's father, and she learned 'as easily as [she] breathed, prayer and praise, and the superb Liturgy'. The curious phrases, descriptions of nature, and mysterious admonitions and assurances in the verses of the rites and services, corresponded to the power and loveliness that would overwhelm her in her encounters with nature and on hearing favourite stories, and later, in reading certain books. Although for much of her life, like many of her generation, she stopped attending church, unlike many, her devotion to what the words tell of never ceased.

Two events dramatized and symbolized the un-making of her childhood home: the burning of her father's books and the selling of the Blakes to pay the death-duties. Mary's brother, Tony, later disputed her story about the loss of Captain Butts's library; whether or not it occurred as she relates, to Mary its destruction represented a triumph of conventionality. Although she is highly critical of her mother, both in this book and in some of her stories and novels where she deplores the harm an insufficiently educated and greatly repressed mind can cause, she understood that many women of her mother's generation were not given enough of importance to think about or do. If her portrait of her mother is not entirely accurate, the grief each caused the other is apparent. This edition of her autobiography includes accounts of her stepfather omitted from the first edition, notably of Mary's mother accusing her of making advances to him, charges the writer denies. Again, whether or not they are true – or indeed, whether *he* made advances to *Mary* – the accusations indicate an impasse between mother and daughter.

Mary Butts is careful to point out that many of the problems she faced as a young person and a student were her own fault, and to deny that she was an exceptional child. Like many girls' schools, the one at St Andrews was designed in part to save women from lives like those of her mother and her stepfather's sisters. Mary pays tribute to some of the excellent teaching she met with, but regrets that there, as at home, the same restriction and distrust of deep inquiry prevailed, an 'impeccable piety, so arid of devotion' that separated life from its loveliness.

Except for a few maps, the walls at her school were bare; but, as if by divine accident, there was a reproduction of the Hermes of Praxiteles, a reminder of another world 'where there was laughter and immortal loveliness and gold weather, an infinite number of memory miles away. No. Not far-off at all – it was inside you, and just – just as one was becoming so miserable as almost to forget, the Gods had remembered.' Such moments sustained her. From her difficulties at school she learned to stand alone and one teacher confirmed her belief that 'the pulse of everything' heard in poetry could silence mediocrity and all sorts of meanness. As a remembrance of what is real, poetry existed outside the dreariness and lovelessness of school and home. Moreover, it enabled her to understand 'those for whom there is no sweetness', especially the many she would meet in London and Paris who had been broken by the war, and who are often the subject of her stories.

When she was little, she read about an eagle that was blinded and put in a cage: 'Suddenly I found myself crying, seized by an utterly new sensation, a helplessness and agony of mind.' It is one of her criticisms of the way children are raised that they are not taught to cope with the evil and unhappiness they see and feel. No one, of course, can meet the demons or go to the Dark Tower for another, but for Mary the inability of her elders to help in this task increased the pain of growing up. Many of her stories deal with living in a world where misfortunes happen, and Bryher, Douglas Goldring, and others have remarked on her proclivity to aid those adrift. This is not the occasion to discuss what the desire to comfort satisfied; however, these efforts do relate profoundly to her poetics. Butts's work maintains that it is possible to transform what is awful – witness the Greeks and Shakespeare – and for her such transformation provided a link with Christianity, particularly as embodied in the admonition to love one's enemies. Referring in part to those who inspire little affection, she writes in a poem, 'And it is not possible to love / Any people but these.' Love is only love where there is transformation. What is hateful or fearsome often falls away before what her characters call 'Hermes', 'Aphrodite', and 'God'.

Though she was largely unsuccessful at such alteration of her own life, Butts did embody it in the writing that increasingly became her life, impelled as much by pain as by desire to find her vision there: to 'make Shelley come true' is one way she puts it. 'Words out of their place in their own heavenly country and entered the ordinary world' unveil what the mind dulled by habit fails to apprehend. As a young woman, Butts was so impressed with the five words 'love and man's unconquerable mind' they became audible to her during an air raid and ensured her safety. Such words, like the building of Asgard and parts of the Bible, were 'a way of telling what was true', as were her encounters with the *numina* in the salt marshes, woods and gardens around her home. She has vivid memories of these contacts – of the thunder of bees, of stones 'full of secrets, with a sap and a pulse and a being' all their own, of a particular starry sky, of one violent wind and of individual trees. Her perception of the separateness of each thing has its counterpart in that imagination which detects the eternal in a moment of time. Summing up her previous experiences of this correspondence of visible and invisible, Badbury Rings, a mysterious set of prehistoric mounded circles not far from Salterns, sealed her destiny as an artist. Like Delphi, the Rings epitomized this double vision. After her initiation there, she revisited the Rings in a dream and gained inspiration that lasted a lifetime. A sacred place like the Rings and an experience like hers in its precinct became a motif in her writings.

A reader of her fiction will discover other events like those recounted in *The Crystal Cabinet*, metamorphosed to be sure, that unite the temporal and the timeless. A masterful writer of supernatural tales, Mary Butts particularly admired M.R. James and Charles Williams. Her stories are permeated with the inevitable, often terrifying justice of the uncanny, as well as with the disturbing beauty of nature so characteristic of Algernon Blackwood's work, which she also knew. The invisible she evokes is not a transcendental dimension of natural power, nor a manifestation of a devil, though it may have attributes of each, as in the stories 'Green' or 'The Saint'. Nor is it 'the goddess', although her characters may so address it, as in 'Mappa Mundi'. Above all, it is not 'the parson's God'. In the abruptly shifting scenes of her novel *Armed with Madness* (1928), the Grail, which is lost and found by a group of young people in England in the 1920s, focuses the power of the hidden that disrupts their lives. In *The Macedonian* (1933), Alexander's daimon is the unsettling element. Whether it is a short story or a novel, whether the setting is ancient Greece or Rome or contemporary London or Paris, her work commemorates occurrences that show one where to look for God. Beginning with the memory of a puddle of yellow mud and ending with a vision of Badbury Rings, *The Crystal Cabinet* re-creates the growth of her imagination as it follows the action of memory, 'winding . . . in and out, like the streams of Poole Harbour', perpetually turning back to her experience of what is unseen.

While it offers reflections from the perspective of her forties, Mary Butts's autobiography, as the subtitle suggests, takes her only to early adulthood. In 1911 she came into her personal inheritance. Living in London, she investigated socialism and got to know, among others, Rebecca West, Nina Hamnett, Roger Fry, and Wyndham Lewis. Through Stella Bowen she met Ford Madox Ford, who, along with Ezra Pound, praised her work. In 1918 she married John Rodker, a writer and protegé of Pound's, and proprietor of the Ovid Press. Her poems, stories, and reviews began to appear in *The Egoist*, *The Little Review*, and *The Dial*, and in 1919 she finished her first novel, *Ashe of Rings*. After the birth of her daughter, Camilla, late in 1920, she and Rodker separated. She was in love with Cecil Maitland, a writer of some promise but little initiative, who probably introduced her to drugs and black magic. They spent some months at Aleister Crowley's 'abbey' in Sicily, and after returning to England, travelled to Germany and Austria. *Speed the Plough*, her first volume of stories, appeared in 1923. In the 1920s Butts travelled and lived in France, where she met French and American writers and artists and their crowd, including Ernest Hemingway, Sylvia Beach, Peggy Guggenheim, Mireille Havet, Eugene McCown, and Robert McAlmon, whose Contact Press published *Ashe of Rings*. She and Maitland parted in 1925, and a little over a year later he died of alcoholism and consumption. Over the next few years Butts had a number of intense relationships with women and men, most of the men homosexual. For extensive periods during 1925-27 she lived at the Hotel Welcome in Villefranche, where Cocteau frequently stayed. His sketches capture her at this time, and his illustrations for her *Imaginary Letters* (1928) are the first he did for a book not his own. Her greatest love of this period was Virgil Thomson, who has extolled her and her work.

In 1928 Mary's Aunt Ada took in Camilla. Mary had never spent much time with her daughter, and saw her infrequently over the next nine years. The most severe blow during her late thirties was the estrangement from her brother, Tony, whom she may have loved more than anyone. They had shared adventures in the countryside around Salterns, and she claims that he too was initiated at the Rings, but he drew closer to his mother. Although he wrote a play and painted, he was not devoted to the world of writing which meant everything to his sister, and he could not be the companion and soulmate she wished him to be. Her battle with poverty and drugs led to a breakdown in 1930, and her mother brought her back to England from Paris. Shortly after, Butts married Gabriel Aitken, a water-colourist and cartoonist, who had been a friend of the Sitwells and of Siegfried Sassoon. After some moving about, the couple settled in a bungalow perched above the Atlantic in Sennen, Cornwall. Over the next two years Butts published two novels, a volume of short stories, and two long essays. Then, at the end of 1934, Gabriel left her. Shortly afterwards, she published her richly textured last novel, *Scenes from the Life of Cleopatra*. She wrote a long introduction for a book about Julian the Apostate and completed *The Crystal Cabinet*, which had gestated for years. Suddenly, on 5 March 1937, she died in a hospital at Penzance of a perforated ulcer, general peritonitis, and an untreated diabetic condition. Alcohol and drug addiction had severely undermined her health, but her life might have been saved had she lived in a less remote spot.

The years of indigence and rejection, though largely self-inflicted, were none the less difficult for the woman who as a child had known affection and plenty; and for one who had enlivened parties in Chelsea and Montparnasse, the last years in the small house at Sennen must have been lonely. There were occasional visitors and a few friends, but mostly her hours were her own. She read widely and constantly, from mysteries and books about gardening to history and mythology. Her journals, which she began in 1916 and which cover her life after the period of her autobiography, include lists of books and notes on what she read. She reviewed for *Time and Tide*, *The Bookman*, and the *Sunday Times*. She gardened and explored the surrounding country. Few trees grow on that windswept coast, but everywhere abounded what she called 'visible Pan'. The ocean, the bones of the land, birds, foxes and the smell of the turf were actors in a drama larger than their own which absorbed her.

Evelyn Waugh mentions that there were many festivities at Butts's house in Belsize Park in the early 1920s, and Elsa Lanchester, who lodged there, provides close-ups of some of the bizarre tenants and noted visitors. Other glimpses of Mary Butts in memoirs of the period suggest how substantially her exuberance and intelligence contributed to gatherings, but she always stood out, a little apart. Not just because of her much-remarked-on bright red hair or original behaviour, but because of her awareness of what lies just at or beyond the edge of the perceptible, an attitude found in her writing as well.

Like Kirchner's brooding paintings, with which she felt an affinity, her work enlarges her modern subjects by placing them in an adventure not entirely personal that has repercussions beyond their own lives. Hugh Ross Williamson observed that her writing combines Lawrence's romanticism and Eliot's classicism, and while her prose is not experimental like that of Proust, Joyce, or Dorothy Richardson, Mary Butts does share the passion of these writers for seeing the confusion of daily life as an occasion for the marvellous. Considering what interested her 'apart from the specific work of writing', she wrote: 'Nothing but spiritual development, the soul living at its fullest capacity.' If one could become a part of what one loved, then writing, like gardening, might be a worship and an entrance to that glory glimpsed in poetry and most potently at the Rings, which told her she could live in its presence. This conviction, perhaps more than anything else, accounts for her not being better known, and it is one of the main reasons her work needs to be read.

Virgil Thomson comments that Gertrude Stein liked Butts's poetry, and early on Ford and Pound encouraged her. She did not cultivate such friendships, nor, when she sought them out – as with T. S. Eliot – was she very successful. It seems the intensity of her personality and of her work got in the way. She writes of being embarrassed by her behaviour with Ford, and Virginia Woolf complained about her perfume and referred to *Ashe of Rings* as 'an indecent book, about the Greeks and the Downs'. Later, Hogarth Press turned down *Armed with Madness*. Butts never became part of any group that could ensure her a place in literary history, and though personal relationships in part may account for her failure to find support, it is more likely that the writing itself, in its uncompromising effort to read *le message indéchiffrable*, proved disconcerting. Such a predicament is not unusual for a woman writer, particularly for one who treats decadence and the sacred with the authority of a male author. The greatest degradation and the greatest sanctity often merge in her work, making both those who believe in God and those who do not uneasy. In addition, her women, while hardly conventional, are not noticeably modern. The spirit of Butts's books – closer to H.D. in *Palimpsest* and *Trilogy* or to Pound in *The Pisan Cantos* and *The Spirit of Romance* than to Katherine Mansfield or Jean Rhys – indicates how disorder may lead to those mansions the heart desires.

In 1984 after much effort, Camilla Bagg added to her mother's gravestone in Sennen churchyard Blake's line from 'The Crystal Cabinet': 'I strove to seize the inmost Form'. Suggesting the distinctiveness of Butts's work as well as its energy, this line points beyond the darkness and brightness of human life. Though she suffered losses and though she was caught up in much of the revelry of the 1920s, she never relinquished what she had seen in poetry or at the Rings. At the end of her autobiography, she tells of falling asleep while reading in Homer about Helen on the walls of Troy. Suddenly she is facing the Rings, and sees enough to inform her life's work. Years after this vision, when dancing in the rue de l'Happe, she meets the young man she had seen in the dream and tells him they are there because of Badbury

Rings. Her work, too, exists because of the Rings. For her there are not two worlds, poetry and the wild, pleasant or forbidding, but only the world alive in a child's memory of a bee and a garden, or beheld in a print of Hermes in an inhospitable schoolroom. Though the night could be long, there would be at last 'a theophany, a shining-out of a God'.

BARBARA WAGSTAFF
Berkeley
California

Appendix

THESE notes are an attempt to clarify and identify some of the allusions that Mary Butts makes, without explanations, in her text. Some of the names she mentions – H.G. Wells, for example – seem too well known to need a note. Regrettably, not a few of the quotations and names cited in passing have escaped the editors' efforts to trace to their source.

The Crystal Cabinet

The title of the book comes from Blake's poem 'The Crystal Cabinet', the last stanzas of which run:

> *I strove to seize the inmost Form*
> *With ardor fierce & hands of flame,*
> *But burst the Crystal Cabinet*
> *And like a Weeping Babe became*
>
> *A Weeping Babe upon the wild*
> *And Weeping Woman pale reclind*
> *And in the outward air again*
> *I filld with woes the passing Wind.*

3 Stones

9 standish   an inkstand
12 Bishop of Ely   Robert Butts, bishop from 1738 to his death in 1748, aged sixty-three.
13 Thomas Butts   1757?-1845, the patron and friend of William Blake. He lived in Fitzroy Square, London.
Emanuel Swedenborg   1688-1772, Swedish scientist, philosopher and theologian. After his death his followers formed the New Jerusalem Church and the English Theosophical Society. His writings greatly influenced Blake, though eventually Blake could not agree with him entirely.

4 *The House*

14 *Poly-Olbion* A long poem by Michael Drayton, begun in 1598. It consists of a 'description of all the tracts, rivers, mountains, forests, and other parts of this renowned isle of Great Britain, with intermixture of the most remarkable stories, antiquities, wonders, rarities, pleasures, and commodities of the same'.

18 Ingoldsby R.H. Barham (1788-1845) English clergyman and poet, published his collection of poems and stories *The Ingoldsby Legends* in 1840, comic and grotesque retellings of medieval legend, very popular.

19 William Rufus second surviving son of William the Conqueror, crowned William II in 1087; killed by an arrow as he was hunting in the New Forest in August 1100.

Kerguelen Kerguelen Land, or Desolation Island, an uninhabited, mountainous island in the Southern Ocean, annexed by the French in 1893.

5 *Fear of Pan*

22 Juliana of Norwich Dame Julian of Norwich, a fourteenth-century mystic, who recorded in *Sixteen Revelations of Divine Love* the visions revealed to her in her illness in 1373.

23 As it happened to Wordsworth it seems likely that MB is referring to *The Prelude* here, with its famous lines, 'Fair seed-time had my soul, and I grew up / Fostered alike by beauty and by fear.'

'every day . . .' this is adapted from the practice of Emile Coué (1857-1926), whose system of cures by 'autosuggestion' was world-renowned.

'Science so loved the world . . .' a parody of St John 3.16: 'So God loved the world, that he gave his only-begotten Son, to the end that all that believe in him should not perish, but have everlasting life.'

Pheidippides *c*. 450 BC, a famous runner who brought to Athens the news of the Greek victory over the Persians at Marathon.

24 'yet in my flesh . . .' 'For I know that my redeemer liveth, and that he shall stand at the latter day upon the earth: And though after my skin worms destroy this body, yet in my flesh shall I see God.' Job 19.25.

25 'Why' the name is a pun on the Latin for 'why', which is 'cur'.

7 *The Two Romances*

33 Malory   Sir Thomas Malory (d.1471) was the author of the *Morte D'Arthur*; the 'matter of Britain' is the term for the Arthurian legends, first used by Jean Bodel in the twelfth century.

34 Louise de Querouaille   (or Kéroualle), Duchess of Portsmouth (1649-1734) and mistress of Charles II. This portrait was destroyed along with the remaining family treasures when a bomb hit the furniture depository in which they were stored during World War II. (The painting is visible in the photograph on p.272.)

36 George Santayana   (1863-1932) was Professor of Philosophy at Harvard until 1912, then resident in France, England and Europe. Apart from his volumes of speculative philosophy, he also published poetry, criticism and memoirs, including *Soliloquies in England* (1922).

39 *Lays of Ancient Rome*   (1842) a collection of poems by Macaulay, dealing with traditional tales of Roman history.

41 pre-Frazer days   MB makes frequent reference to the work of Sir James Frazer (1854-1941), the eminent anthropologist, who is best known for *The Golden Bough* (1890-1915). This analysis of fertility rites, the dying god myths, ritual murders etc was immensely influential in the literature of the 1920s, notably in T.S. Eliot's *Waste Land*.

42 Yggdrasil   in old Norse mythology, the ash-tree which binds together heaven, earth and hell. Its roots run in three directions and under each root is a fountain of wonderful virtues. At the bottom of the tree lies the serpent, gnawing the roots, while the squirrel runs up and down the tree to sow strife between the serpent and the eagle at the top. It is also called the Tree of the Universe.
the Hesperidean   the three Hesperides live in the far-western orchard which Mother Earth gave to Hera, where the golden apples hang.
the Irminsul   or Column of Herman, was the object of the old Saxons' worship (Herman was the hero of Teutonic independence), in defence of which they fought desperately against Charlemagne and his Christianised Franks.
Adonis   in Greek mythology a model of beauty, beloved of Aphrodite. He died after hunting, wounded by a boar's tusk. At Aphrodite's intercession, Zeus allowed him to spend half the year in the upper world and half in the lower. He typifies the withering

of nature in winter and its resurgence in spring; his cult came by way of Asia Minor to Greece, Egypt and Rome.

Atys   the Phrygian counterpart of Adonis.

Osiris   in Egyptian mythology is the spirit of the first half of the year, his rival and twin, Set, the spirit of the second half, and they perpetually contend for the favours of their sister, the moon-goddess Isis.

8 Our Children

44 Zadig   the hero of Voltaire's short novel *Zadig, ou la Destinée* (1748), in which he is an honest but naïve young man whose well-intentioned plans often go wrong because of a destiny beyond human control.

47 Pascal   'Nous brûlons de désir de trouver une assiette ferme, et une dernière base constante pour y édifier une tour qui s'élève à l'infini; mais tout notre fondement craque, et la terre s'ouvre jusqu'aux abîmes.' *Pensées*, II, 72.

52 *Landslide*   a book by Monica Curtis, published by Gollancz in 1937.

Charles Williams   (1886-1945), poet, novelist and theological writer, member of C.S. Lewis's group 'the Inklings'. His novels have been described as 'supernatural thrillers'; his cycle of poems on the Arthurian legend, *Taliessin through Logres*, was published after MB's death, but he lent her the poems in 1935, during a three-year correspondence up to her death.

Spengler   Oswald Spengler (1880-1936), the German writer of *The Decline of the West* (translated into English 1926-29), in which he argues that all civilizations go through the same cycles of growth and decay.

53 Father Knox   Ronald Knox (1888-1957), distinguished Roman Catholic priest and author of apologetics, also translated the Bible. His book *Broadcast Minds* (1932) was a reply to recent works such as Julian Huxley's *Religion without Revelation* (1927), Bertrand Russell's *Conquest of Happiness*, Gerald Heard's *The Emergence of Man* and Langdon Davies's *Science and Common Sense*. Knox detected the belief that churchmen discouraged inquiry in the natural sciences, and that 'science' was somehow destructive of theology – this misconception was the theme of his book.

The Chaplet of Pearls   subtitled 'The White and Black Ribaumont (a romance of French history, 1572)', by the immensely popular novelist Charlotte Mary Yonge (1823-1901), published in 1868.

54 *Ladies Whose Bright Eyes*   a novel by Ford Madox Ford (who knew and encouraged MB), first published in 1911 and reissued in 1935 with a much revised ending.

9   Brother Aubrey

58 Fenrir's chain   in Norse mythology, Fenrir was the offspring of Loki, the god of destruction, and a giantess. He grew so fierce he had to be chained, but nothing could hold him until a chain was forged which no force could break, made of the roots of a mountain, the noise of a moving cat, and the breath of a fish.

10   Aunt Monica

60 'Arethusa'   poem by Shelley

63 'A savage place! . . .'   lines 14-15 of Coleridge's 'Kubla Khan'.

66 'Warrior Dead'   from Tennyson's *The Princess*: 'Home they brought her warrior dead. / She nor swoon'd, nor utter'd cry: / All her maidens, watching, said, / "She must weep or she will die."'

11   The Heroes

73 The Heroes of Asgard   in Norse mythology, Asgard is the equivalent of Olympus in Greek mythology, reached only by the Rainbow Bridge, Bifrost. Heimdall guards the bridge against the giants.
Fenrir   the wolf-son of Loki and the brother of Hel, queen of the dead and goddess of the underworld. Odin – the chief god of Norse mythology – sought in vain to chain him, for he represented the goading of a guilty conscience.

74 Mimir   a water-demon in the form of a giant, who lived under the root of Yggdrasil, at the well which was the source of all wisdom. Odin, to obtain a drink from the well, was obliged to leave one of his eyes in pawn.

The Edda was compiled in about 1270, but some of the poems in it belong to a much earlier age (there is also a Prose Edda). They concern legendary Germanic heroes, and the Norse myths.

75 Dodona a city of Epirus, seat of the oldest oracle, dedicated to Zeus.

Max Müller Friederich Max Müller (1823-1900) was a German-born British philologist, best known for his *Sacred Books of the East*. A major influence, not only on linguistic studies but also on comparative religion and mythology.

77 Roger Fry (1866-1934) art critic and painter, influential through his essays and his organization of two important exhibitions of Post-Impressionist paintings at the Grafton Galleries, London, in 1910 and 1912.

79 the Bluebird Prince Maurice Maeterlinck (1862-1949), a Belgian poet, dramatist and essayist; *The Blue Bird* (1909) embodies his faith in the spiritual life of all living things.

Andrew Lang (1844-1912), educated at St Andrews University, was a prolific and versatile writer; besides poetry, translations, anthropology and *belles-lettres*, he wrote and collected fairy tales, of which the volume *The Blue Fairy Book* (1889) was the first in a series.

the Wounded Prince thought to be a reference to MB's lover, Cecil Maitland.

12 The Stump

84 'Tout est dangereux...' quoted from *Zadig*, 'Tout est dangereux ici-bas, et tout est nécessaire' in the context of a discussion of the passions.

13 Cousin Henry

88 The Newcome touch the lovable Colonel Thomas Newcome is a man of simple, unworldly tastes and the utmost honour in William Thackeray's novel, *The Newcomes* (1855).

89 'the glorious liberty ...' 'Because the creature itself also shall be delivered from the bondage of corruption into the glorious liberty of the children of God.' Romans 8.21.

90 Naboth in Biblical times, he was the owner of a vineyard desired by Ahab, king of Samaria, but he would not give it to the king.

14 The Wasted Land

91 William Beckford (see also p.109) an extremely wealthy traveller and connoisseur (1759-1844), whose chief creation was Fonthill Abbey, west of Salisbury, a Gothic extravaganza.

92 *Nichée de gentilshommes* taken from the title of Turgenev's novel, *A Nest of the Gentry* (1859).

93 Trevelyan the historian G.M. Trevelyan (1876-1962), whose *History of England* was published in 1926.

95 Coles and Postgates George Cole, his wife Margaret and her brother Raymond Postgate collaborated in writing books on socialism; they were active in the Fabian socialist movement.

15 Intellectualis Amor

98 'Nullum numen habes . . .' you have no divinity/godhead if you apply wisdom; it is we, we who make of you a goddess, Fortune. Heimarmenê the personification of Fate.

17 Murder in the Woods

110 Wards in Chancery a colloquial expression of the age, referring to money left to minors under the terms of a settlement. The Chancery Court was empowered to oversee such arrangements up to 1925.

18 Shelley

114 'Ah did you once . . .' from Robert Browning's poem 'Memorabilia'.
ἐν τούτῳ νίκη in this is victory.

115 'To suffer woes . . .' from Shelley's *Prometheus Unbound* IV. Jane Harrison (1850-1928), classical scholar and anthropologist, author of *Themis, a study of the social origins of Greek religion* (1912).

116 'Revenge and Wrong . . .' from Shelley's poem 'Hellas'. 'I met Murder on the way –' from Shelley's 'The Masque of Anarchy'; Lord Castlereagh was Foreign Secretary during the Napoleonic Wars, and extremely unpopular because of the disastrous condition of home affairs.

118 'I should like to see, and this will be the last and the most ardent of my desires, I should like to see the last king strangled with the guts of the last priest.' From the Will of Jean Messelier, 1733, published by Voltaire.

19 Odd Man Out

128 'The Three Ravens' In her manuscript MB wrote 'The Twa Corbies,' but quoted from 'The Three Ravens'. When she later speaks of 'those cruel birds', she is surely referring to the corbies, who pick out the eyes of a dead knight; by comparison, 'The Three Ravens' is not so awful.
Percy *Reliques* Thomas Percy (1729-1811), poet, scholar and antiquarian, whose eclectic collection of old ballads, political songs from the seventeenth century and ballads by himself and his contemporaries reawakened a taste for English balladry, and influenced the Romantics.

20 In Sleep

132 Apollo god of the arts, of medicine, music, poetry and eloquence; as Phoebus Apollo god of light though not properly of the sun. Twin brother of Artemis.
Artemis goddess of hunting and of light.
134 Hecate in Greek mythology a goddess akin to Artemis. She practised and taught, through her emissaries, sorcery and witchcraft. She appears in the later cult of demonology.
Loki god of destruction in Norse mythology, father of the Fenris-wolf. Of handsome appearance but evil disposition.
a man without a heart thought to be a reference to MB's first husband, the writer John Rodker.
135 Cabestan A Provençal poet who lived near the end of the twelfth century and was killed from jealousy by Raymond de Roussillon. According to the legend, Raymond caused his wife to eat, unwittingly, the heart of Cabestan. When she discovered what she had done she vowed that, after such noble food, her lips should touch no other, and she died of starvation.

'Kilmeny'   a poem by James Hogg (1770-1835) about the bonnie sinless maiden who disappeared to the land of the spirits. She asked to go home to see her people but when she came back seven years had passed. No one knew if it was she herself or a ghost, and she soon returned to 'the land of thought'.

137   Mr Dunne   J.W. Dunne (1875-1919), author of *An Experiment with Time* (1927) and *The Serial Universe* (1934), proposing theories of time to account for such phenomena as precognition and previsional dreaming.

139   'Scio, Domine . . .'   I know, Lord, and I know in truth, that I am not worthy to approach so great a mystery, because of my too many sins and infinite negligence. But I know that Thou art able to make me worthy.

21   *Two Drawing-Rooms*

143   It is curious that MB should have remembered the chair with two whole lions when the traditional style is for a lion and a lamb, as can be seen in the photograph on p.272.

22   *Death-Duties*

154   Lord Peter Wimsey   the aristocratic detective hero of Dorothy Sayers' mystery novels.
Ellis and Yeats   W.B. Yeats edited *The Poems of William Blake* (1893), and with F.J. Ellis edited *The Works of William Blake* (3 vols, 1893), which included a memoir and interpretation of the mythology.

155   Young's *Night Thoughts*   Blake's engravings for Edward Young's popular poem *The Complaint*, or *Night Thoughts on Life, Death and Immortality* were published in 1796-7, and not well received at the time.
Blair's *Grave*   Blake's engravings of Robert Blair's *The Grave*, another poem of the 'graveyard school', were published in 1808, and attacked by Leigh Hunt.

158   the Longwood sale   Napoleon spent his last years in Longwood House, on the island of St. Helena in the Atlantic.

23 *Tiger-Tiger*

162 Sindal   This place could not be found until a suggestion was made that it might be Syndale Park, near Faversham. On reading the history of the house (now a motel) it was learnt that John Hyde bought it in 1848. He was High Sherriff of the county but left it before the end of the century to move, presumably, to Bournemouth.

the Clarendon Hydes   Edward Hyde, Lord Clarendon, was Chancellor of England in the reign of Charles II. His daughter, Ann, was the first wife of James II. (This is possibly how Mary Colville-Hyde came to own a watch which had belonged to Charles I, and also furniture from that period.)

Vesta Tilley   (1864-1952) the professional name of Lady de Frece, English commedienne and the most celebrated of all female impersonators.

164 'Jeune homme . . .'   from the poem 'A Adolphe Gaïffe' by Théodore de Banville (1823-91).

shikari   a hunter (from the Urdu).

165 Empress Elizabeth   of Austria, also a celebrated horsewoman, who came to England and Ireland (1876-80) during the hunting season. She was piloted in the field by Captain George ('Bay') Middleton.

Experiences of an Irish R.M.   the two very successful novels *Some Experiences of an Irish R.M.* and *Further Experiences . . .*, published in 1899 and 1908, written by the cousins Edith Somerville and Martin Ross (Violet Martin).

166 Horace Annesley Vachell   (1861-1955) a prolific and popular English novelist, best remembered for his novel *The Hill* (1905) about public-schoolboys' life at Harrow.

167 *Little Henry and his Bearer*   a novel by Mrs Mary Martha Sherwood (1775-1851), a prolific author of children's books and tracts. One edition of *Little Henry* was published along with A. MacNeil and Theophilus Smith's tale *The Last Days of Boosy*.

168 Napier of Magdala   the British under Sir Robert Napier captured the Abyssinian stronghold of Magdala in 1868, and he was created Baron Napier of Magdala.

Mr Knox's Country   (1915), the third of the series by Somerville and Ross; but the characters Lucine and Louisa do not appear in it.

169 The Anson Trophy   perhaps something acquired on Anson's famous journey round the world, accompanied by Jack Byron (1723-86), later Admiral and grandfather of the poet. It may have been left behind when Newstead Abbey was sold to Colonel Wildman, a Hyde ancestor.

24   Départ pour Cythère

178 'One stiff blind horse, his every bone a-stare . . . I never saw a brute I hated so; / He must be wicked to deserve such pain.' Robert Browning *Childe Roland*.
'Quaere reliqua . . .'   Seek the rest of this material/subject among more secret things/places.

25   Regiment of Women

187 'The Spring comes slowly . . .'   ''Tis a month before the month of May, / And the Spring comes slowly up this way.' Coleridge, *Christabel*.
Leto   the mother of Apollo and Artemis by Zeus.
190 *L'Homme Qui Rit*   an historical romance by Victor Hugo (1869).

26   Cheiron's Pupil

193 Cheiron   the most learned of the Centaurs, a race half horses, half men, who lived in the region of Mount Pelion.
194 Ran   a water-demon, destructive goddess of the sea, where she caught drowning men in her net.
196 λεπτον γαρ ὁ ποιητης και πτηνον και ἱερον;   the poet is a subtle, winged and holy thing.
199 the little song of Kipling's   the poem 'Norman and Saxon'.
200 Κουροτροφοι.   nurse of young men (said of certain places).

27 Atthis

201 Atthis   goddess of the rugged coast, seems to have been a title of the Attic Triple-goddess.
'à l'ombre des jeunes filles en fleurs'   Proust, *A la Recherche du temps perdu*, vol. II.

202 Erckmann-Chatrian   Emile Erckmann (1822-99) and Alexandre Chatrian (1826-90),authors of historical novels – popular school-prize literature – about the revolution and the Napoleonic wars.
e.g. *Madame Thérèse ou les Volontaires de 1792* (1863), *Waterloo* (1865), etc.

28 Night and Day

216 E. Nesbit   (1858-1924), author of much-loved children's books, including *The Story of the Treasure-Seekers* (1899), *Five Children and It* (1902) and *The Railway Children* (1906).
Sredni Vashtar   a short story by Saki (H.H. Munro), involving a boy's vengeance on his hated guardian aunt, through the agency of a ferret.

219 Axel Münthe   (1857-1949) Swedish physician and writer, who retired to Capri and wrote his best-selling autobiography, *The Story of San Michele* (1929).

221 'The Wife of Usher's Well'   an old ballad, in which a woman's dead sons come home to her for one night, wearing hats made of the bark of a birch that grew 'at the gates o' Paradise'.

29 Origin of Species

222 Mrs Inchbald   Mrs Elizabeth Inchbald (1753-1821), novelist, dramatist and actress. Wrote prose romances *A Simple Story* (1791) *Nature and Art* (1796), also *The Child of Nature* – illustrating her belief in a simple education, and in man's natural goodness until corrupted by 'civilization'.

227 'Hub of a wheel...'   lines from a poem by MB, 'Corfe', reprinted in the 1979 edition of her book *Imaginary Letters*.

228 Surt   In Norse mythology, a fire-giant in the destruction of the
world by fire, when the gods are in battle with the powers of evil.
It is followed by the regeneration of all things.
Aesir   the race of the gods.
Norn   the three Fates, Past, Present and the Future, who
determine the destinies of gods and men.

234 the Flying Scotsman   this train was not put into service until
1923. Perhaps by the 1930s it was forgotten, and any fast train to
Scotland was so called.

30   Crystal Cabinet

242 Bellepheron   in Greek mythology the rider of Pegasus, the
winged horse, and slayer of the Chimaera, a fire-breathing
monster, part lion, goat and dragon. His pride so increased with
his achievements that he tried to mount to Heaven on Pegasus,
but Zeus maddened the horse with a gadfly and Bellepheron fell
to earth.

31   The Weeping Babe

245 Primrose League   in Great Britain, a league pledged to
principles of conservatism, as represented by Benjamin Disraeli
(1804-81), and opposed to the 'revolutionary tendencies of
radicalism'. Founded in 1883.

246 'The soldier-saints, who row on row, / Burn upward each to his
point of bliss.' Robert Browning, 'The Statue and the Bust'.

248 'Comes this way sailing . . .'   lines 713f. of *Samson Agonistes*.
'Oh no man knows . . .'   from Walter de la Mare's poem 'All
That's Past'.

253 The Graiae   sisters of the Gorgons, with one eye among the three
of them, which they passed around.

255 the Jacquerie   the name given to an insurrection of French
peasants against the nobles in the Ile de France, 1358.

32 The Rings

258 More   Henry More (1614-87) was one of the group of 'Cambridge Platonists', who held that to search for truth was to search for God. His works included *Divine Dialogues* and *Philosophicall Poems*.

259 Semele   courted by Zeus, but at his wife Hera's request he appeared to Semele in thunder and lightning, which terrified her into giving premature birth to Dionysus, and she died. She was later rescued from Hades by her son, and came to represent Spring.

261 the Cabiri   mystic divinities of crops and vines, who also gave protection at sea.

263 Coventry Patmore   (1823-96) a poet whose work was much admired by the Pre-Raphaelites. Known especially for his series of poems in praise of marriage, *The Angel in the House*.

264 Morgan le Fay   in Arthurian legend played the part of Arthur's evil fairy, bent on his destruction and spoiling his court's reputation.

266 In a bungalow near Java Head . . .   the people referred to in this paragraph may be cautiously identified as follows: the young Scotsman as MB's lover, Cecil Maitland; the young man from the grim north as Gabriel Aitken, MB's second husband; the pale lad as MB's first husband (and father of Camilla), John Rodker (the connection with the next sentence is obscure); a pageboy as MB's lover Sergey Maslennikoff; the college boy perhaps as Ezra Pound, and the couple as Scott and Zelda Fitzgerald; and the boy of supernatural beauty as Cocteau.

267 Πολυν Χρονον άλγεα πασχειν   to suffer griefs for a long time.